WHO DIES?

WHO DIES?

*An Investigation
of Conscious Living
and Conscious Dying*

STEPHEN LEVINE

ANCHOR BOOKS
Anchor Press/Doubleday
Garden City, New York

Although the case histories in this book are true, the patients' names have been changed to honor the privacy of their families and loved ones.

Acknowledgments are made to the following for their kind permission to reprint copyrighted material:

From AT THE EDGE OF THE BODY by Erica Jong. Copyright © 1979 by Erica Mann Jong. Reprinted by permission of Holt, Rinehart and Winston, Publishers.

From THE WAY OF CHUANG TZU by Thomas Merton. Copyright © 1965 by The Abbey of Gethsemani. Reprinted by permission of New Directions Publishing Corporation.

From THE WHEEL OF DEATH edited by Philip Kapleau. Copyright © 1971 by Philip Kapleau. Reprinted by permission of Harper & Row, Publishers, Inc.

From THE KABIR BOOK translated by Robert Bly. Copyright © 1974 by Robert Bly. Reprinted by permission of Robert Bly.

From THE COLLECTED WORKS OF RAMANA MAHARSHI edited by Arthur Osborne. Reprinted by permission of Samuel Weiser, Inc.

From RAMAYANA by William Buck. Reprinted by permission of the University of California Press.

From ZEN MIND, BEGINNER'S MIND by Shunryu Suzuki. Reprinted by permission of John Weatherhill, Inc.

From "Death in the Open" from THE LIVES OF A CELL by Lewis Thomas. Copyright © 1973 by the Massachusetts Medical Society. Reprinted by permission of Viking-Penguin Inc.

The Anchor Books edition is
the first publication of WHO DIES?

Anchor Books edition: 1982

Library of Congress Cataloging in Publication Data
Levine, Stephen.
Who dies?
Includes index.
1. Death. I. Title.
HQ1073.L48   306
AACR2
ISBN 0-385-17010-6 (pbk.)
Library of Congress Catalog Card Number 81–43214

To my wife, and spiritual partner, Ondrea, who worked page by page with me on this manuscript and whose love reminds me again and again to let go of the mind and die into the heart.

PREFACE

Not so long ago I attended a birth for the first time since my own. To breathe with the mother, to watch the child's head appear, to experience the entire process moment by moment allowed me to touch a primordial element in my being. I laughed, and cried, experienced fear, empathetic pain, and deep joy. I was standing at the doorway of existence, feeling, as deeply as I had ever felt, the connectedness of my humanity to the rest of nature with her cycles of spring and winter, creation and decay. The moment was filled with an awe-full grace, a sense of living spirit. Here was a ritual in which participation renewed my deepest sense of the human family.

And now not only birth but death has come out of the closet. As recently as the past ten years, spearheaded by the work of Cecily Saunders and her Hospice movement in England and Elisabeth Kübler-Ross in the United States, a far more humane psychological milieu is being provided for those undergoing the death process. Further impetus has been given this movement by the medical community's increasing recognition that its intensive-care and life-support technologies are sorely in need of deeper investigation of their appropriate application, an investigation of our humanity. To place an individual who is obviously approaching death in a sterile environment that separates that person from family, friends, children, pets, and a familiar environment is a particularly barbaric way of expiating our fear and guilt about death by imagining in the use of the technologies and sterile mechanics of our time that "we have done all we could."

This new Hospice movement focuses on providing a warm, supportive, and open environment for the individual undergoing the dying process. There is help provided in getting one's affairs in order, help for the grieving family, and help with the day-to-day needs of the patient.

Perhaps the most important contribution this movement makes, however, is that it supports the acknowledgment by all involved that dying is indeed the business at hand. How refreshing, after the almost total conspiracy of denial of death generally surrounding those facing dying in the past.

As admirable as this burgeoning movement is, it still represents only the first, faltering steps in a transformation of our relationship to the dying process. It still treats death as "unfortunate" and sees its business as attempting to make the best of an unpleasant situation. This movement is still rooted in denial: not denial of death, however, but, rather, a denial of our own intuition.

Science in its zeal for objectivity tells us we are our bodies, the product of Darwinian evolution, originating in a chance concatenation of molecular gases, our growth and decay dictated by genetic DNA codes. Thus death is the end. But there is something in the collective unconscious of the human species that intuitively knows that this "objective" definition does not embrace the totality of who we are. We have convinced ourselves that our intellect, rather than our intuition, must guide our lives and thus we must only acknowledge that which we can know we know. But intuitive wisdom does not fill that criterion. It seems to arise from beyond this rational, objective mind, so we have largely denied what it tells us, though every great world religion and many profound philosophers have been rooted in just this deeper wisdom.

In recent years intuitive ways of knowing seem to be gaining some legitimacy. Indeed, Albert Einstein, in speaking of the source of his inspiration for the theory of relativity, said, "I didn't arrive at an understanding of these fundamental laws of the universe through my rational mind." He recognized another way of knowing, previously pointed to by such philosophers as William James, who spoke of ways of knowing the universe of realities that lie hidden until we acknowledge them.

Once our culture begins to honor intuition, it will expiate the doubt that usually robs intuition of its power, and much of our world view will change. And paramount among these changes is our attitude toward death. There is an aspect of us—call it "being" or "awareness" or "pure mind" or "I"—that lies behind all the apparent phenomena (our body, emotions, senses, and thinking mind) which appear in the matrix of time and space. We intuit that even when we leave our body at death, this deeper part of our being is unaffected. With this basic change in identity, in the sense of who we are, death is converted from being a frightening enemy, a defeat, an unfortunate error in the universe, into another transformation through which we move, an adventure to surpass all adventures, an opening, an incredible moment of growth, a graduation.

Perhaps this is somewhat analogous to how the early explorers felt after the theory that the world was flat and that one could disappear over its edge was replaced by the spherical concept of our planet. What courage that theory must have released, thus allowing explorers to go fearlessly into the unknown.

Most people experience only intuitive "flashes" or brief moments of clarity about the deeper nature of self, followed almost immediately by the reassertion of dominance of our habitual ways of thinking. For us to be able to profit from our own rich, intuitive wisdom, we must cultivate this deeper way of knowing. We do this by learning to listen: listen to what the Quakers, for example, call "the still small voice within"; listen to the patterns, laws, and harmonies of the cosmos of which we are a part; listen with a delicate balance of a quiet meditative mind and an open loving, heart. This work of listening must be done by all of us, the living and the dying, the healers and the patients. Our service to each other must be rooted in just this work on ourselves. It is through this work of deepening our recognition of the intuitive heart-mind that the door so recently opened to death can lead into light, rather than more darkness.

Several years ago I asked Stephen Levine if he would become director of the Hanuman Foundation Dying Project. The purpose of the project is to create a context for the process of dying in which the work on oneself would be the central focus for all in-volved—be they healers, helpers, families, or the individuals approaching death. This collaborative endeavor is proving to be of immense benefit in transforming the dying process into one of spacious, loving growth.

And now out of Stephen's work with this project comes *Who Dies?* Because it is rooted in our collective intuitive wisdom, gleaned from a quiet mind, it is a definite departure from the plethora of books that the new dying movement has spawned. This book has addressed itself to the many aspects of the dying process with refreshing insight, candor, and lightness. It invites us to look directly at "what is," with clarity and without judgment. It divests the incredible melodrama called "death" of its frightful power, supplanting fear with calm, simple, compassionate under-standing.

Stephen Levine is a poet, longtime practitioner of Buddhist meditation, and meditation teacher who in close collaboration with his wife, Ondrea, is a dedicated servant to those facing death. In this book he integrates all these areas of expertise in a man-ner that at moments assumes classic proportions. I honor this effort and invite you to share in the richness of this offering.

In love,

Ram Dass

ACKNOWLEDGMENTS

There is really no way I can adequately acknowledge the years of learning and collaboration with my dear friend Ram Dass, but this book, as the last, is greatly the outcome of his consistent encouragement and love.

Indeed, this work contains the voices and hearts of many fine teachers:

Many of the unattributed quotes in this book are from the teachings of Sri Nisargadatta (whose name loosely translates as Mr. Natural), whom I have not met but whose works, through his two volumes *I Am That,* have had a profound influence on this investigation.

Also the teachings and presence of Neem Karoli Baba (known as Maharaji) and Ramana Maharshi permeate this sharing, as do years of Buddhist practice and teaching.

My close association with Joseph Goldstein and Jack Kornfield have also influenced this transmission.

As have the early years of this work when teaching with Elisabeth Kübler-Ross and our ongoing warmth and friendship.

This book is as much a product of the surrender and lucidity of those I have been with in the dying process as it is the teachings of spiritual friends who have lent their kindness and fierce clarity to guide me on the path of insight.

What follows is a weaving of many years of spiritual practice and sharing with dying patients as recorded and transcribed from various workshops and retreats. And but for the heartfelt labors of Jakki Walters, Jean Thompson, and Al Strickland I would still be hunting and pecking my way through the first chapter.

CONTENTS

AUTHOR'S
PREFATORY NOTE

When reading this book,
Listen to it
with your heart.
Let it be a mirror
of your own great nature.

Understanding is the
ultimate seduction of the mind.
Go to the truth
beyond the mind.
Love is the bridge.

1
OPENING TO DEATH

Today, approximately 200,000 people died. Some died by accident. Others by murder. Some by overeating. Others from starvation. Some died while still in the womb. Others of old age. Some died of thirst. Others of drowning. Each died their death as they must. Some died in surrender with their minds open and their hearts at peace. Others died in confusion, suffering from a life that remained unlived, from a death they could not accept.

It is as Lewis Thomas wrote in *The Lives of a Cell:* "The obituary pages tell us of the news that we are dying away while the birth announcements in finer print, off at the side of the page, inform us of our replacements, but we get no grasp from this of the enormity of the scale. There are 3 billion of us on the earth and all 3 billion must be dead, on a schedule, within this lifetime. The vast mortality, involving something over 50 million of us each year, takes place in relative secrecy . . .*

"Less than half a century from now, our replacements will have more than doubled the numbers. It is hard to see how we can continue to keep the secret with such multitudes doing the dying.

---

* Updated figures show that now there are nearly 4½ billion of us, and the annual mortality rate is about 70 million.

We will have to give up the notion that death is catastrophe, or detestable, or avoidable, or even strange. We will need to learn more about the cycling of life in the rest of the system, and about our connection to the process. Everything that comes alive seems to be in trade for something that dies, cell for cell."

We live in a society conditioned to deny death. It may be for this reason that many, at the time of their dying, feel so confused and guilty. Like sex, death has been whispered about behind closed doors. We feel guilty for dying, not knowing how to live. The ways of a lifetime are focused in our death.

Those who live in what are called "material societies," whose technology has allowed the acquirement of goods and less effort for survival, who have measured self-value by wealth, perhaps have a somewhat stronger tendency to identify themselves with the body. Our society spends billions of dollars each year on cosmetics, girdles, toupees, face lifts and hair dyes, pushing away the lessons that the decay of the body would have us comprehend. Indeed, in a world where starvation is one of its greatest agonies, this country spends more than four hundred million dollars a year just to lose weight.

Observing the body's decay, the change in metabolism as we age, the middle-age paunch, the lowering of energy, the graying at the temples, the lessening of muscle tone, the loss of hair, how can we deny the inevitability of the falling away of the body. Experiencing the loss of loved ones, seeing that all we have ever known is in constant change, that we are the stuff of history, how can we disregard death?

How often, for instance, is one encouraged to contemplate the aches and pains of the flu as a preparation for death, as a means of melting the resistance to life? Struggling for satisfaction from moment to moment, we think of ourselves as either fortunate or unfortunate, little realizing the teachings of impermanence.

We seldom use illness as an opportunity to investigate our relationship to life or to explore our fear of death. Illness is considered bad fortune. We hold to models of good health and Pepsi-Cola vitality. We only think we are O.K. if we are healthy. But how, in this fixed idea of the acceptable, do we learn to open to the impossible? How do we allow ourselves to come into the un-known with an openheartedness and courage that allow life its fullness.

In the funeral home we put rouge on death. Even in the casket we deny our transiency.

At home in our favorite easy chair, we read in the newspaper of five dying in a hotel fire in Cleveland, of ten killed in a bus accident on the freeway. Of three thousand crushed in an earth-quake in Italy. Of the death of Nobel laureates in their labora-tories. And of murderers in the electric chair. We partake of the "survivor's news," reinforcing the idea that "everyone dies but me." Sitting there, reading of the death of others, reassures us of our survivorship, of our immortality. The misfortune of others makes up a large percentage of the front page, creating the illu-sion of our good fortune. Seldom do we use the news of another's death as a recognition of the impermanence of all things, that all changes as it will.

And yet the acknowledgment of impermanence holds within it the key to life itself. The confrontation with death tunes us deeply to the life we imagine we will lose with the extinction of the body. But what is the truth of this sense of presence we experience, of timeless being, which seems to have no beginning, in which we sense no end? We imagine we will die only because we believe we were born. We don't trust that sense of endlessness, of edge-lessness within.

Our suffering is caused by holding to how things might have been, should have been, could have been. Grief is part of our daily existence. But we seldom recognize that pain in our heart that one fellow called "a deep weeping, a mourning for everything we have left behind."

A friend, reflecting on the time her cancer had been diagnosed as terminal, said, "Being terminal just meant that at last I ac-knowledged that death was real. It did not mean that I would die in six months or even die before the doctor who had just given me the prognosis. It simply meant that I acknowledged that I would die at all." In a society based on material gain, which imagines itself to be the body, which holds health so precious and fears death so much, it is often hard to understand that death is natural, even necessary for the continuance of life, both inner and outer.

In the Egyptian *Book of the Dead,* there are long narratives that tell about the spirit of the deceased descending into the underworld where it is met by the Great Judge who weighs the heart against a feather. It is the feather of truth. And one wonders whose heart is light enough to be measured against the truth.

Seventy-five per cent of the population take their last breath in a convalescent home or hospital. Most die in institutions where death is considered the enemy. I have seen many approach death in physical and spiritual isolation, seldom encouraged to open past their imaginings and fears, cut off in heart and mind from the loved ones who might share this precious moment. Unable to trust their inner nature, removed from life itself, they enter with painful insecurity and confusion into another realm of being.

I have watched many cling desperately to a rapidly degenerating body, hoping for some incredible miracle, anguished by a deep longing for fulfillment never found in life. I have also met those whose death was an inspiration to all about them. Who died with so much love and compassion that all were left filled with an unnamed joy for weeks afterward.

Few participate in their life so fully that death is not a threat, is not the grim reaper stalking just beyond the dark windowpane. Most fight death as they fought life, struggling for a foothold, for some control over the incessant flow of change that exemplifies this plane of existence. Few die in wholeness. Most live a life of partiality and confusion. Most think they own the body. Few recognize it as just a temporarily rented domicile from which they must eventually be evicted. Those who see themselves as passengers in the body are more able to let go lightly.

In this culture we look at life as though it were a straight line. The longer the line the more we imagine we have lived, the wholer we suppose ourselves to be, and the less horrendous we imagine the end point. The death of the young is seen as tragic and shakes the faith of many. But in the American Indian culture one is not seen linearly but rather as a circle which becomes complete at about puberty with the rites of passage. From that time on one is seen as a wholeness that continues to expand outward. But once "the hoop" has formed, any time one dies, one dies in wholeness. As the American Indian sage Crazy Horse commented, "Today is a good day to die for all the things of my life are present." In the American Indian wisdom wholeness is not seen as the duration one has lived but rather the fullness with which one enters each complete moment.

Unlike our culture which encourages little preparation for death, in the American Indian culture at the time of death a naturally formed crystal is often offered for use as a meditation object. Gazing into the fissures within the crystal that create prismatic rainbow lines, one projects one's consciousness into the rainbow, letting go of all that keeps the mind from focusing beyond itself. At death one is guided into the rainbow body, melting out of temporal form with ease and wise preparation.

There seems to be much less suffering for those who live life in the wholeness that includes death. Not a morbid preoccupation with death but rather a staying in the loving present, a life that focuses on each precious moment. I see few whose participation in life has prepared them for death. Few who have explored their heart and mind as perfect preparation for whatever might come next be it death or sickness, grief or joy.

Who is prepared to die? Who has lived so fully that they are not threatened by their imaginings of nonexistence? For it is only the idea of death that frightens us. It is the unknown we pull back from.

How often are we like the battered child on the front page of the Los Angeles *Times,* being carried gently from the room by the compassionate matron, who reaches out over the matron's shoulder shouting, "Mama, Mama," to the woman in custody between the policemen on the other side of the room, arrested for burning the flesh and breaking the bones of this child? How many reach back for the hellishness of the known rather than opening into the unknown, with the patience and warmth that make room in our heart for ourselves and all others?

In some societies, death brings the whole tribe or family together in celebration and acknowledgment of the continual changing nature of life. During these celebrations, often a deeply spiritual context for this passing allows many to have profound experiences of their own true nature. For these societies, death is a continual opportunity to let go of the illusions of life, to see it as it is, and open in love to all about.

In Hebrew culture, as in East Indian society, the body is most often disposed of within twenty-four hours. In the Orthodox Hebrew tradition, one sits shiva for a week, mourning the loss with lamentations and prayers, yet respecting the passage of the other, wishing that being well in whatever newness may approach it. In India the corpse is carried on a litter by the family to the burning ground. On the first part of the journey, chanting *"Ram Nam Satya Hey"* (The Name of God is Truth), the family carries the deceased with its head still pointing toward the home it has just departed. Halfway to the funeral grounds, the litter is turned about so that the head no longer faces the life just left, but instead approaches what is to come. At the burning ground, with the family all around, the body is placed on a large stack of wood and covered with flowers and incense and set ablaze. If the deceased is the father of the family, as the bones disintegrate, as the body begins to fall apart, the eldest son stirs the burning bones with a large staff, and, if necessary, with a stout whack, caves in the top of his father's skull so that his spirit may be released in joy to whatever realms await.

In Mexico, in November, there is celebrated *"La Día de la Muerte,"* the Day of the Dead. Children buy paper skeletons and insert firecrackers to blow them apart, or eat candy skulls as the parents go to celebrate the nature of change picnicking in the cemeteries that adjoin each small town.

I've been with those whose death has brought them fully into life and strengthened their confidence in something sensed to be ongoing and untouched by the demise of the body. I have seen those whose lives have been fearful come to the moment of death with a new openness that allowed them a sense of completion they had seldom known.

I have been with people at the time of their death whose pain and fear had so closed them that they could not say good-by to those they loved most. So much business was left unfinished that all about were bereft of the contact they so desired.

I have also seen those who cried out, "God, not me!" when they received a terminal prognosis, after a few months of deep investigation, quietly close their eyes and whisper, "Sweet Jesus" as they died.

2
GETTING BORN

When we think of our death, we imagine ourselves surrounded by loving friends, the room filled with a serene quietude that comes from nothing more to say, all business finished; our eyes shining with love and with a whisper of profound wisdom as to the transiency of life, we settle back into the pillow, the last breath escaping like a vast "Ahh!" as we depart gently into the light.

But what if just as you are about to "Ahh!" out of the body, your mate turns to you and confesses they have been having an affair with your best friend? Or your angry child comes bursting into the room saying, "You've always been a jerk, why don't you stop playing your games!"? Would your heart slam shut like a stone door, would your mind whirl with confusion and self-doubt, would you need to say something in return to try to defend yourself, would you contract in painful agreement?

How can we die in wholeness when we have lived our lives in such partiality? When we have lived our lives so much in the mind's precious idea of itself, how can we die with our hearts wide open to the mystery of it all? Where will we take refuge?

Where will the confidence in the perfection of the moment come from when we have so often pulled back from what we feared?

It is difficult to think of dying consciously when we notice how incomplete we feel, how frightened we are of life. It is almost as though we were never completely born, so much of ourselves is suppressed and compacted just beneath the surface. So much of ourselves postponed. So little have we investigated what has caused us to retract in pain from our lives. So often our inquiries into who we are have been "called on account of rain" because it was too painful to go deeper.

We speak of dying in wholeness yet we see there are aspects of ourselves that have never fully seen the light of day. We see how much of ourselves is submerged, feels yet unborn, how much we push away life. It is as though we had never fully touched the ground of being. Never placed our two feet squarely in the present. Always shuffling and toe tapping, waiting for the next moment to arrive.

If we examine our fear of death we see in it a fear of the moment to follow, over which we have no control. In it is a fear of impermanence itself, of the next unknown changing moment of life.

To become wholly born, whole beings, we must stop postponing life. To the degree we postpone life, we postpone death. We deny death and life in one fell swoop.

There is so much of ourselves we wish not to experience. So much fear, guilt, anger, confusion, and self-pity. So much self-doubt, so many weak excuses. Is it any wonder, considering the bizarre insistence of our conditioning—the conflict of one value system with another in the mind—that we feel so incomplete. One moment the mind is saying, "Take a big piece," and then the next it says, "I wouldn't have done that if I were you." No wonder we are all crazy, so fractured, trying to protect ourselves from who we fear we are. We dare not share our minds with anyone, even ourselves. We are so frightened of who we might be, of not being loved or lovable for the convolutions of our thoughts.

But states of mind, though uninvited, are constantly coming and going, and some we wish would never come again. They do, and we find ourselves scrambling for leverage to keep our fear down, experiencing the nausea of our immense insecurity and self-loathing.

This persistent elimination from awareness of unwanted states of mind leaves us constantly feeling threatened as we look and say regretfully, "That can't be me, that fear isn't really who I am. Anger isn't me. That self-hatred, that guilt, can't be who I am." But there it is. And you wonder who you really are. How do you open to that which you deny? That which you think somehow shouldn't be there even though it is?

We wish we were otherwise and that is our hell, our resistance to life.

Coming to the end of our life, we look at our participation in the past and wonder how we can die fully when our life has been lived in such partialness. We wonder who, beyond all our self-projections, it really is that dies.

It is almost as though we have become a fractured image of our original being. Our experience with the world has become like looking into a mirror that a great stone has fallen on and shattered into hundreds of pieces, broken from a single unified reality into some splintered reflection of what is seen, of what is imagined to exist. As we look at this fractured reality, we notice with dismay certain parts of the reflection are not what we wish to see or want to be seen. "I don't want anyone to see my lust; that's not such a good thing to have. I'm not supposed to be like that. No one's mind is as crazy as mine." So we take a piece out. "Oh, there I am really sorry for myself. If they only knew what my life had been like! Ah, but they don't." And that piece is removed as well. You notice your greed and self-interest, the sexual fantasies, the competition and confusion of the mind. And you start picking these pieces out. Because these are unacceptable parts of who you think you are supposed to be.

But I think it is very useful, and indeed more accurate, to call it *"the* mind" instead of *"my* mind."

Because when you call it "my mind," you start removing so many pieces that when you look down at this fractured mirror it reflects back very little of what is real. It only displays those qualities you wish to project as being who you are, eliminating all the rest, eluding your wholeness. We think we have something to hide. Yet this self-protection is our imprisonment. Imagine if for the next twenty-four hours you had to wear a cap that amplified your thoughts so that everyone within a hundred yards of you could hear every thought that passed through your head. Imagine if the mind were broadcast so that all about you could overhear "your" thoughts and fantasies, "your" dreams and fears. How embarrassed or fearful would you be to go outside? How long would you let your fear of the mind continue to isolate you from the hearts of others? And though this experiment sounds like one which few might care to participate in, imagine how freeing it would be at last to have nothing to hide. And how miraculous it would be to see that all others' minds too were filled with the same confusion and fantasies, the same insecurity and doubt. How long would it take the judgmental mind to begin to release its grasp, to see through the illusion of separateness, to recognize with some humor the craziness of all beings' minds, the craziness of mind itself?

To be whole we must deny nothing.

We think we have something to lose, and the reinforcement of that feeling that there is something to protect cuts us off from life, leaves us a fractured reality through which we attempt to express our naturalness. But life becomes confusing when we eliminate the truth. And we wonder, how do I live my life or die my death with room for the whole being, no matter what is arising in the mind. Because we see that when we wish not to experience certain qualities in ourselves, our heart closes whenever these qualities arise.

We wonder, how can I keep my heart open when what I am experiencing isn't pleasant, when I see my self-interest, my fear, guilt, my doubt? When the predominant state of mind is confusion, can I still stay open to the moment? Or do I have to escape elsewhere? We show so little mercy to ourselves. We barricade the heart and feel alone in a hostile world. We seldom let go of our judgment and make room in our heart for ourselves. How can we so lack compassion for this being we feel suffering in our heart? If, without self-pity, we fully acknowledge our pain, it would be difficult not to be swept with a care and compassion for our own well-being. The very nature of having to pull away from what is, of having to be someone else, makes life hellish. It is a resistance. And we live a great deal of our life in hell.

Anger arises in the mind and we become confused. "If I'm a spiritual person, I shouldn't have anger. I guess I'm not so spiritual after all. I mustn't show this anger." But anger is the truth of that moment, and if we push it away, if we pretend that it's not there, we've lost another opportunity for freedom, another reflection on who we really are and who we really aren't. Because we don't know what anger is, though we may have experienced it thousands of times. Just as we don't know what fear is, or doubt is—because each time they arise, instead of using this mental state as an opportunity for investigation, it becomes an emergency, a threat to our self-image. Very seldom, as we're walking down the road, if something arises which threatens us, do we go straight into it. Instead we attempt to dodge to the right or to the left, to elude the next moment, to escape. We wish to rush away to the safety of a false reality, a fractured being, in which we somehow feel safe. We are constantly attempting to escape from the truth. We are frightened of the open space of investigation, frightened of becoming vulnerable to the truth of the moment, open to what is. We want to capture the world, to control reality and turn it into some image of ourselves.

It's that very attempt at control that is at the root of much of our suffering. Attempting to re-create the pleasures of the past, to barricade the future from the pains of unfulfilled yearnings. But events are, in a very real way, beyond our control. They are this way one minute, and another way the next. And sometimes the truth is that there is anger or fear or greed, that there is lust or ignorance in the mind. All of which is O.K., because these too are opportunities for seeing deeper, for going beyond the identification with these states as being all we are.

But if it isn't O.K. that these states arise, there you are pulling back from the present, acting your life instead of opening to it—in a conspiracy to deny the truth with each person you meet. Pretending that both of you have your feet planted solidly on the ground, neither admitting the groundlessness of the other. It is the social game. Because it's not polite to admit that both of you are hiding the truth of your being. In the same way that it is not polite to be angry or frightened. In the same way that we fear we will not be loved if others knew how our mind worked, if we were real.

Anger is a good example of how we hide our experience from ourselves. For many people, anger is a very unacceptable phenomenon on the one hand, and a very compulsive way of acting on the other. But when anger stimulates investigation, it becomes a meditation on life rather than a distraction from it—then the escape syndrome, the resistance to life, becomes recognizable and we start to come out of hiding. We start to emerge into the light.

The mind compares itself with images of Buddha or Jesus, with saints and selfless beings of which we have read. And the mind finds itself wanting in the balance. The mind condemns itself for being what it is, though it fears letting go into the spacious freedom that would release it from its bondage. Like the battered child carried gently from its mother, its tormentor, the mind cries out in pain for what it is leaving, fearful of what is yet to come. To the mind, even hell is acceptable and preferable to the unknown.

We berate ourselves for the contents of the mind, for the anger and doubt, for the fear and loathing. And it is this very act of judgment that continues the judgment of the mind, that causes us to feel separate from ourselves and all else. It is constantly rating us on our behavior and participation, and seldom disappears long enough for us to merge with our experience, to become one with life.

I have met several very clear beings, yet I don't believe I've met anyone who is completely without anger. To be without anger means we have no desires, no models of how things should or must be. No desires means no frustration. No frustration, no anger. (And yet this, too, is a model which if we hold to can lead to frustration and confusion.) If the mind doesn't cling to anything being any way at all, then there's no anger. Our anger is a kind of spontaneous combustion that occurs when our idea of things becomes cramped by reality.

Our models, our ideas of who we are and how the world is supposed to be, create a cage. Each concept becomes a bar that blocks the reception of the truth. Each idea of how things are limits our ability to experience them as they really may be. We can't go beyond our idea of the world to actually touch the world. When we move beyond our models and ideas, we feel threatened and defensive. Confronting some reality which opposes our self-image, our sureness confuses and upsets us. We don't know who we are because we think of ourselves as our ideas and old models. The world is constantly confronting us with the truth. We are constantly withdrawing. Our experience is pain.

Confronted with a reality which does not confirm our image of how things are, we begin to panic. We look for someplace to hide. Often I am with people who are dying while still attempting to conceal themselves. Indeed, I suspect many beings die in hiding. They are still relating to death and life as though it were outside of them. Just as they relate to anger and fear and their difficulty with others as though it were coming from outside, as though they were a victim of their feelings and their thoughts, rather than the space in which all this mind-stuff is unfolding. We choose to trade off reality for the safety of our cage. No matter how small. No matter how painfully we have withdrawn from life.

Our fear of death is directly equatable to our fear of life. When we think of dying we think of losing something called "me." We wish to protect this thing at all costs though we have very little direct experience of what this "I" refers to other than as some idea which seems constantly to be changing. In death, we fear we will lose our "I," our "me-ness." And we notice that the stronger this idea of "I," the more distinct is the feeling of a separation from life and a fear of death. The more we attempt to protect this idea of "I," the less we experience anything beyond that concept. The more we have invested in protecting something of "me," the more we have to lose and the less we open to a deeper perception of what dies, of what really exists. The more we hide or posture or postpone life, the more we fear death.

Protecting this precious "I" we push life away, and wonder at its meaninglessness.

Until we have nothing to hide, we cannot be free. If we are still considering the contents of the mind as the enemy, we become frightened, thinking we have something especially wrong with us.

Not recognizing the mind as just the result of previous conditioning, nothing special. That all these states of mind which we fear so much can actually be mulched back into ourselves to become fertilizer, the manure for further growth. Which means that in order to allow these materials to compost, to become rich fertilizers for growth, we must begin to make room in our hearts for ourselves. We must begin to cultivate the compassion that allows the moment to be as it is, in the clear light of awareness, without the least postponement of the truth.

Indeed, we often relate to ourselves as a puzzle from which many pieces have been removed. We gaze at a very distorted and confusing image we have constructed and are bewildered. We look at this puzzle of ourselves and notice only the fractures, only the surface mind of separation and partiality, and wonder, "Who is this really that I am?" When we focus and identify with our fracturedness, we become afraid of ourselves. But as we allow ourselves to penetrate deeper, working to acknowledge these things, to let go of our partialness and hiding, the fractures no longer obscure the whole picture. It is like going beneath the surface of a wind-torn sea, to the stillness that is untouched by surface conditions.

And we begin to penetrate the surface commotion and find that guilt and fear and anger, and all the mental smorgasbord that has been stashed there, are nothing to be afraid of. We imagine that these things we have suppressed are who we really are. But by starting to acknowledge these qualities, to bring them into awareness, to open to them with some compassion for this human condition we find ourselves in, allows us to go deeper to what underlies this seemingly solid reality. As long as we are pushing parts of ourselves away, we cannot go deeper. "Self-knowledge is bad news," as a frightened friend put it. Or as one Tibetan teacher said of the penetration of this layer of suppressed material, "It is just one insult after another." Most people are afraid of confronting all the stuff they have pushed down because they still think of it as being who they are. We are frightened of all the forbidden mind states that we have pushed below the surface of awareness to protect our self-image.

Yet we see that we must suppress nothing. In suppression we

push below awareness what we imagine is unacceptable. In this very act of suppression we enslave ourselves. We have postponed life once again. Nothing can be free of its prison of darkness until it has been brought out into the light of awareness. Suppression pushes things out of awareness where they become inaccessible. Tendencies that motivate us are still present but we no longer have access to them because they have been forced below the level of awareness. So each feeling must be acknowledged in its turn, allowed to exist without judgment or fear in clear awareness where it may be seen for what it is, an impermanent, oddly impersonal state of mind passing through. We imagine that we are caught in some unworkable situation, that life is a punishment instead of a gift.

Each time we identify with anger as "I," or with doubt or guilt as being who we really are, we suppress that state of mind and can go no deeper. Whenever you call anything "I," that's where you stop. That's the depth of penetration. That's where you get off the elevator. But if you stay open to anger, and let anger be there, you go deeper. You begin to experience the space in which these things arise and into which they dissolve. You begin to experience the space anger is floating in. That moment is not a moment of anger, but a moment of clear awareness. And then you stop identifying with yourself as anger. You are observing anger, but not becoming lost in it.

We begin to stop thinking of these different qualities of mind as being "I" and start to open to the space, the wholeness, within which the events are occurring: a nonjudging, exquisitely merciful space that we have access to in the heart, that doesn't cling or condemn any object of the mind. This space is the essence of mind itself. It doesn't call itself Susan or Fred or Ondrea or "I." It just is. It is the space of is-ness itself. It is the root of that which we refer to when we say "I am." It is the awareness that we mistakenly call "I."

We have gotten so used to looking outside of ourselves that we have forgotten to ask who it is that's looking.

We participate in our natural spaciousness so seldom that we have come to believe we are whatever arises in the mind. When our confusion arises in the mind, we contract into an incomplete puzzle of things. We lose our natural spaciousness. When we think of dying, we think of losing who we are. We think we will no longer be able to be this or that which we imagine ourselves to be. Yet if we pay close attention, we notice that whenever we say, "I am this," or "I am that," there is to some degree a feeling of being an impostor. That whenever the "I am" of just being is attached to this or that in the world, there is a feeling of falsity, of incompleteness, of somehow not quite telling the whole truth. When I say "I am happy" or "I am sad," "I am smart" or "I am fair," we see that all the things we attach to this "I am" are constantly in change; that one moment we are happy, and then the next we are proud, and in the next judgmental of that pride, and in the next confused, and then once again, remembering and coming back to the "I am," and then again lost in the this's and that's which we so often attach this "I am" of pure being to. "I am this" or "I am that" somehow feels untrue. Because there is nothing within this universe of change that I can call myself for very long, nothing I can say I am that is the whole truth. In fact, much of the time we feel like we are pretending to be someone else simply by pretending to be anything at all. But we notice that when we simply say "I am" that there is just space, just being; that this "I" does not refer to something separate, to something outside of ourselves, or even to the body or the mind. It is just a sense of presence, of being. When you say "I am" and when I say "I am," we are referring to the same being. We are referring to being itself. Everybody's "I" is the same "I." It only becomes separate, and a religious war, when we attach a this or that to it. When you say "I am this," the universality of being is lost. When you say "I am this joy or this fear or this mind or this body," the truth is shattered like the rock hitting the mirror. The One is broken into the many.

We are constantly trying to become someone or something. "I am this" conveys the idea that I am not that. But if there is envy in the mind, or fear or guilt, how do you incorporate these qualities into your self-image? Or can you just let go of that imagined self long enough to open to the contents of the moment, no matter what they are? How can you open and go beyond what Zorba the Greek calls "the whole catastrophe"? For it's only a catastrophe if there's something to elude. How, when jealousy or envy comes up, instead of closing the heart, can you begin investigating that denseness in the mind, seeing how isolating such heavy emotion can be and how quickly these states of mind attract the idea of "I"? How seldom we go beyond the emotions, thinking we must either express them or suppress them, never sensing that we are the spaciousness of being itself.

How, seeing the compulsive response of the mind to its contents, can you not feel compassion for that being momentarily caught in such pain? We cheat ourselves with so little compassion. We treat ourselves in ways that we would never treat another. Somehow we think it's O.K. to do it to ourselves because we've lost the sense of who we are. We've forgotten we too are the truth.

Such forgetfulness causes great pain. When we speak of our grief, that is much of what we are referring to. The loss of touch with our original nature. We've suppressed so much, so many parts of ourselves have been found unacceptable and frightening, that when these qualities arise we squash them down and tend to feel that this tangled mass is our "hidden identity." Because these states of mind so conflict with our models, they become yet more bars in our cage. Each instance of suppression makes the cage smaller.

We are cultivating ignorance by attempting to keep awareness from touching what is deeper in our "industrial dump site."

We fear that is where our "real nature" lies because we don't see how anger or fear or jealousy can take us to the living truth. Not what I say to you, or what Krishnamurti says to you, or what Buddha says to you, or what Jesus says to you. Discover yourself. Because you are the truth. And no one can take you there except you. Buddha left a road map, Jesus left a road map, Krishna left a road map, Rand McNally left a road map. But you still have to travel the road yourself. It is like a friend of mine who approached a Zen master to request the teachings that would help free her from the superficial illusions of separateness and fear. She said, "I have come to learn the path." The Zen master, silent for a moment, pointed to her with loving ferocity and said, "You are the path!"

When you begin to recognize that you are the path, that all of life is but a reflection of the mind, then each experience becomes an opportunity to free yourself from your prison. At this point, you begin to see that life is an opportunity for wholeness, for opening to the truth. You start investigating "What closes me from this essential spaciousness of being? Who am I, really?"

There is a meditation master in Thailand by the name of Achaan Chaa, who in his early years became a monk because his priority was to try, more than anything else, to understand what it is that sits here, who it is that exists. To understand as he puts it, "just this much," just this moment of being as it unfolds. After practicing for a few years, he heard rumors about a meditation master in the northern part of Thailand who was reputed to have no anger. No anger is quite an accomplishment; think of what that means. It means a mind that clings nowhere. It means the being has tuned into their original nature to such an extent that they see no object in mind, even anger, as who they really are. They don't identify with anything that comes up as being separate from the truth.

When he heard of this great teacher, he left the monastery where he had been practicing and went to ask the teacher if he might become his student. He spent about a year and a half with this teacher, and the fellow never seemed angry. Very impressive. Then one day, out of sight of the teacher, in an L-shaped kitchen where they were both working, he looked over as a dog came into the room and jumped up on the counter to grab some tasty morsel. The meditation master looked both ways and then kicked the dog. Achaan Chaa got the teaching! Imagine the painfulness, the incredible mercilessness to pretend for any reason at all that what is present in the mind isn't there. Yet we all perpetrate this same execution on ourselves, pretending to be something we aren't, partially born, partially alive, wondering so at the heaviness of life.

To be whole, to live life fully, to die fully, we can deny nothing. I am told the American Indians had a tradition called the "Eater of Impurities": on a high holy day, like a solstice, the shaman, the wise man of the tribe, would sit with each member of the tribe individually and suggest something like, "Bring into your mind some thought, some feeling that you have that you wish no one else to know; some idea or fantasy, something you feel is aberrant or abhorrent; that you feel you must suppress and hide away." Often that person would be so frightened that he would hardly be able to allow that thought to arise in his mind for fear that it might somehow leak out his ears and be heard. That someone would overhear the fearful content of his mind. But the shaman encouraged the individual to see how frightened he was of exposing himself, of being vulnerable, of approaching wholeness. And he would say, after some time, "Now, give me that thought." And the thought or image would be brought out and shared between them. And the darkness in which it was held would be dispelled in the light of the trust and compassion of the moment. And each, once again, saw how little there was to protect, how much room the heart has for all the mind's meanderings. As one teacher put it, "The mind creates the abyss; the heart crosses it."

It might be useful to sit down with the following exercise and investigate the mind and heart which closes.

Letting the Mind Float in the Heart

[This is a guided meditation which can be read slowly to a friend or repeated silently to oneself.]

Bring some unacceptable thought into your mind. Some thought you wish no one else knew you had.

Just let it be there.

But let it be there with compassion.

Feel how the mind constricts around that thought, how it wishes to squeeze it out of existence. See how frightened the mind is of itself. Feel the texture of the fear. See how we live our life before a mirror.

Now take that thought and, instead of surrounding it with denial and tension, allow it to float free in the mind. Just let it be there.

Allow that thought to be experienced as a sensation in the mind.

Feel its denseness, its sharp edges.

Now, begin to allow that thought to sink into the heart. Bring that sensation down through the throat and into your body. Let it settle into the heart-space in the center of your chest. Let the thought just think itself there, in the spaciousness where there is room for everything and judgment of nothing.

Whether it is the thought of masturbation, homosexuality, violence, fear, dishonesty. Whatever thought you fear is totally unacceptable in the mind, allow it to sink gently into the extraordinary openness of the heart, where it is welcomed in warmth and patience.

The natural spaciousness of the heart excludes nothing. It experiences each thought compassionately as just another movement in the mind, just another feeling.

Experience that now, floating in this soft compassion. See how fear is like a prison in the mind. Come out into the warmth and love of your essential nature.

What is there to fear?

What is worth the imprisonment of self-protection?

● ● ●

We think we are our thoughts. We call our thoughts "I." In letting go of thought, we go beyond ourselves, beyond who we imagine we are. Behind the restless movement of the mind is the stillness of being, the stillness that has no name, no reputation, nothing to protect. It is the natural mind.

Focusing attention on the sensations in the heart center, we notice each flicker of the mind's contractions, the momentary stagnation we think of so much as "I." Each contraction in mind, each feeling and thought is felt like a shadow crossing the heart; each time mind draws attention to itself it reminds us to let go lightly of what obstructs our connectedness with our underlying nature. Then each previously threatening state of mind, so often thought of as the enemy, becomes an ally. Each fluctuation of the heart reminds us to let go gently into yet a deeper level of being. When the mind becomes full with itself, its denseness is so obvious it causes us to recall the freedom glowing in the heart and we open into it. Then the heavier the emotion, the more intense the self-interest and confusion, the more these states become teachings which remind us that we are not these painful densities (painful because we fear and resist them, dense because they coagulate the flow), that we are rather the light that shines beyond.

Even the thinnest sheet of tinfoil held before your eyes can block the warmth and light of the immensity of the sun.

In the Sufi tradition, there is a saying, "Overcome any bitterness that may have come because you were not up to the magnitude of the pain that was entrusted to you. Like the mother of the world, who carries the pain of the world in her heart, each of us is part of her heart and therefore endowed with a certain measure of cosmic pain. You are sharing in the totality of that pain. You are called upon to meet it in joy, instead of self-pity. The secret: offer your heart as a vehicle to transform cosmic suffering into joy."

We have pushed so much of our life away, held it captive so deep within us that when we begin to let go we notice how much our expectations, concepts, and preconceptions have limited our experience. As the self-protection of the mind is no longer encouraged, we begin to see all that we have suppressed come into consciousness once again. All these old holdings rise once again into awareness. But the priority has changed. We are no longer trying to create "someone or something of value" out of this constant changing flow of mind. We are instead attempting to investigate the truth. In this investigation, no state of mind is preferable to any other. Only the clarity of seeing is of importance. It is not what is seen so much as how clearly it is perceived. Then the investigation becomes what is the truth, who am I really, what is it that I call "I," what dies? Am I these thoughts? Am I this mind? Am I this body?

The more we allow of the mind to exist within clarity and compassion, the less we are tempted to call any fleeting moment "I." The less we are lost in identification with the superficiality of "I am this or that." The more we experience just consciousness itself, no longer so distraught with its contents or clinging desperately to its joys. We experience just the spacious stillness of being, without any need to define *who* it is that is being. Or perhaps, more accurately, *what* is being. Though the mind may scramble for a dozen definitions and limitations, the experience itself is limitless. And the small mind is seen floating within the vastness.

Then one day there comes a moment when you're angry and all

of a sudden you recognize anger. And you open to it in investigation: "What is it to be angry? How does it feel in my body? What does my mind do?" And settling back into a chair, closing our eyes, we begin to move toward that which blocks the heart, instead of pulling away from it and allowing it to mechanically close us to a fuller experience of the present. Examining anger or fear or guilt or doubt, we begin to see the impersonality of what seemed so much "I." We see that the mind has a mind of its own. That anger and fear and all these states of mind have their own personality, their own momentum. And we notice that it is not "I" that wishes to do harm to another but that the state of mind we call anger is by its nature aggressive and often wishes to insult or humiliate its object. We watch the fantasized conversations and arguments of the mind, the shadow-boxing that has so often left us breathless and alone and at last we begin to relinquish our suffering.

Then we begin not to cling to states of mind that barricade the wisdom of the heart. Once again love and trust open between beings. Then all which previously kept us isolated in mind—our doubt and anger and fear acting like watchdogs that warned of the threatening approach of others—become reminders of the painfulness of not loving and become a means of opening to, rather than withdrawing from, life. We see how our fear of, and identification with, the ramblings of the mind has made life shallow. We begin gently letting go of all that rises into awareness. We just let the mind be without closing in judgment, and begin to recognize the ongoing process of arising and dissolution in the mind. In recognizing the impermanence of each thought, each feeling, each moment of experience, we come to see there is nothing we can hold to that will give us lasting satisfaction. There is no place we can solidly plant our feet and say, "This is who I am." It is a constantly changing flow, in which, moment to moment, who we think we are is born and dies. All that we would project ourselves as being is seen as transient and essentially empty of any abiding entity. There is no person in there, there is just process. Who we think we are is just another bubble in the stream. And the awareness which illuminates this process is seen for the light it is. We begin to give up identification with the mind as "I" and become the pure light of awareness, the namelessness of being.

The body dies, the mind is constantly changing. But somehow, behind it all there is a presence, called by some "the deathless," that is unchanging, that simply is as it is.

To become fully born is to touch this deathlessness. To experience, even for a moment, the spaciousness which goes beyond birth and death. To emerge into a world of paradox and mystery with no weapons but awareness and love.

3

"BE ALSO READY"

Remember, friends, as you pass by
as you are now, so once was I.
As I am now, so you must be.
Prepare yourself to follow me.

from a headstone
in Ashby, Massachusetts

A friend who had been meditating for some time, approached a
Zen master recently arrived in this country. He asked the roshi if
he might study with him. To which the roshi replied, "Are you
prepared to die?" My friend shook his head in bewilderment and
said, "I didn't come here to die. I came here to learn Zen." The
roshi said, "If you are not willing to die, you are not ready to
let go into life. Come back when you are ready to enter directly,
excluding nothing."

If we are not open to anything that might happen, if we are
closed to any possibility, any event whatsoever, our perceptions
narrow to a kind of tunnel vision that excludes the unacceptable.
The unacceptable being anything that does not reinforce our fantasy of our imagined self. The fantasy of some solid permanence.
We exclude quite a bit, approaching most events with a kind of
drowsy blindness.

The American Indians developed an extraordinary technique to
prepare for death. They cultivated an openness to death by using
a death chant. Upon entrance into adolescence, they undertook

the rites of passage, going out into the wilderness alone for several days of fasting and prayer, to open to the unknown and receive some guiding message for their life to come. Often they experienced a vision of wholeness from which arose spontaneously a healing or a death chant, a means of maintaining contact with the Great Spirit in time of threat or stress. Others came to their death chant from a grandfather or a dream. Or perhaps from tuning into an animal they had just killed. It was an instant centering technique to keep the heart open and the mind clear even in great adversity. When you started to fall from your horse or were confronted by a dangerous animal, or lay aching with food poisoning or burning with a fever, immediately the death chant came into the mind. It became a part of themselves, always available in a time of need. It created a familiarity with the unfamiliar, with death.

Imagine, after having sung your death chant perhaps a hundred times in various close calls, when one day you find yourself immobile in the shade of a great boulder, your body burning with snake venom and no one there to help you as the poison begins to paralyze your limbs. But you are not helpless. You've got a powerful channel, a path you can follow, each moment unto death. Having made this technique a part of their life, many Native Americans died with great clarity. Because they had practiced a technique that integrated life and death, focusing on their vision, they went beyond the known.

In the Hasidic tradition—a somewhat mystical branch of Orthodox Judaism—there is a teaching that has to do with being ready for whatever the moment might offer. It is believed that you are born for a specific event that will occur at some point in your life. But you never know when. You have to always be on your toes, so that when the test comes you will be prepared. It means an opening to a kind of not-knowing, to just being. There is nothing you can do to elude any moment but cultivate an openness to the unknown so that whatever occurs you will be fully present for it.

In that kind of not-knowing, we are always present. Because when you allow that you don't know, you become very awake.

You become like a hunter who doesn't know what's going to happen next. He's not making anything happen. He is just stillness in the midst of activity. He is an open space through which anything can move. He is no longer a noun. He's become a verb. He's the act of standing.

That kind of presence for our life is the perfect preparation for death. It means being open to whatever happens, excluding nothing. Because if everything is O.K. except death, then eventually you notice that everything's O.K. but death and loss. And then everything's O.K. but death and loss and a bad pastrami sandwich. Then everything's O.K. but death, loss, a bad pastrami sandwich, and the plumber coming. The limiting of what is acceptable narrows down the cage of self-protection in which we fitfully live so much of our life. Until "security" means nobody entering our cage. We are isolated. Nobody is rattling our bars.

In the Hindu tradition, there is another instance of this kind of presence for life/death. It is taught and practiced that to die with God's name on your lips is a way of consciously returning to the source. In an instant, you can drop the mind's projections of the world and just be with it as it is. When Mahatma Gandhi was assassinated, he walked out into the garden early one evening and a fellow came up to him and shot him through the heart. As he fell, he said, "Ram." Ram is one of the names of God in the Hindu tradition. Millions of Hindus focus their life on God so they may be able to die with his name filling their heart and mind. Just as I have been with those who whispered "Sweet Mother of Heaven" as they died. Their death was a soft passage into the light. How many people are so connected to some essential part of themselves that even death could not distract them? That's something you don't wait until death to find out. That's something you cultivate right now. There's no other moment to begin preparing for death.

It might be noted here that the word "God" is not equally useful to all. I use "God" out of exasperation for a way to denote the whole of things, the underlying reality. Nature or Tao, or Dharma, or just truth would equally suffice yet remain insufficient for the indescribable. For many "Jesus" is not the historic personage so much as a term to describe the perfected heart; "Buddha" not the prince of ancient India but the nature of the translucent mind.

Occasionally I hear people say, "Oh, don't worry, when the time comes, I'll do the proper meditations." Good luck! Because when it comes time, the energies you have now may very well not be present. It may be difficult for the mind to concentrate. Fear may close the heart. Imagine trying to meditate with two huge hi-fi speakers blasting cacophonous music on either side of you. Though it's a rather oversimplified analogy, it gives some idea of how disquieting extreme pain and the fear of dying might be at that moment.

If you should die in extreme pain, how will you have prepared to keep your mind soft and open? To be with whatever the moment offers? What have you done to keep your mind present, so that you don't block precious opportunity with a concept, with some idea of what's happening? Open to experience the suchness, the living truth, of the next unknown moment.

Your bank account and reputation do not prepare you for death any more than your wardrobe or your cleverness does. What are you doing in life that prepares you for death?

Whatever prepares you for death enhances life. Gandhi's closeness to God, the death chant, the Hasidic openness to the unknown all make life a richer, more joyous experience.

Glen Mullins writes of a Tibetan monk who, sensing that death was approaching, asked the Dalai Lama for guidance. The Dalai Lama wrote, "When comes the time to carry the load of life through death's door, one can take neither relatives, friends, servants, nor possessions. Attached mind is animal mind. Abandon attachment.

"No matter how intense the pleasure one may gain on the peaks of illusion, again shall one fall to suffering, spinning on the wheel of unknowing, no shelter. Abandon grasping.

"The limitless beings around us, parents who kindly nurtured us, are creatures seeking only happiness. Abandon the unkind mind.

"All that appears to the senses in ultimate nature is empty. Yet, in fallacious and illusory images, we continue to grasp for truth. Abandon self-imprisonment.

"When death's moment falls, withdraw the mind from distortion, fear, and superstition. Avoid illusory hopes and fears . . . after the subtle energies of the body have gradually dissolved, the subtle mind of death arises. Transform it into the essence of the path of clear light and abide there unwaveringly."

To sense how difficult it might be to "abide there unwaveringly," notice even with a healthy mind and energy how often it is difficult to stay present, how readily the latent tendencies toward judgment or fear sweep the mind away in a torrent of agitation and attempted control.

How much more distracting would it be if your pancreas were pulsating with pain? Or if bone cancer had made it impossible to find any comfortable position? Lying there in a bed of hot embers.

How difficult might it be to stay with the death chant or with feelings of love and acceptance in the midst of considerable discomfort and the surrounding confusion of loved ones?

I've been with many people as they have approached their death and seen how much clarity and openheartedness it takes to stay soft with the distraction in the mind and body. To stay with the fear that arises uninvited. To keep so open that when fear comes up, they can say, "Yes, that's fear all right." But the spacious acknowledgment is unafraid, because the separate "I" is not the predominant experience, there's little for that fear to stick to.

Clearly, a practice that would be useful is to cultivate an openness to what is unpleasant, to acknowledge resistance and fear, to soften and open around it, to let it float free, to let it go. If you wrote down a list of your resistances and holdings, it would nearly be a sketch of your personality. If you identify with that personality as who you are, you amplify the fear of death: the imagined loss of imagined individuality.

If you made a list of everything you own, everything you think of as you, everything you prefer, that list would be the distance between you and the living truth. Because these are the places where you'll cling. You'll focus there instead of looking beyond.

Instead of seeing the context in which you are happening, you will grasp onto the happening as the only reality. It is the essence of shortsightedness. It is the tendency that keeps us caught in our melodrama, the holding that makes it so difficult to let go of our suffering.

Buddha said that fortune changes like the swish of a horse's tail. Tomorrow could be the first day of thirty years of quadriplegia. What preparations have you made to open to an inner life so full that whatever happens can be used as a means of enriching your focus? It's an ongoing process of opening to life. The more you open to life, the less death becomes the enemy. When you start using death as a means of focusing on life, then everything becomes just as it is, just this moment, an extraordinary opportunity to be really alive.

Then the investigation becomes "Who is dying?" And the first thing you answer is, "It is I that am dying." Then it becomes, "Well, if it is 'I' that am dying, what is this 'I'?" You wonder at the condition by which this "I" does not seem fully to refer to any of the mind's images, to any sound or any taste of any of the senses. And you ask, "Am I just this impermanent flow of minute impressions? But I have a name, a face, a reputation." Then you see that "I have a name" is just another momentary thought, a bubble that passes through the vastness of mind. And a moment later the mind is thinking about something else. You notice "I" is only an idea. Where is this "I" when it is not being thought about?

Indeed, what's interesting when you watch thoughts is to see that all thoughts are old. Perception is based on memory. Take away memory, your collection box of concepts and symbolism coded to represent reality, and when you walk down a path, there is just walking. And when you look, there is just seeing. You feel what you feel. You don't experience everything secondhand. You experience the thing itself, without some afterthought casting a shadow of "someone" walking, seeing, experiencing.

If you walked into a room and all of a sudden your memory dissolved, you would experience "a new loveliness" in each previously familiar object. You would be seeing with fresh eyes a glistening reality. Your familiarity gone, knowing nothing, all would have a new life. In each moment, you would see the miraculous.

It is our "familiarity" with things that keeps us from seeing the things themselves. Instead we project a concept of what they are. When awareness is focused in the present we experience the suchness of each thing as we meet it. We see a tree and don't experience "tree," but a living, vibrating reality, unfiltered by concept and past preference. We meet each thing without an image of that thing to diminish its reality. And then we begin to see how little of life is actually experienced. How we meet death as life with an image that keeps us at arm's length from touching its reality.

Some years ago I managed an animal sanctuary in southern Arizona, an extraordinary migratory stopover for about 125 species of birds, the southernmost reach of some Arctic fowl and the northernmost of some South American. It was a very rich oasis, a mandala of brilliant colors and songs and flight. I came to the sanctuary knowing very little about birds, but part of my job was to show expert ornithologists about because I knew the various habitats as well as where rattlesnakes and other potentially dangerous situations might arise. Walking with experts, they would say, "Ah, look at that vermilion flycatcher" or "Ah, there's a Canadian marsh hawk." And I started noticing, walking in the woods, that I would see "vermilion flycatcher" instead of the crimson, living reality. "Marsh hawk" instead of the truth. I realized that the way the mind had of turning each thing into itself, of naming it, killed the clarity of just being with each new meeting. How the mind pushed away the scintillating suchness of things.

It is this tendency of the conditioned mind to turn reality into ideas and images that keeps us from meeting life head on. We trade off reality for the shadows it casts.

So we see that whatever we say or think about death, we really don't know. The idea that you pass out of the body and the Great Ice Cream Cone in the Sky is waiting for you is still just an idea. Whether it is the truth or not is inconsequential at that point, because whatever it is, it is still just an idea. If we substitute concepts for the living truth of the moment, we live in shadow and confusion. Even an idea such as "the body dies and consciousness continues" is still just another bubble floating in the mind. But if our experience is of our ideas of things, rather than the things themselves, how are we to stay open to a reality that turns out to be quite different from what we imagined? What happens when life conflicts with what we are absolutely certain is "real"? Because of this difficulty in keeping the mind and heart open when something conflicts with an idea of what it is supposed to be, we see less of the miraculous in life. Because it was "impossible," its perception will quickly be rationalized and discarded as unreal.

How can you stay open to the impossible? What if you die and Jesus is standing there saying, "I'm an atheist"? What do you do when it isn't the way you imagined? Expectation. If you are reading this expecting to come away with some quick-cook recipe for how to live or die, then all the suggestions that the only work we have to do is on ourselves will seem beside the point.

If you go to a restaurant that you believe has the best Chinese food in town and it turns out to be a German restaurant, you may well be thinking your food instead of tasting it. Because expectation increases tunnel vision. You can see only between those few bars in your cage where you are focusing. How can you stay open to "Ah, sauerbraten!"

In a way, it seems strange that we are so unprepared for death, considering how many opportunities we have to open to what is unexpected or even disagreeable. Each time we don't feel well, each time we have the flu or a kidney stone or a pain and stiffness in the back, we have the opportunity to see that sooner or later some pain or illness is going to arise that won't diminish but will increase until it displaces us from the body. We can use each such situation as an extraordinary opportunity to practice the death chant, to practice Gandhi's closeness with God. We are reminded again and again of the process we are. Continually opportunities arise to practice letting go of this solidness, to tune to the ongoing process, to sense the spaciousness in which it's all unfolding.

Why wait until the pain is too great to focus the mind? Why not use each moment of sickness, each flu, each cold, each slight injury, as a reminder to let go, to open to the intensity arising?

When pain or sickness arises I see there is the option to open to it, not holding or pushing it away, not blocking it, not intensifying it. When I open to it as a teacher it no longer reinforces identification with "the sufferer," "the victim of circumstances." It's just what is. And as I try to open to it, I see how it is a perfect preparation for whatever might come next, a deeper letting go. It shows me how I hold to any expectation that life has to be any way at all. Being sick or accidentally hitting my thumb with a hammer becomes preparation for the impossible, for dying, for living in the next unknown moment of life.

As Achaan Chaa said, holding his thumb and forefinger about an inch apart, "All you have to understand is just this much, just this moment." If you can participate in this moment openly, then you'll more likely be present for the next. If that next moment turns out to be on your deathbed, then you'll be open to that too. There is no other preparation for death except opening to the present. If you are here now, you'll be there then.

In Carlos Casteneda's books about receiving the teachings from Don Juan, he mentions again and again how his teacher tries to bring this point to his attention. But Casteneda's rational mind is throwing up a million ideas about how life is supposed to be. Don Juan uses every trick in the book, including Casteneda's fear of the unknown, to bring Carlos' attention to the very moment in which life is unfolding. He pushes Carlos beyond the mind: "A man of knowledge chooses a path with a heart and follows it . . . He knows that his life will be over altogether too soon . . . He knows because he sees that nothing is more important than anything else. In other words, a man of knowledge has no honor, no dignity, no family, no country. But only life to live."

Who is close enough to the truth to live without honor, without dignity? Who trusts this moment so much that they have no need to create some arbitrary morality? Because they know that who they are is the essence of morality itself. They recognize that they are the shining awareness by which life is perceived. Who trusts the light of their original nature sufficiently to allow oneself to respond appropriately in the moment to whatever is called for?

A man very close to death was told that it looked like something might have occurred which would change his condition. He

might be in the process of remission. Waiting to hear the lab results as to whether he would be dead in a few weeks or perhaps
up and around, he turned to his wife and said, "You know,
whether I die or not, it's clear to me that I have exactly the same
work to do."

To acknowledge the moment, to live fully in this instant, participating in one's life moment to moment, compassionately observing what is felt, seen, heard. Not in the analytical mind of
why, where, or how it relates to some self-image, some model of
the universe. But with the keen light of investigation, with a new
wonderment at each unfolding.

Most people begin to open to their life not because there is joy,
but because there is pain. Pain often denotes the limit of the territory of the imagined self, the "safe ground" of the self-image, beyond which a kind of queasiness arises at being in the midst of
the uncontrollable. This is our edge, our resistance to life, the
place the heart closes in self-protection. Our edge is the foundation to which the walls of our cage are secured. Playing the edge
means being willing to go into the unknown. It means approaching that place where real growth occurs. When you are near your
edge, you are near the truth. When we start playing the edge, we
don't just hang out in safe territory any more. Fear becomes the
beacon of the truth and we cut through our resistance by the investigation of what is real and who indeed is holding to some
false sense of security. We see that our pain arises in pulling back
from the unknown and the imagined. It is by playing this edge
that we expand beyond the fear of death, beyond the idea of
"someone" dying, and come into the wholeness of being, the
deathless.

If you sit down with yourself each morning and allow the mind
to quiet, you will begin to see that edge. You will see the place
that starts muttering and commenting on everything that arises in
the mind. If you are paying attention to your relationships with
your mate or children or boss or parents, you will probably start
seeing your edge. It is holding to our edge that obscures death,
that makes death seem so real and solid, rather than another transition into the next unknown.

An example of how each person's edge is different was clearly demonstrated one day when a number of us in southern California began to climb the pinnacle peaks at the Joshua Tree National Monument. Of the two dozen people who began scrambling up the rocks, after a few moments it could be noticed that some stopped at a hundred feet while others continued on. Some halted at two hundred and fifty feet, others continued on. On a ledge at four hundred feet sat a number of others. Most had come to the level where fear halted further advance while a few dropped to their hands and knees crawling against their trepidation, heads down as though butting against their edge. At the very top of the pinnacle several danced and shouted and yodeled off into the echoing wilderness. It was interesting to note at the time that those who had climbed to even the first hundred-foot level may well have done more playing of their edge than those who went all the way to the top, unafraid of the precipitous fall, their particular edge untouched in this instance. You could see each person's edge as clearly defined as strata in the sheer rock wall.

Our edges differ and are constantly changing, as is all else in the universe. We notice that our cage has varying capacities and available space. We move to that edge with compassion. And each step beyond is taken slowly and mindfully. Each step is taken with love, not forcing the edge but softly penetrating our imagined limitations and going beyond, step by step, into the freedom of nonholding.

I received a call not long ago from a woman I have known for some years who has been a prostitute and a heroin addict. She had been involved in this life for about twelve years, until her best friend died in her arms of an overdose of heroin two years before. She said she just couldn't hide any more. The pain was too great, and she decided not to pull back, but to go right to the edge of her holding and play it for all it was worth. She moved out of downtown San Francisco and found an apartment in the suburbs where she got a job in a large office and began, as someone put it, "to take herself apart, bone by bone," not to let anything go by unexamined.

Now this kind of fierceness, which attempts to compensate for years of hiding, also has a tendency to breed certain qualities of self-judgment, which she discovered too had to be worked with, had to be seen as an edge, had to be let go of.

Her commitment is so great, because the pain in her life has been so intense. She has been brought to a place where she is willing to stop deadening the pain with temporary satisfactions so she can go to the root of what or who is suffering. She said that she had to come to a point where there was no place to turn, except inward.

So, the unexpected or unwanted brings each of us to the edge of our pain. But we begin to investigate what causes the pain and posturing. We come to the fear, the doubt, the anger that we usually withdraw from, and gently enter into it. We often find that we don't know what anger is or guilt is or fear is. Because we have always pushed these qualities away or compulsively acted them out, with very little awareness of what was happening. We don't know what these qualities of mind are because as we have approached our edge we have withdrawn into the drowsy blindness of a life only partially lived. We have judged these qualities as unworthy of our fantasy of our imagined self. And, in order to protect that mirage of some separate worthy solidity, instead of using the signal of our attachment, our pain, as a notice to go beyond our cage, we have withdrawn from the edge of life. We have postponed our life in the same way we are attempting to postpone our death.

A friend, taking robes as a Buddhist monk in Thailand, went to study with one of the great meditation masters. When he met with the teacher, the teacher said, "I hope you are not afraid to suffer." Because if you want to find the truth, you cannot allow your resistance to continually motivate you. We are constantly hiding and posturing, inventing an acceptable reality, instead of meeting with the pain and resistance which so cloud understanding. We continually elude our liberation because of an unwillingness to open to the stuff which has been locked in by years of postponing life. All the encrustations of the heart, all the mercilessness to ourselves, all our fear of letting go of who we think we are.

And this is the condition we find ourselves in. It's not something to judge. It's just something to notice. Here we all are, with so many unwanted states of mind. And we pull back. Our reaction limits our openness to what comes next. Fear arises, we close. Doubt arises, we close. Anger arises, we close. Death arises, we close.

To some, this encouragement to acknowledge the blockages of the heart and the confusion of the mind may seem quite negative. But actually what we are speaking about is the path of joy. The acknowledgment of the stuff which closes us allows a softening, a melting away at the edges. And the spaciousness which results illuminates that which has always been there, our original nature shining through, the joy of pure being, the stillness of the underlying reality we all share.

Indeed, the mind is always dreaming itself. So we start coming to the edge of the dream, start cultivating the compassion to let go. We relearn the ability to experience life as it unfolds, to play lightly without force or judgment. It is not a war. It is at last a kindness to ourselves, which gives rise in time, with constancy, to a spacious participation in the flow of change, beyond ideas of loss and gain, beyond ideas of life and death; opening into just this much, the vastness of what is.

We begin to open to awareness itself, threatened by nothing, withdrawing from nothing, becoming one with life. Perfectly prepared for death, knowing that nothing can separate us from our true nature and that only our forgetfulness can obscure it.

IS LIFE THE INCURABLE DISEASE?

Is life the incurable disease?
The infant is born howling
& we laugh,
the dead man smiles
& we cry,
resisting the passage,
always resisting the passage,
that turns life
into eternity.

Blake sang alleluias
on his deathbed.
My own grandmother,
hardly a poet at all,
smiled
as we'd never seen her smile
before.
Perhaps the dress of flesh
is no more than a familiar garment
that grows looser as one diets
on death, & perhaps we discard it
or give it to the poor in spirit,
who have not learned yet
what blessing it is
to go naked?

Erica Jong

4
THE THIRSTY MIND

We seem to be born with a thirst, a craving for life contacts and sensations. A leaning toward pleasure. A pulling back from pain.

The mind longs for what it imagines will allow the experience called satisfaction, a feeling of wholeness. We call this thirst, desire.

This thirst for experience reminds one of a person stumbling in the desert without water, yearning for satiation. Again and again, we view the mirage oasis, shimmering just over the next dune. We see the objects of desire and run toward them, forgetting all else, imagining that at last the thirst will be slaked. We run to the mirage only to find there is no end to this thirst. Each desire seems like another mirage beckoning just over the next rise.

Each mirage only intensifies our thirst, only sharpens our desire. We see that the satisfaction of desire does not make desire disappear but only hones its cutting edge. Eventually, like that man wandering in the desert, we come to see that the mirage is a mirage. Only a dream of satisfaction. Even as we awaken from this dream, seeing that lasting satisfaction is not to be found in the ever-changing mind, the mirage yet remains. Though we run to it less often for satisfaction.

When at last we recognize the emptiness of such visions, though desire still arises in the mind, we no longer cling to it as the only reality. We notice how our thirst creates the mirage and maintain our direction without falling, without losing our path.

When desire is present it narrows the mind's capacity. It causes mind to contract in expectation to a single goal. Acquisition of the objects of thought and imagination causes temporary satisfaction and increasing thirstiness. Letting go of thought and imagination is called freedom. It is a going to the wellsprings within, in which satisfaction may be found. Freedom seeks to satisfy nothing. No thirst.

Desire is unfinished business. Whatever has its goal in the future is an incomplete transaction with life. But if thirst is seen as thirst, business becomes finished in the moment of letting go. The mirage is broken. It no longer seems like "my" desire. Something solid about which something must be done. Seeing the impersonality of desire, we are less likely to become lost in the compulsion to satisfy.

An interesting quality that can be noticed about desire, about wanting, is that what is called satisfaction only occurs in the moving from not having to having. Satisfaction is a moment of release from the pressure of wanting.

Indeed, when desire or any object draws our attention in the mind, it is so seductive, so magnetic, that the awareness, the spaciousness of the natural mind, closes around it. Then the whole of our experience is of that desire, a thirst for that object only.

But it is the edgeless space of awareness we refer to when we say "I." Whatever awareness touches, there our experience arises. Deeply involved in reading a book, for instance, we do not notice a friend entering the room offering us a cup of tea, because, we say, "I was reading; I couldn't hear." Though all of the elements for hearing were present—sound and the ear's ability to hear—because awareness did not touch that sound, hearing did not arise in our experience. Wherever awareness is, "I" experiences. When awareness touches hearing, we hear. When it touches seeing, we see. When it touches tasting, we taste. When awareness makes contact with an object of the senses, we say we experience that sense. Without that contact, no experience arises. When we say, "I am here," we mean awareness is present.

When there is desire in the mind, this vast awareness contracts around that thought or feeling, and our innate spaciousness is lost from view. Whether it is the thought of an apple or a feeling of fear, the mind implodes, becomes hermetically sealed around that object, and the sense of the natural mind is lost. This process is called identification. When the spacious "I" of awareness is contracted to the shape of some object in the mind, we mistake that thought or feeling for "I." It is this state of identification with the contents of mind that results in our imagining that the mind is "I." It is another case of mistaken identity. Much of our experience of ourselves is a dull solidity of mind. All the ever-changing flow, the immensity of original mind, is lost in that single object of desire, in that thirst, in that mirage.

Unable to differentiate between the object of awareness and awareness itself, we think of all the content of mind as our own, as "me."

Desire is a cloud in the mind. It obscures our real nature.

The mind is continually contracting around its contents. Moment to moment, we are identifying who we are with what is floating in the mind, seldom noticing the space in which it floats, seldom recognizing our true nature. Instead we stumble from mirage to mirage, from mind-moment to mind-moment, lost in a sense of "I am this desire," "I am this mind," "I am this thirst."

The experience of the mind losing its inherent spaciousness is called suffering. A heaviness, an isolation we notice in strong desires or heavy emotions. When we become lost, thinking that object "me," it becomes our predominant reality. It is the loss of context that causes pain in our lives, that causes the feeling of confusion and bewilderment that we so often feel.

We don't know who we are or where we're going because our whole world is mind. We are constantly absorbed into thought, imagination, fear, and desire, seldom experiencing the depth of awareness which meets each object in clarity and peace, without wanting, without goal.

Attempting to satisfy the directives of the mind, we notice that even the objects of desire exist within change. Satisfaction is short-lived. The object of desire decays, grows old, evaporates, and disappears. Sometimes in years, sometimes in a split second. And we are left with an unfulfilled emptiness. A life guided by desire, a life contracted to the mind's thirst, seldom has the spaciousness of being. That pure awareness which wants nothing, which yearns for nothing, which simply takes on the shape of whatever form comes within its natural spaciousness.

Awareness could be said to be like water. It takes on the shape of any vessel that contains it. If one mistakes this awareness for its various temporary forms, life becomes a ponderous plodding from one moment of desire, from one object of the mind, to the next. Life becomes filled with urgency and the strategies of fear, instead of lightly experiencing all these forms, recognizing that water is water no matter what its form.

The recognition, the acknowledgment of desire, allows the mind to open around its content, some space is experienced, and desire no longer becomes the sole motivating force. It instead becomes a reminder of awareness, a mirror of how we hold, how readily we sink into the mind's content and forget our true nature, how we stay shallow. When the mind closes around desire, the heart is often not accessible.

So we start to relate *to* the content of the mind instead of *from* it. We observe the observer. We begin to relate from the heart. Watching whatever passes through the mind, observing for instance the thought "apple" without "apple-ing," without becoming lost in thought as though it were reality. We begin to notice that a thought is a thought, just another bubble passing through. You see you can't take a bite out of the thought "apple" any more than you can be bloodied by the fearful imaginings of a car crash. With the thought of an apple, this seems not so momentous. But when the mind is closed around fear or desire, the encouragement to stay open allows a moment of clear seeing, an opportunity to experience the freedom with which we can live our lives.

When we relate *to* the mind instead of *from* it, we relate to desire not from desire. Relating to fear we are not frightened, relating from fear all that we see theatens us. Relating to confusion there is clarity, relating from it there is disorder. Each moment of relating from the mind is a moment of ignorance: each state of mind, each feeling becomes a tinted lens through which we perceive the world. When we are angry, we see a world of aggression and injustice. When frightened, we see only our fears, a menacing world. In our confusion, the whole world seems upside down. When we relate from the heart, we see a world of awareness and effortless activity. When we relate from the mind, our perception of the world is imprisoned by our preferences and thirsts.

How much of our life is lived with a kind of deadness, with a mechanicalness, with a compulsivity?

When the mind wants, when it views its goal, we can almost feel the magnetic pull. It leans toward the next moment, a moment of possible satisfaction. It often seems as though we are pulled from action to action because there is so little room, so little choice in our lives. So little space in which we consciously participate in being. When we relate to the mind from the heart, all the changing flow is seen as just passing show. When we relate from the mind, change becomes our prison.

Often when we begin to recognize the thirst of the mind, we become a little awed at its power, its capacity to cause us to act blindly. We have a tendency to go at it with an ax, but obviously it is desire itself swinging the ax. Watching the avalanche of desire in the mind, we see how conditioned we are. How compulsively we react to each thought as though it were the only possible option in a flow of unceasing possibilities. We notice that the more the mind wants, the more pain it is in. We see that the very nature of wanting is a feeling of incompleteness, of not having. An impatient waiting for another moment of satisfaction.

What we usually call happiness is the ability to re-create previous pleasures. The pursuit of happiness is the attempt to satisfy old desires. The very nature of desire is a feeling of unwholeness, of being incomplete. We see that this thirst creates what could be called the "if only" mind. The yearning that says, "If only I could get my sports car, I'd be happy." "If only I could get that job, or that date, or that money I need, then everything would be O.K."

But to the degree the mind wants that object yet unmaterialized in its world, the less it can be present for what is happening. It is drifting off in future pleasures or musing on satisfactions past. The whole world narrows to just that desire, just that sports car, that prize, that pretty face. The whole world disappears into expectation and life is missed once again, traded off for a mirage floating in the mind. We seldom make direct contact with reality, but instead live only in the flat silhouettes that it casts in the mind.

Desire can be quite painful because it is a feeling of not having, a wish for something more. The present is unsatisfactory because it does not contain the desired object. The greater the desire, the more dissatisfaction is experienced.

Desire can be very subtle. It does not have to be the obvious self-satisfaction of the sports car or first prize. It can be the subtle desire for our children to be well. It can be the desire for a healthy body. It can even be the desire for clarity. It doesn't matter what the object of desire is, it is the closing of awareness around that object which causes us to lose our spaciousness, the loss of ease in our life. It is not the object of desire that matters, it is desire itself that closes the mind, that creates pain. The desire for sex or the desire for happiness causes the same contraction in the mind. It doesn't matter whether the object of desire is gold or peace. Ironically, the happiness that is sought is lost when the natural mind condenses around the form of some momentary shadow. We lose our happiness by grasping at it.

The nature of thirst is to push away the moment in search of "something else." Your search for "the perfect mango" or "the hottest sports car" has at its core a feeling of unsatisfactoriness. Then there comes the moment of satisfaction. The moving from not having to having that comes as you catch a glimpse of that longed-for mango. You become exhilarated. "Oh, it's yellow. Oh, what a beautiful mango!" And the mango is in your hand and there is a moment of peace. For a split second there is no desire in the mind and the body feels very light. Peace is experienced not because of the object in our hand but because for a moment desire does not obstruct the joy and quietude of our underlying nature. What we call satisfaction is the momentary experience of the vastness which lies beneath. All of a sudden the clouds part and the sun shines through. The painfulness of desire does not exist. The mind for a moment experiences its wholeness. In that moment of nonwanting, the mind becomes like a clear pool no longer ruffled by the prevailing winds and we can see through the still water to what lies beneath. We experience a moment's participation in the joyousness that arises as we approach our true nature.

In a split second this satisfaction disappears as other desires arise to protect what it has just acquired. To hide the mango, to plant its seed, to get as much out of it as possible. Freedom is lost in the density of yet more wanting, of yet more protection and self-interest.

We've got the new sports car and are freed for a moment from wanting. We experience a lightness, a happiness, a joy, even love for that object that allowed a moment of liberation. But then, down the street we hear the rumbling of a steam roller and we run to the window, the stomach tightens: "Oh no, not my new car. I should have put it in the driveway. I hope I have enough insurance. Oh, I never should have gotten it in the first place." Desire arises, fear arises, dissatisfaction arises. Our sense of wholeness is lost in the attempt to protect the object of desire from the flow of change.

Desire is a product of latent tendencies in the mind. Old imprints left from previous experience. A memory of the pleasant which the mind attempts to re-create. A pulling away from remembrances of dissatisfaction. Memory creates desire as well as fear, a yearning for things to be other than they are. Every thought or feeling or perception that arises in the mind passes through this filter of unconscious preferences and tendencies. The mind is in a constant roller-coaster state of reaching out for and pushing away its contents. In restless agitation, mind seeks the peace that it knows only in the momentary satisfaction of the absence of desire. We notice in that moment that we have somehow groped our way by a kind of braille method into a spacious feeling of peace. The desire for satisfaction is perhaps motivated by an innate momentum toward the truth which some call "a homesickness for God." A desire to participate in the One. The difficulty with our desires is just that they are too small. They are the desires of me and mine. They do not include the universe. They are a desire for what we want, not for who we are.

From moment to moment, we are in search of satisfaction. From day to day, yearning for some completeness which mind does not experience in its constant clinging and condemning. Leading us from lifetime to lifetime thinking, "If only I could find a sweet one." These unconscious tendencies are subtle holdings in the mind accumulated over billions of moments of experience. They are the preferences that create expectation and the models into which we attempt to squeeze reality. But when these tendencies arise in a mind that remembers, that cultivates a reliance on its own spaciousness, then awareness does not contract into identification but instead remains open and spacious. Awareness notices each object as it passes through, but never forgets itself. Recognizing the spaciousness through which the mental circus passes. The lions and tigers, the clowns and high-wire acts are all present, but are seen as the mind's game only. Projections of the past experienced in the present. But because there is no identification, because the circus is not thought of as "mine," it is observed like any parade. The pomp and flourish, the color and motion are appreciated, but are recognized as a staged event, essentially unreal, the momentary celebration of some forgotten imprint. Then these unconscious tendencies, though they may continue to create form upon form in the shadow-play of the mind, no longer attract identification. And we watch these tendencies burn themselves out, like watching the marchers disperse at the end of the parade route. And we are left with a mind that is present, steady, and peaceful. Indeed, long after it does not matter what the content of the mind might be, desires may still be seen to arise and dissolve, propelled by the momentum of previous graspings and fears, lusts, and repulsions.

And the question arises, "Why keep playing with the fulfillment of every desire? Why not cut out the middleman and go directly to the source of satisfaction within?"

As we begin to let go of identification with the mind, we discover that there are other means of uncovering the natural satisfactoriness of the mind's essential spaciousness. Occasionally, in deep introspection, in meditation, or in a moment of quiet, we open beyond our clinging and the mind becomes so unclouded that nothing blocks its inherent joy. Its expanse is so great that waves of energy wash through the body making any satisfaction we've ever had, even our profoundest sexual gratification, pale by comparison. The natural energy of the mind is released. Grasping has stilled long enough so that we experience the immensity and intensity of our deepest nature. We experience the joy of what in Zen is called the One Mind, shining through.

Our work is not to acquire new goodies or even to "be a better person," but simply to let go of the seeming solidity of the mind. Desire has been so deeply cultivated by our constant attention and mistaken identity with it that as we awaken we see how deeply entrenched this thirstiness is and how fearfully the mind reacts to a life without desire to guide it. Our desires give us something to do in an arbitrary world where only our doing seems of any value. Letting go of what blocks our being means to begin to play lightly with desire. Not to make it such a serious business.

Quietly observing desire, we notice how the mind imagines that if only it could get something more, somehow it would be enough. We see the mirage of the "if only" mind, fantasizing "a beautiful life." But we notice when we meet people who are actually happy that they are not happy because of what they have, but rather because of what they are. They are lighthearted because they have touched within themselves the great source of satisfaction.

There is a story about a fellow who dies and, leaving his body, finds himself in a glistening realm. Standing in the midst of shining flowers and an iridescent sky, he looks about and thinks to himself, "Wow, I was better than I thought. I've gone to heaven. How about that! But I need someplace to live." And with that thought, his dream house materializes a few feet away. As he approaches the door, it swings open to reveal the décor he has always wished to live in. Sitting down on the perfectly comfortable couch, he looks about at his perfectly beautiful house and thinks, "I'd really like something to eat," just as one of the living room walls slides back to reveal shelves filled with all his favorite dishes prepared just the way he likes them. Sitting there, musing and bemused by his surroundings, he thinks, "I'd sure like to hear

some music right now." And at that very moment, his favorite
Bach toccata exudes from the walls. "This is really far out," he
thinks. "'Just what I've always wanted." Hanging out in this lux-
urious space for a few days, he feels very relaxed and comfortable.
When he thinks, "This is very nice, but I'd really like somebody
to share it with," there comes a knock on the door. The door
swings open and standing there is his perfect sexual-intellectual-
emotional-spiritual partner. "Come right in!" he says. And there
they are, living out their desires week after week. One after another his desires materialize the moment he wishes for them. But
after about six months he notices that, though he's getting all he
wants, he doesn't really feel more fulfilled in any deeper sense.
He notices that the mind still holds fear. He recognizes that if all
this were to disappear he would be devastated. Noticing how attached he has become to all this luxury he thought, "I've always
imagined that if only I could get what I want, I'd be happy. But
how can I be happy if I depend so much on what is given to
create my happiness? How can I depend so much on external
conditions for my peace of mind?

"All this gratification isn't really making me any lighter, any
wiser, any quieter in the mind. There is less stress from not getting what I want, but there is really not any more peace."

Another couple of ice cream sodas, another couple of lovemak-
ings, and after a month or so he starts to question whether this is
really very useful for him. None of this has taken him beyond his
desires. He has not in the least dealt with that place within him
that only feels comfortable when it gets what it wants. He has not
touched the yearning, the root that had made life such pain at
times. In fact, he feels as though he's feeding this root by the
escalation of all his desires. And he begins to wonder if there
might not be someplace in the universe where he could work
more deeply on the latent fears and separateness that have always
caused him difficulty.

After a while he goes to the head man and says, "I don't mean
to sound ungrateful, and this may sound preposterous, but I think
I'd rather transfer to hell." The head man turns slowly to him and
says, "And where do you think you are!"

There is a song that has a line, "I've not seen one rich man in a thousand with a satisfied mind." Happiness is not bought. Happiness is our very nature. It comes from the constant letting go of what causes suffering. It seems to come to those who dive deeply into life, into the investigation of being itself. As we grow, we become like a man crossing a frozen lake in spring, learning to walk lightly. As the ice begins to thaw, the going becomes more precarious. And we learn to distribute our weight in a more balanced manner so that our density is well dispersed, rather than concentrated on a single thin area through which we will fall if we are not mindful.

Examining the possibility of walking lightly in this world is the recognition that life need not be suffering, need not be grasping. We begin to make an art of life, to walk, as the American Indian said, in "a sacred manner," to develop a reverence for life which does not seek self-satisfaction, but simply is as it is, edgeless and unending, containing everything, lacking nothing. It is in recognition of the pain caused by our thirst for the little satisfactions of little desires that we are led to the great satisfaction of the great desire: freedom from the mind's incessant wandering and thirst.

I have been with those people at the time of their death who looked back and said, "It was all empty, what was that all for? Every satisfaction has passed. Nothing remains that makes me feel any more whole, any more fulfilled. Nothing I have done has prepared me for this moment. And now as my death approaches, I wonder if my life had any meaning at all."

Sometimes in retreats, as we share around the circle, there will be sitting next to each other two people who offer very different life stories. One says, "My life has been very difficult. I've lost my husband. My son was killed in an accident when he was a teenager. I've experienced the death of many loved ones. But somehow through this, I've seen that I'm not going to find lasting satisfaction in the outside world and I have gone within, seeking some sense of what or who I really might be. As each longing has been shattered, I have seen how painful desire is, and I've come to grasp less. I've gotten some inkling of what it might be about. And all these things, which at one time seemed such hardships, seem great teachings to me now. I've learned to live my life with greater ease and appreciation of what is given. Although I've lost my child, I have found something of importance in myself."

I don't feel sorry for this person. I see the incredible grace of what so many consider tragedy. I see how much connectedness with something deeper has ensued from the investigation of such suffering. I see that her heart has never been so open.

Next to this woman sits a rather stiff college professor, who says, "This stuff has nothing to do with me. I've never lost anyone. I just came here to decide whether to teach a course on Death and Dying next semester. I don't need any help finding out who I am. I get pretty much what I want in the world: My wife keeps a good house and my kids do what I tell them."

This being I almost feel sorry for, because the real tragedy is not the loss of loved ones. The real tragedy is forgetting what connects us in love to all beings. The greatest loss is never touching the essence of fulfillment, our original nature, the source of peace in one's life. What brings pain to my heart is seeing beings who have lost the most important loved ones: themselves. Who have lost their contact with their humanness, with compassion and kindness for themselves and those around them. Theirs is not the more noticeable anguish of deep grief. It is the silent smoldering that burns through life. The confusion that destroys the nutrients of the rich dark soil in which we flourish, that leaves the fields fallow, the flowers and trees dwarfed and starving. It takes what was once a forest and turns it into a desert. It is the longing which causes us to die of thirst.

The search for happiness is the seeking of our original nature. It is the search for fulfillment that goes beyond a limited sense of self, an identification with the bubbles of the mind. A life led by satisfaction of little desires is a life of suffering. We might even say that satisfaction cannot be found in the world of desires, but is only to be found in the uncovering of our true nature.

We come to see the difference between the desire for self-satisfaction, the identification with the mind, and another quality of mind which is a motivation toward freedom. For lack of a better term, we can call this motivation desire as well. But it is not the little desire of old preferences, it is the great desire of liberation. The desire which reminds itself to let go of desires. It is a sense of presence that does not look elsewhere for satisfaction. It investigates the mind without judgment or force. Desires are seen within this patient openness, without the least identification, arising and passing away all by themselves.

Nonattachment is not the elimination of desire. It is the spaciousness to allow any quality of mind, any thought or feeling, to arise without closing around it, without eliminating the pure witness of being. It is an active receptivity to life.

When the truth becomes the priority, our whole life is open to investigation and we soon recognize the power of patience, which is so different from impatience, the quality of waiting for fulfillment that desire usually breeds. We see that patience is simply a presence for what is, a constancy of attention for all that arises. But because it is in the nature of desire to seek its goal, even the great desire for liberation can create pitfalls, what one Tibetan teacher calls "spiritual materialism," a longing for clarity or "deeper experiences," which slow the process of letting go into our original nature. To be free, we must eventually let go of even the desire for freedom so that the underlying nature may present itself free of the mind's clingings.

Desire wants what it does not have. Freedom is the uncovering of what has always been there.

Ramana Maharshi, the great Indian teacher and saint, spoke of making use of the Great Desire to burn out lesser desires. He speaks of using the desire for the truth, a motivation for coming into wholeness, in the same way that in India the tender of the burning grounds uses his great staff to stir the fire on which the corpse is cremated. One uses the Great Desire for liberation to stir up the fire that conflagrates the little desires that draw one into a mind of bondage. One watches the bones of desire disintegrate in the flames of awareness, consciously stirring the remnants with the great stick. The stirring up of the embers allows the fire to consume all the tissue, muscle, and ligaments that bind together the body of desire. And eventually as the bones and flesh and organs of our holding, of our seeming solidity, are dissolved in the great blaze of purification, the stick that we use to stir the fire, the desire for freedom itself, is thrown into the blaze as well. So that nothing remains to obstruct the reception of the truth.

Albert Einstein proffered the theory that the edge of the universe is constantly expanding. Being complete nothingness, a perfect vacuum, the universe is expanding into what Einstein imagined to be "less than nothing." He posited that if a rocket ship were to approach the edge of the universe, exceeding the speed of expansion, it would disintegrate, because apparently even "nothing" has an edge, a solidity to it. Letting go of the contents of mind, of desire, leaves nothing to obstruct the entrance into "less than nothing." The actual experience of "less than nothing" cannot be accurately imagined because even that moment of imagining is "just another something" in the mind. The experience of our edgelessness is beyond the mind. Holding even to the thought of our vastness blocks the experience. We see that freedom is not a thought. That satisfaction does not come from acquirement or holding. That to expand into "less than nothing," nothing must be held, not even an idea of emptiness. Any solidity, any closing of mind, will keep us from experiencing the space within which our life momentarily exists. When desire does not shape the mind and limit it to thought, consciousness becomes translucent. Entering into the spaciousness of the original mind, we become the vastness itself. Inseparable from all else, at one with all that is.

5

MODELS

We see the world through our idea of who we think we are. Our model of the universe is based on our model of ourselves. When we look at the world, all we see is our mind. When we look at a tree, a face, a building, a painting—all act as mirrors for who we think we are. Seldom do we experience an object directly. Instead we experience our preferences, our fears, our hopes, our doubts, our preconceptions. We experience our ideas of how things are. All is created in our image and likeness. Little is allowed independent existence.

As Krishnamurti continues to point out, "The observed is the observer." What is perceived is a function of the models we have. The mold into which we pour molten reality. The newness of each moment is compressed to fit our idea of ourselves.

Our models freeze-dry the flow of experience into a "manageable" reality. They are our idea of the truth, not the truth itself. The truth is what is. It is this moment, without the least trace of the last or any expectation of the next. Our models are a prison. They are the limit to which we can accept the molten flow of change. They act as filters that accept what we believe and reject what seems otherwise. We don't so much receive reality, as we *perceive* it. We pre-receive it. It is precast in concrete. Usually all that we see are memory and expectation.

Models create such expectation by preconceiving, like any philosophy or idea, a sort of tunnel vision of the mystery. Because we seldom touch the heart of what is happening. We experience only our idea, our dream of what is real.

Models can cause suffering. Holding to them, we miss the truth. We create a world of desire and fear.

Working with people during the process of their dying, I have seen how much suffering is created by our models and resistance to the givens of the present. A kind of mental cramping develops from holding to the models of who we think we are and how the world is "supposed" to be.

Imagine that you are brought to a time when illness has caused the energy in your body no longer to be sufficient for you to participate in the world in the ways you have become used to. The ways that have nurtured your self-image. The ways you have cultivated to reaffirm this imagined self that you keep building and rebuilding like an armor about you. Imagine that your energy isn't sufficient to keep up the doing that maintains the mirage of solidity and separateness. What happens when you can no longer keep up the kind of employment that brought money into your home and created your self-image as a good provider? What happens when you are no longer able to keep up your image of yourself as a valuable member of society? When you can no longer maintain your identity as a teacher or plumber or poet or parent? What happens when you can no longer be someone with "responsibilities" to the family and community?

Imagine your body deteriorating and energy diminishing so that you find it increasingly more difficult to support that mirage of self. Imagine the pain of resisting and saying, "No, I've got to be a great lover" or "I'm an athlete; I've got to go running" or "I can't be sick; I'm supposed to be taking care of the kids today; I want to take them to the park, but I can't" or "I've got to get out; I'm a helper; I'm of use to people; I've got to get going; I've got to be there."

There you are, lying in bed, with your new car parked in the driveway just outside the window, realizing that you may never again drive that car of which you were once so proud. Your shoes are sitting by the closet; you know you may never wear them again. Your children are playing in the next room, but you are too weak to get up and join them. Your mate is cooking supper in the kitchen for the children and another meal for you, which she will have to spoon-feed you because you are too weak to feed yourself. Your digestive system no longer able to withstand the food you so much enjoyed in the past. You want to get up and help, as you always have, but it is no longer possible. Indeed, you sense that in a year from now your mate may well be making love to another and that, in a short time, someone else might be raising your children. Looking over at your closet, you see hanging there the clothes you so enjoyed, clothes you sense you will never wear again and which someday may be worn by someone you've never met. And you ask yourself, "Who was that stylish person who bought those clothes?" Because it's not you any more. All the motivation for buying those clothes, and adorning the body, seems so confusing as the body dwindles, losing twenty, thirty, forty, fifty pounds or more. Who was it that went out and bought those clothes?

Can you sense how your resistance, your desire for things to be other than they are, would be like a vise closing in on you? "Oh, this is terrible, this is awful; I've got to gain weight; I've got to be able to go out dancing; I've got to be a good parent; I've got to be a good worker. I've got to be that person I have worked so hard to become: someone who knows what it's all about."

But that model is no longer available to you. How painful our models are when we can no longer fulfill that imagined reality. We wonder to ourselves, "Who am I? Who is it lying here in this bed? Who is dying? Who was living?"

We don't know who we are because we can't play out our specialty any longer. Our sense of being someone in the world is greatly threatened. And the confusion that comes about burns the mind and contracts the heart to an ember.

We have become so identified with our doing, with our model of who we are, that we become incredibly insecure at the time of death. We no longer know who we are, because we have always traded off our true being for some stance in the world, for some

position of authority. We have traded grace for the mask of someone doing something in a world of arbitrary values.

The self-cruelty of our holding to models can be seen in the
eyes of those on their deathbed unable to continue manifesting
the roles they have spent their whole life polishing and developing, guilty and confused at the condition they find themselves in,
wondering what is real and who they really are.

Their resistance is hell. The resistance is so painful, the pushing
away of the present so isolating and fearful, that a feeling of helplessness arises. The more they resist, the more they contract, and
the less space they have in which to live their life and die their
death. The more painful it gets, the more restless they become.

Reflect on what it would be like to be bedridden with so little
energy to move and yet an incredible restlessness that made you
feel, as one person put it, "like climbing the wall, like jumping
out of your skin." It touches on the levels of hell that Dante described. Holding to models creates this hell. The difficulty of
opening to the truth of the moment that denies the opportunity
for a direct participation in this mysterious unfolding, beyond the
mind's calcified preconceptions and fanciful ideas. It is the resistance to life that causes such suffering at death.

Imagine, as sickness continues, that you find yourself unable to
move your bowels. Someone has to give you an enema, and then
wipe your behind. But even then, sometimes you are so impacted
that someone has to pick the feces from your anus. Who are you
then? Where is the social creature who had all those faces, all
those postures, all those gestures, lying there now, on your side,
while someone is painfully picking the shit out of you. Who is the
person who doesn't have the strength to chew the food? Who has
to concentrate just to swallow? Where is that being who had all
those social and sexual, intellectual and physical identities?
You're watching your body get weaker and weaker. You can't
take care of the children. You can't make love. You can't earn a
living. You can't even go to the bathroom by yourself. Who are
you now?

The confusion and suffering arise from our attachments to how
it used to be and how we thought it always would be. For these

people, dying is hell. It is a tearing away of all that seemed so real and substantial.

But dying doesn't have to be hell. It can be a remarkable opportunity for spiritual awakening. I have been with many people who have experienced this falling away of energy, this same wearing away of the body, this same inability to be the individual they thought they were, who, instead of tightening into even greater suffering, began to let go of the root of their contraction. As their self-image began to melt, I saw them begin to have a little more space in which to experience themselves.

When this occurs there is an opening to a whole new participation in life as an investigation, because somehow, though you can't maintain who you thought you were, there is a sense that who you really are is still there. Such people notice that even though the energy decreases, though they may never leave their bed or work again, or do what they have done to be who they thought they were, even though they are watching their body deteriorate, somehow their spirit and their participation in the moment are getting stronger and stronger.

Finally, these things they used to present themselves to be in the world are seen as bars in a cage. They see they have lived their whole life in a prison made of models and ideas of how things are, should be, must be, will be, instead of allowing themselves the vastness of what is. They are no longer kept captive by their models of the world. They see that everything they are is present in each moment. There is nothing absent in their predicament, nothing that blocks them from their liberation. They see how identifying awareness with the fantasies of the future and dreams of the past has kept them imprisoned their whole life, rather than allowing them a full participation in their being as it presents itself moment to moment.

I shared some time with a fellow from Los Angeles who was dying of ALS. ALS is a degenerative nerve disease, also known as "Lou Gehrig's syndrome," which results in a gradual deterioration and paralysis of the body. About two years ago, when my friend Aaron was thirty-six years old, living with his wife and two children, he was a singer, dancer, and virtuoso guitarist. But now

he finds himself strapped into a wheel chair, unable even to support his body weight. His lung capacity so decreased that he must
consciously breathe in sufficient air to push back past his voice
box to create those few words he is able to communicate. Nothing
comes automatically any longer. Nothing is guaranteed to him.
His flesh is literally rotting on his bones. His legs, arms, and body
are no longer able to move of their own volition.

One day Aaron, with much difficulty said, "You know, two
years ago I was healthy and strong. I had a very well-tuned body.
In fact, I was an athlete. I used to run five miles a day. I made
my living by singing and dancing. But now I can't even hold my
guitar. I can hardly speak, much less sing. I can't even stand up
by myself. I need a lot of help just to go to the bathroom. Yet
I've never felt so alive in my whole life, because, ironically, I see
that I am not just this body. As my body gets weaker, somehow I
get stronger. Now that I can no longer do all the things I used to
do to be someone in the world, I see how unreal all those things
were. I see, in fact, that all that doing separated me from everyone and everything in a way that made life a kind of dullness, a
kind of separation from the vitality of things.

"It seems to me that people's lives become such an oddity. So
much time is spent polishing the personality, strengthening the
body, honing, and even having pride in, the separateness, the
competitiveness, the painfulness. No one seems to play lightly
with it. Nor did I. Everyone makes it such serious business. But
now I can't involve myself in that serious business any more. I'm
not this body. This body is rotting off its skeleton. Even so my
heart has never been so open, and I have never felt so much love
for so many beings. It's not even feeling love *for* other beings. I
just feel love. Everyone who enters this space, I love—not being to
being, not out of separateness. It's just that I am *in* love with
them. We exist in love together. I'm touching the place inside of
me I've never looked at before, a place I never knew."

Aaron said that all his singing and dancing, and all the plaudits
he received, all the praise, the money, never really brought such a
deep satisfaction as he was experiencing right now.

He mentioned that, in the large healing group he participates in
a few times a week, there are many patients and therapists who

exchange insights and investigations of what their disease is and how it came about. He said, "It's strange. I used to look to them for answers. But, when I began to look to myself, I saw that everything I needed was right here and now. Instead of me calling the therapists to ask them questions, now the therapists call me. Sometimes they even come over late at night and sit with me and ask my advice. I don't so much have some idea of how it is any more. All I can do is hang out with it. All I can do is be here with it as it is."

One day, sitting in a circle with this healing group, we were talking about the extraordinary voyage Aaron had undertaken. Some of the people in the group, feeling so much love for him, spoke of their wishes for his well-being, of how much they loved him. And he, with his characteristic cackle, said, "Well, you know, I'm worth it." How many people open to themselves so fully that they can honestly respond that they are worth loving?

When Aaron first realized how sick he was becoming, that indeed he might die, he became lost in ideas of how things were and feelings of resentment and diminishment. But with much inward looking, a never imagined freedom often arose as he let go of these old models. Now he says he is free to just be.

Yet even now he is not beyond the possibility of replacing his old models with new ones. The mind until it is liberated from its clinging still has the potential of closing around a less obvious self-imagery. The work never stops. Even the subtlest identification with some model can diminish the experience of being. Still he must remain aware of the mind settling on some new image of itself. That he not become "someone dying beautifully"—that his old clingings don't just go up an octave to resonate with some more acceptable model, some further suffering.

Many people say that they have never been so alive as at the time they are dying. Perhaps this is because at last the investigation of what is real has given their life meaning. And when life has meaning, it has vibrancy. The investigation becomes "Who am I?" Life's energy is not used to confine reality to old models. The preoccupations of a lifetime no longer obstruct, filter, and dull the mystery. Indeed, these beings are participating in their life, not just thinking it. They have become alive by not trying to

make life what they wish it to be. Their life is an investigation of
the truth as they drop models to discover what lies beneath.
"Who is it that dies?" The meaning that comes into their life is
the uncovering of who they always thought they had to be and
what it is within that they have never allowed to emerge.

When I am with such people, I see that their work and my
work are precisely the same: To let go of self-protective control,
to let go of that kind of holding and suffering that keeps us separate; to open, now; to die into the present moment. To live fully
with what is given with an open heart and a mind that no longer
clings to models.

In the last few years, I have shared time with various people
who, instead of lamenting their predicament, have begun to use it
as a means of awakening. These people have discovered that even
pain and the loss of who they imagined they were, were workable.
They have seen through the suffering of their illness and the
clinging to models. As they let go more and more, life becomes
more spacious. They're not picking up anything. They're letting it
all go. And, as they let things go, they experience the timelessness
that is not "them" or "me," but just is. It is a process of letting go
of what some call the "snags," those tendencies in the mind which
attempt to capture and control the ceaseless flow of being.

They often begin by investigating the psychological elements,
the contents of the mind. And, to a certain degree, that seems
useful. Examining states of mind makes them more aware of the
blockages to clarity, though it doesn't necessarily remove them.
But, instead of working through each psychological knot, trying
to finish business with themselves as a personality, they begin to
diminish the identification with these knots. Starting to let go of
themselves as a psychological entity, as a personality, as something or someone separate, they begin to recognize that they are
the space within which all these mind states occur. And, as they
penetrate more deeply into their being, their priorities change.
They start to relate to the mind, instead of from it, which allows a
whole new dimension of participation in being, in life itself.

They come to the edge of the mind. They see that they are
none of the objects of thought or mood. They begin to relate to
the light by which all this mind-stuff is seen. They come to recog-

nize that they are awareness itself, beyond any model of solidity or expectation. They no longer confuse the light of awareness for the objects which reflect the light. In the silent "I am" of the mind, consciousness itself is revealed. And they no longer mistake themselves for the objects of awareness, but instead recognize themselves as the vast space of awareness itself.

They have touched the deathless.

One woman said that usually she related to the world from her conditioning, from her mind, from her psychological reality, from her models, identifying with her personality, her psyche, her name, her reputation, her honorableness. But this created such suffering that she could no longer allow herself to hold on to these ideas. She could no longer allow herself to live a second-hand life, experiencing her thoughts of things instead of the things themselves. And in that letting go, she felt such spaciousness and ease, opening to a direct experience of what is, beyond life, beyond death.

Each time we remember, each time we encourage ourselves to penetrate past our attachments, we start to relate to the mind and feel a greater expanse of being. We start to see that what we called "our experience," what we called "me"—"our" seeing, "our" hearing, "our" tasting, "our" smelling, "our" thinking—is actually just bubbles floating through vast spaciousness, changing from instant to instant. And that we are none of these. These experiences are like an old movie, playing to an empty house. It's all happening by itself. Thoughts are thinking themselves. And any kind of control introduces force, and force closes the heart and creates suffering.

When I am with people whose greatest priority is the truth and work to let go of all that blocks their understanding, I don't hear them say, "God, I've got to get my energy back; I've got to be someone in the world." Instead, they say, "I don't have to be anything or anyone to be who I really am." It is a considerable insight for beings who have lived so much of their life, as we all have, in ideas and models of a universe of "shoulds" and "musts" that doesn't exist. I see them touch the real. I see them become part of what is.

Those beings who live with such insight are the most openhearted and clear-minded people I know. They say, "I don't have to be anything special to investigate the truth, to find real freedom. I don't have to worry about being anyone or anything. I don't have to worry about anything, because I'm not that, either." As they approach death, they discover life.

If I might share a composite of what I hear many say, it goes something like this: "This is strange to say, but I've never been so happy in my life, because I've never had so little resistance, or self-doubt. I don't really know who I am but it doesn't matter, because nothing I think of myself as being seems to hold it for long anyway. Somehow I am always something else, and I don't know what that is. But it certainly is the most fulfilling exploration I have ever undertaken, because I am not going into it with a lot of knowing. I am going into it not knowing. My knowing has always blocked my understanding, filled me up, confused me. But now I am vulnerable to the truth, because I have nothing to lose. I had to lose it all to see that little of it was worth having in the first place. Somehow there is more to me than I ever imagined."

These people have let go of their limiting models and the archaic insistence of their conditioning and opened into the fresh, fearless present.

They touch the underlying deathlessness of pure awareness—that which neither comes nor goes, but simply is as it is.

These are the people who I see die in wholeness, without struggle, just evaporating out of their body. They die into their true nature. Their death is like the rain falling gently back into the ocean.

The truth is inside you, and also inside me;
you know the sprout is hidden inside the seed.
We are all struggling; none of us has gone far.
Let your arrogance go, and look around inside.

The blue sky opens out farther and farther,
the daily sense of failure goes away,
the damage I have done to myself fades,
a million suns come forward with light,
when I sit firmly in that world.

I hear bells ringing that no one has shaken,
inside "love" there is more joy than we know of,
rain pours down, although the sky is clear of clouds,
there are whole rivers of light.
The universe is shot through in all parts by a single sort of love.
How hard it is to feel that joy in all our four bodies!

Those who hope to be reasonable about it fail.
The arrogance of reason has separated us from that love.
With the word "reason" you already feel miles away.

How lucky Kabir is, that surrounded by all this joy
he sings inside his own little boat.
His poems amount to one soul meeting another.
These songs are about forgetting dying and loss.
They rise above both coming in and going out.

Kabir, via Bly

6
HEAVEN/HELL

Most people live their lives in an incessant alternation between heaven and hell. Getting what they want, they are in heaven. Losing it, or never getting it at all, they drop to hell. Hell is the stiff resistance to what is. Heaven is our loving openness. Hell is resistance. Heaven is acceptance.

Heaven is the opened heart. Hell is the tightened gut. Usually we hover somewhere between the heart and the stomach. The stomach turns everything into itself; the whole world is seen as food, as existing for it alone: gut ego. The heart is where opposites coincide and preferences dissolve into the One, like a crucible into which ornamental bangles are thrown to retrieve the pure gold.

There is a story of a great Samurai who comes to visit the Zen master, Hakuin. The Samurai approaches the Zen master and bows dutifully, asking, "Sir, I wish to understand the differences between heaven and hell." The Zen master looks at the Samurai and, eying him from head to toe, says, "I would tell you, but I doubt that you have the keenness of wit to understand." The Samurai pulls back in astonishment. "Do you know who you are speaking to?" he huffs. "Not much," says the Zen master, "I really think you are probably too dull to understand." "What?" says the Samurai. "How can you talk to me like this?" "Oh, don't be silly," says the Zen master. "Who do you think you are? And that thing hanging by your waist. You call that a sword? It's more like a butter knife." The Samurai, becoming enraged, draws his sword and raises it over his head to strike the Zen master. "Ah," says the Zen master. "That is hell." The Samurai's eyes shine with recognition as he bows and sheathes his sword. "And that," says the Zen master, "is heaven."

When anger arises in the mind, when fear becomes present, it can either make life hell or reveal another opportunity to enter into heaven. It can be another moment of resistance, of pushing away, of becoming lost in the mind. Or it can be a reminder to let go gently into the vastness, into the openness of the heart, into the essence of acceptance itself.

At one point, Don Juan suggests to Carlos Casteneda that he live his life like a warrior, that he use his life as an opportunity for awakening instead of maintaining the constant refusal of the mind to open beyond itself. He says, "To the ordinary man, everything that happens to him is either a curse or a blessing. To a warrior, each thing is a challenge."

The variance between heaven and hell is the fluctuation of the mind between thinking itself fortunate or unfortunate. We weigh each perception against what we desire. An example is the story of the well-to-do insurance broker who lives with his family in a big house, in a "nice neighborhood." His two children are on the honor roll and he thinks of himself as very fortunate. But the company he works for goes bankrupt and he loses his job and has to sell his house, and considers himself very unfortunate.

However, having to give up his house he thinks, "I might as well do what I've always wanted to." And with the equity from his home, buys a small farm in the country, from which he derives great peace of mind. And once again, he thinks of himself as fortunate.

Then, some weeks later his son, plowing the field, is thrown from the tractor and badly injured. Once again he feels unfortu-

nate. However, the quick action of doctors and the proximity of
the hospital saves his son's life and, once again, he considers himself fortunate.

But as it turns out, his son's leg is so badly injured that it must
be amputated. And again he is certain life is indeed unfortunate.

As it turns out, his son heals rapidly and the insurance covers
all of the hospital expenses and, once again, the fellow is considering himself quite fortunate.

After the operation, the boy returns to school on crutches, and
can no longer maintain his position on the basketball team or
play any sport at all, which the father considers to be most unfortunate.

However, as the boy's sensitivity grows from his new one-
legged relationship to the world, he begins to visit the hospital
where he had the operation and to spend time with other young
people who have had similar operations and mentions to his father that, at last, he has found his life's work. Once again his father thinks of it all as fortunate indeed. The story could go on
forever. And usually does.

Life is not in itself hellish or heavenly. These are the mind's
conditions. Its openness or closedness to events.

As it is the nature of the hand to be soft and open and pliant,
able to support whatever is placed within it, so the natural mind
is a spacious awareness that clings nowhere. But the conditioned mind due to the millions or billions of moments of grasping we have imagined necessary to maintain some false security in
the world has lost much of its original openness. It is like having
to carry some heavy baggage for a period of time. Perhaps running to catch a plane or bus on schedule, clinging to our luggage
for all we're worth, till at last we settle down into our seats. But
as we begin to open our hand, we find it cramped around the
handle of that old baggage. It is difficult, even painful, to return
the hand to its natural openness, because the force of holding has
so contracted it. Cramped by its holding, its return to the natural
state is slow and occasionally discomforting. Because we so fear
pain, we prefer to remain contracted rather than allow the release
of ancient tension.

We prefer the cramped space of our isolated self, of our old holding to the possible freedom beyond our cage. We prefer the familiarity of hell to the pain of letting go into the vast unknown.

There is a story of a fellow who dies and, leaving his body, finds himself in a shimmering realm. He thinks to himself, "I guess I was better than I thought I was." He is approached by a glistening being who ushers him through an archway into a regal banquet hall in which an immense table is laid out with unimaginable delicacies. He is seated at the banquet table with many others, and a choice selection of food is served to him. As he picks up his fork, someone approaches from behind and straps a thin board to the back of his arms so he cannot bend his elbows. Trying to pick up the food, he sees that he can't get it to his mouth because he cannot maneuver his stiff arms to feed himself. Looking about, he notices that all the other people around the table have their arms bound straight so they cannot bend them. All are grunting and groaning as they attempt to stuff the food into their mouths but they cannot reach and there is a great wailing and moaning at their predicament. Going to the being who had shown him to this place, he says, "This must be hell. But then what is heaven?" And the glistening being shows him through the archway and, across the hall, into another huge banquet hall in which there sits another great table, filled with the same array of foods. "Ah, this is more like it," he thinks. And sitting down at the dinner table he is about to dig in when someone comes and ties a board to the back of his arms so, once again, he cannot bend his elbows to feed himself. Lamenting that this is the same unworkable situation as hell, he looks about in dismay to notice that, at this table, there is something different occurring. Instead of people trying to force the food into their mouths, straining against the rigidity of their arms, each being is holding his arm out straight to feed the person on either side of him. Each person is feeding the person next to him. The conditions are the same, but the response is totally different.

Thinking in terms of "I" and self-gratification, we live a life of stiff-armed hell, denying the process we share with all who exist. Recognizing ourselves as part of this whole, we feed each other and are so fed in the doing.

Most of the moments of satisfaction in our life are clung to,

making a temporary heaven into an increasing hell. We fear that
we will lose our short-lived paradise and crouch in the dark
corner, denying the inevitable. Grasping at heaven creates a life
of hell. We keep involving ourselves in old patterns, thinking that
somehow they will bear fruit in a way they never have before.

It's like the much told story of the Sufi crazy wisdom teaching
figure Nasrudin, who comes back from the marketplace with a
huge basket of hot chili peppers. While he is sitting in his room
eating one pepper after another, a student enters and asks why he
is eating what are obviously burning hot peppers. His eyes are
tearing, his lips are swollen and chapped, his tongue swells in his
mouth. "How can you eat those awful hot peppers, one after another?" he asks. To which Nasrudin replies, "Well, I saw them in
the marketplace and they were so pretty I couldn't pass them by."
"But," his student asks, "how can you do that to yourself? How
can you keep eating one burning pepper after another?" And
Nasrudin answers, "Oh, I keep thinking I'll find a sweet one."

Our long search for lasting satisfaction confuses us. The path
bends and turns, there is pain at each departure from our goal.
We are like phantoms attempting to grasp the world in trans-
parent, shadow hands. Like a hungry ghost, the conditioning in
the mind clamors for satisfaction, wanting what it does not have
or cannot make to stay. The mind is misshapen by painful yearning. Desire tears at each tasty morsel, though it has lost the ability
to swallow. We strangle on that next bite of cake. When desire is
great and there is no satisfaction, we think ourselves in hell. Hell
is our inability to play lightly with the hungry ghost of past fears
and temporary satisfactions, the inability to surrender. It is when
we find ourselves backing into a corner to elude the unpleasant
and try to pull back yet farther from the fire of our unsatisfied
longing that we establish residence in hell. And there we are with
nowhere to turn, "no exit," trapped by our longing, unwilling to
let go. Our heart constricted by fear and doubt. And it is then,
when the suffering gets great enough, when we simply can't resist
any longer, that we begin to open to our predicament. When the
heart sighs and begins to surrender its suffering, hell dissolves before our eyes. It is as Thomas Merton said: "True prayer and
love are learned in the moment when prayer has become impossi-

ble and the heart has turned to stone." It is in letting go of hell that we surpass heaven, entering the light beyond the mind.

In the Old Testament it says, "Though I make my bed in hell, thou art with me."

Out of that desperation of "What do I do now?" may come the answer. Because, perhaps, for once there is no quick resolution. At last we don't know. We've known so much for so long that the space in which the truth might spontaneously arise has become too full. There is little room for our true nature. It is in this "don't know" mind that heaven and hell are dissolved. It is in this open, choiceless investigation of the truth that reality presents itself.

There is an extraordinary translation by Richard B. Clarke of a short tract by the third Zen patriarch entitled "Hsin Hsin Ming." In Chinese, the word for heart and mind is the same—*Hsin*. For when the heart is open and the mind is clear they are of one substance, of one essence. In this recognition of the merging of the heart and mind, he begins his tract with these words:

> *The Great Way is not difficult*
> *for those who have no preferences.*
> *When love and hate are both absent*
> *everything becomes clear and undisguised.*
> *Make the smallest distinction, however,*
> *and heaven and earth are set infinitely apart.*
> *If you wish to see the truth*
> *then hold no opinions for or against anything.*
> *To set up what you like against what you dislike*
> *is the disease of the mind.*
> *When the deep meaning of things is not understood*
> *the mind's essential peace is disturbed to no avail.*

Confusion is a pushing against what is, a result of our compulsively seeking answers to fill the mind and block the inconsistency of our preferences and models. Confusion is the state of not being who you really are. A painful wondering at existence. And yet, one could be liberated exploring the confused mind. Recognizing that the silent witness is not itself in confusion. It is in the space that does not cling to "understanding," that does not try to fill itself up as a means of self-definition, that the truth may present itself. It is in the "don't know" mind that the truth is experienced in a spacious, timeless participation in being. Confusion is a pushing against a flow, a grasping at an answer, any answer. "Don't know" is just space, it has room for everything, even confusion itself. There is no force in "don't know." The mind is in no way amenable to force, the least bit of force closes the heart.

Perhaps the essence of the teaching is, "Can you keep your heart open in hell?" When we are closing down from anger, from resistance, from fear, can we still have some openness to ourselves? When we are frightened, can we still have some space within which we allow fright to be without closing. Or is it all so suppressed, so pushed down, that many of the old patterns just keep running off and we find ourselves tight and guarded, life becoming a meaningless jumble, some awful prank?

There is a story about one of the great Tibetan lamas who, as he approached death, prayed that he be reborn in hell. For it was in hell that he sensed the truth would be most useful. It was in hell that he suspected the Dharma was most needed. Some days later he dreamed of heaven realms, to which his merit would take him. And upon waking he cried.

Meister Eckhart was nearly burned at the stake for saying, "I prefer a hell with Jesus to a heaven without."

Our minds are so full. We are constantly rushing to answer each question that arises. We seldom allow the mind to not know. We wish to answer the question and thereby stop asking, "Who am I?" Most answers that the mind comes up with are just excuses not to go deeper. It is the mind's answers that cause confusion. There is no confusion in "don't know." There is just the truth.

As always there is a story of an ancient Zen master; this one approached by a knowledgeable scientist and philosopher who requested his teaching, saying, "I understand much of the physical laws of the universe and the way of things, but there may be something you could add. May I have the teaching?" The Zen master invited him to sit and offered him tea. The scientist held out his cup as the Zen master began to fill it and continued pouring as the tea spilled over onto the floor. Looking up at the Zen master, he said, "This is no good. My cup is too full." And the Zen master, smiling, replied, "That is right. Like this cup, your mind is too full. Empty your cup and then come back for the teaching. Perhaps then you will have room to receive the truth."

Our cups are so full, we know so much, that we understand nothing. We are all so together! In fact, we are altogether too together. And we notice that there is a pain in our heart because of this. Our togetherness is our false knowing. A very expensive trade-off for the freedom inherent in being.

It is in letting go of old models, opening into "don't know," that we discover life. It means getting out of our own way in the same manner that a healer gets out of his own way and lets the extraordinary nature of the universe manifest through him. He's not doing anything. As a matter of fact, for a moment his self-oriented doing has ceased so that he may become a conduit for the energy of wholeness. So, too, in the openness of "don't know" we watch the healing come about. We experience the melting away of old knowings and expectations. We begin to experience the joy of simply being, in love with all that is.

When we no longer cling to our knowing, but simply open to the truth of each moment as it is, life goes beyond heaven and hell, beyond the mind's constant angling for satisfaction.

Anger in the mind—who's angry? Don't know, just is! Fear in the mind—don't know; it's O.K. Jealousy in the mind—don't know, but it's all right. Because if you think it's not O.K., it closes your heart. Which is O.K. too, but it's so painful. There's no should in "don't know," there is just endless don't know.

When I was working with Elisabeth Kübler-Ross, she used to muse that someday she would like to write a book entitled, *I'm Not O.K. and You're Not O.K. and That's O.K.*

So much space for discovery. So little holding to old confusion, to old mirages of comfort and safety. Focusing on the natural openness of the heart, we begin to see that there's nothing to push away, nothing to be, nowhere to go. That we are infinitely undefined. We have been so busy being "someone" for so long that we don't know who we are or who/what we really might be. Letting go of our knowing, we open into being itself. We experience the deathless. Our fear of death and our longing for life merge in being; heaven and hell are resolved in the moment. The richness, the suchness of life becomes evident. Nothing to protect, nothing to hide. Just a renewed vitality and openness to life.

Don Juan leans back in his chair and smiles at Carlos, "The basic difference between an ordinary person and a warrior is that a warrior takes everything as a challenge whereas an ordinary person takes everything as a blessing or a curse."

The warrior has the wisdom to approach each event as it is, not knowing its outcome. Not forcing results. His "don't know" is the joy and courage that fill his life.

7
FINISHING BUSINESS

Imagine that you are lying in an emergency room, critically injured, unable to speak or move, the concerned faces of loved ones floating above you, the pain beginning to dull from the morphine just injected. You wish to reach out to tell them something, to finish your business, to say good-by, to cut through years of partial communication.

What would you say? Think of what has remained unsaid and share that each day with those you love. Don't hesitate. Tomorrow is just a dream.

Finishing business does not necessarily mean you clear up all the particulars of a lifetime of incomplete trust and fractured communication. Many think of finishing business as a totaling of accounts, coming to bottom-line-zero, balancing out the predicaments of the past in a long talking through of events. In my experience there is often not enough time or trust or self-confidence or simply not enough energy to deal with such old holdings and resentments, fears, and doubts.

Finishing business means that I open my heart to you, that whatever blocks my heart with resentment or fear, that whatever I still want from you, is let go of and I just send love. I let go of

what obstructs our deepest sharing. That I open to you as you are
in love. Not as I wish you to be or as I wish me to be. An opening into the oneness beyond the need to settle accounts. No
longer looking to be forgiven or to show others how unfair they
were. To finish our business, we must begin to stop holding back.
Gradually love replaces clinging. As we begin to open past our
image of some separate "me" in relationship to some separate
"other" and just be there with ourselves in soft openness, our business is finished.

If we are grooming our children to be "good adults" but they
turn out to be as confused as we are, and we resent it, how much
are we losing of our contact with them? How would it be a year
from now, if you looked down into the casket and saw your dearest one lying there? If the connection between you and your loved
one hasn't been maintained in love, you will feel the broken edge
of that incomplete touching, a feeling that there is "business to
finish" and you may come away from the experience feeling guilty
and confused. But if you have finished your business, if you have
opened in love to the full range of feelings that arise in every relationship, then you will come away with a sense of completion,
a feeling of wholeness.

Most of our relationships are rather shallow because we deny
so much of ourselves. But how are you going to open to another
if you are attempting to present a façade? How are you really
going to become whole if you are only pretending to be whole?

As you look at your relationships one by one, how much do
you sense you would have to work out before you could say
good-by? How incomplete, how partial is the touching of your
heart with another. How many times did you, for some "reason,"
not surrender into the heart of your closest companion.

We use the word "love" but we have no more understanding of
love than we do of anger or fear or jealousy or even joy, because
we have seldom investigated what that state of mind is. What are
the feelings we so quickly label as love? For many what is called
love is not lovely at all but is a tangle of needs and desires, of
momentary ecstasies and bewilderment—moments of unity, of intense feelings of closeness, occur in a mind so fragile that the
least squint or sideways glance shatters its oneness into a dozen

ghostly paranoias. When we say love we usually mean some emotion, some deep feeling for an object or a person, that momentarily allows us to open to another. But in such emotional love, self-protection is never far away. Still there is "business" to the relationship: clouds of jealousy, possessiveness, guilt, intentional and unintentional manipulation, separateness and the shadow of all previous "loves" darken the light of oneness. But what I mean by love is not an emotion, it is a state of being. True love has no object. Many speak of their unconditional love for another. But in truth one does not have unconditional love for another. Unconditional love is the experience of being, there is no "I" and "other" and anyone or anything it touches is experienced in love. You cannot unconditionally love someone. You can only *be* unconditional love. It is not a dualistic emotion. It is a sense of oneness with all that is. The experience of love arises when we surrender our separateness into the universal. It is a feeling of unity. You don't love another, you *are* another. There is no fear because there is no separation. It is not so much that "two are as one" so much as it is "the One manifested as two." In such love there can be no unfinished business.

But how often did you maintain your separateness, nurture it, cultivate it like a poison weed until the gulf between you and another seemed insurmountable and, instead of love, a socially acceptable communication was substituted, a kind of coping?

But finishing business does not so much mean a totaling of old accounts as it does a canceling of them. It means finishing relationships as business. No longer relating to others on a profit or loss scale. Letting go of accounts which magnify the separatism and pain.

Most people maintain relationships like they are doing business. "I'll give you five if you give me five. If you give me three, I'll give you two. But if you give me two, I'm taking my marbles and going home."

I shared recently with a glowing, thirty-one-year-old woman who has a brain tumor. She said, "You don't have a moment to lose to tell people how much you love them. In a way I am freer to express my love now than I ever was before. All my life I wanted to tell people how much I loved them but I felt I couldn't.

I felt vulnerable and frightened. I feared they wouldn't listen. It
seemed like the time was just never right. But now I see I don't
have a moment to lose." No more doing business. Just loving.

You don't have a moment to lose to share the anger and the
love. So you can go beyond and arrive together at a place of
oneness. You don't have a moment to lose to start letting go of
what keeps you separate. Indeed, you can measure the degree you
push away others by the degree you push yourself away. How
often do you hide your thoughts and feelings? How often do you
deny yourself?

It's not easy. We must be very kind to ourselves and let go of
"the urgency of our imperfections." We are so encouraged to be
closed and self-protective. To guard some imagined idea of who
we are, which is constantly creating the world we see. We seldom
touch the truth because we are cultivating and manicuring a barrier, polishing a personality, damning and varying whatever we
suspect would cause us pain. How often do we touch our innate
connectedness with others?

But when we start to touch that caring, we see that there is
nothing to lose and no one to protect. That protection *is*
unfinished business. Our holding back from life, from death, from
love.

As my dying friend said, there isn't a moment to lose. And as
the great Tibetan saint Milarepa remarked, "Hasten slowly."

When you can look at your mind and still keep your heart
open, business is finished. It isn't that anger or fear, doubt or confusion are absent. There's just no pulling or pushing. No loss or
gain. But just a going beyond holding, in a soft awareness that
meets each moment with compassion instead of fright. With
quietude and stillness instead of agitation and grief for a life
that has dissolved behind us.

We've seen how much being "sweet" is a trade-off in personal
relationships. How it can be the death of real sharing. Most people relate from a kind of protectiveness of themselves and others
that keeps the living truth buried. Because, for most people, truth
is not the priority. We protect ourselves in ways that obscure the
truth of what we feel, seldom deeply touching that other being.
Much of our sweetness comes from a confusion, a difficulty in

revealing ourselves. A feeling that others can't be trusted to understand and still give us the love we so much want from them. Most are still doing business.

People who seem to have no unfinished business are people who live right now, in just this moment. The Zen master Suzuki Roshi said, "One should live their life like a very hot fire, so there is no trace left behind. Everything is burned to white ash." Each act is done so fully and so completely there is being shared in each moment. There is nothing left to do but be.

. A good example of our undoneness is the gulf that separates many from their parents or children. We insist we will open our heart when the other opens theirs. We say we will expose ourselves as soon as they do. But they can't, or don't, and our confusion and pain become everyone's loss. Our inability to tune into them or with them keeps us light-years apart.

Many people, for instance, are judgmental of their parents, feeling they "just don't understand." And they wish their parents to change. We argue they should be different, that they should conform to our models of the universe in the same way our parents may have scolded us as children, to be good little boys or girls. The tables are turned, but it is still the same old table that separates us in the same old way.

When I was a teen-ager, I was a bit of a hellion. Hot rods, black leather jacket, street fights. It was not at all the way of my middle-class Jewish parents. And as I got more into the heat of adolescence and had a half dozen brushes with the law, my mother, in great disappointment, would occasionally shake her head hoping someday I might "straighten out," and say, "I should only live to see the day!" There seemed an immense gulf between us.

But, as time passed, and the adventures of life changed, as my heart opened a bit more, I found that, coming on my yearly visits from California, instead of sitting at the dinner table in deep contention with my father, I was more of an openness that did not close around their value system or attempt to defend my own. Each visit I found more space in which to honor them as they were. Not so much seeking their approval as being open to them in love. A bit less attached to how I saw things. As the years unfolded, I visited just to be with them, just to love them. And I could see how my desire for their approval had always been a fire between us, had closed my heart because, as they disapproved, I pulled back yet further. But now I was no longer doing business. I was just there, sharing to whatever extent I could. Recognizing the deep conditioning that could so easily close my heart in a moment of clinging and confusion.

I began to see all that separated us as work on myself. Attempting to stay above the high water mark of my deepest fears and confusion. In the years that followed, as we opened to each other more and more, one day my mother turned to me and said, "Well, I've lived to see the day!" And as wonderful as that was, it still was not the finishing of business. For whenever my heart fluctuates, withdraws, I notice those places where yet I can become caught. Where love can be blocked by the mind's desires and old holdings. Finishing business is opening unconditionally into love.

There is a story about an old fellow who had worked his whole life to develop a farm that would support his family. The old man, having worked many years tilling the land and fighting the elements to feed and shelter his family, came to a time when he felt it was appropriate to retire, to sit on the porch and contemplate the universe. His son was strong and able, and having a family of his own, it seemed time for him to take over. So the old man handed the farm over to his son and settled into a comfortable chair on the porch to enjoy his remaining years after a life of backbreaking toil. His son was, at first, proud that finally he was master of his own farm. But as the months went by, working in the fields, he began to resent his father's inactivity. His father sat on the porch, bouncing his grandchildren on his knee, while he had to work all day. Resentment began to arise in the son's mind and he began to look at his father as just another mouth to feed. He thought to himself, "I have my wife and children to take care of now. The old man doesn't understand. He just sits there. It doesn't matter what came before. This is hard work and I wish I didn't have to take care of him too." So his son went on hoeing and planting, getting angrier and angrier, until at harvest time he began to think that he didn't want to share his food with "that useless old man on the porch." He wanted it all for himself and his family and thought, "His time is over." He doesn't need to be around any more." So the son built a great wooden box of heavy teak and, when it was complete, he put the box on a wheelbarrow and wheeled it over to the porch and said firmly to his father, "Dad, I want you to get in this box. Do it now." His father bowed and, without a word, climbed off the porch and into the box. The son closed the heavy lid over his father and snapped the great brass hinge. Wheeling the box to a cliff, he was just about to tip it in the chasm below when he heard a knocking from within. "What do you want?" he said gruffly. From within the box came his father's soft voice, "You know, I understand. If you want to get rid of me, that's O.K. You think I'm just a useless old man. But if you want to throw me over the cliff, what I would do is take me out of the box and just throw my body over. I would save this box if I were you. I think your children may have use for it someday!"

On several occasions, people have shared that they would like to have been able to finish business with someone who has since died. They wish they could have communicated the love, the connection between them, but now they feel it's too late. Often this recognition of the incompleteness of relationship leads one to identify with feelings of helplessness and guilt. And we are asked, How do you finish business with someone who is no longer around? Of course the answer is always the same—one need not see that person to send them love. To finish business the other doesn't even need to acknowledge your presence, much less the process you are sharing. It is our work to open in love to another. This work is independent of results. It is done of its own and for its own sake.

In the course of workshops, some have spoken of going outside on a clear evening and sitting or lying on the ground, looking up at the sky, and choosing one star as if it were their long departed loved one and beginning a dialogue with that being personified by that star. Speaking from the heart and listening from the stillness beyond the rational mind, they communicate that which they feel still separates them. And even though the passing of that loved one may have been twenty years before, many speak of a new

clearing, a new openness between them. The gulf that they felt
separated them for years has dissolved in love. Often, just ten or
twenty minutes of such communication allows the separateness of
years to fall away and only their essential contact remains. Indeed, this finishing of old business once again reminds one that
when two people are pulling on either end of a rope, it takes only
one of them to let go of his end to release all of the tension between them.

The separation and antagonism of a lifetime dissolve in a moment of love. Letting go of the account, we trust our heart and
touch on what Jesus may have meant when he said, "Faith can
move mountains." For we see that this love, like faith, is the natural space of the open heart and mind. And that like faith, love is
a much used but seldom understood term that attempts to name
the essentially unnamable wholeness of being in which we each
dissolve out of our separateness.

It is so easy for us, caught in our melodrama, to forget that we
are part of a process. We are like cells in a single organism that
share consciousness and motion.

One of the great teachings of that personification of our original nature we call Jesus is forgiveness. Forgiveness is the quality
of letting go of resentment and holding to a separate identity. It
means going into your heart so that you can feel the pain of another and let go of it. Forgiveness occurs when the holding mind
sinks into the spacious heart and is dissolved. The Indian saint,
and teacher of many close friends, Maharaji, used to say, "Don't
put anyone out of your heart." Because when you put someone
out of your heart, you remove yourself as well. This truth is perhaps reflected in Jesus' statement "Judge not lest ye be judged."
For the more you identify with the voice of judgment the more
you cultivate the judging mind, which glares on all things equally.
It is an old habit of the conditioned mind. The judging mind
plays no favorites, it can't tell the difference between "you" and
"other." It coddles or condemns all that it views with merciless
impartiality. To the degree you judge another, the mind will be
encouraged to judge itself.

"If only I could have seen it the way I see it now. How stiff my
life has been. Of so little importance are the disagreements and

opinions. How seldom has frustration led to remembering what we share rather than creating barriers against the deeper communication of the heart. How forgetful I have been of the simple beauties of shared love and forgiveness."

Self-forgiveness Meditation

[To be read slowly to a friend or silently to oneself.]

Reflect for a moment on that quality we call forgiveness. Bring into your mind, actually into your heart, the image of someone for whom you have much resentment.

Take a moment to feel that person right there at the center of your chest in the heart center.

And in your heart say to that person, "I forgive you for anything you may have done in the past, either intentionally or unintentionally, through your thoughts, words, or actions that caused me pain. I forgive you."

Slowly allow that person to settle into your heart.

Don't judge yourself for how difficult it is.

No force, just opening slowly to them at your own pace.

Say to them, "I forgive you. I forgive you for the pain you caused me in the past, intentionally or unintentionally, by your thoughts, your deeds, your words. I forgive you."

Gently, gently open to them. If it hurts, let it hurt. Gradually open to that person. That resentment, that incredible anger, even if it burns, ever so gently though. Forgiveness.

"I forgive you."

Let your heart open to them.

It is so painful to hold someone out of your heart.

"I forgive you."

Let your heart open just a bit more to them. Just a moment of opening, of forgiveness, letting go of resentment.

Allow them to be forgiven.

Now opening more to forgiveness, bring into your heart the image of someone from whom you wish to ask forgiveness.

Speak to them in your heart. "I ask your forgiveness for anything I may have done in the past that caused you pain, either by my thoughts or my actions or my words. Even for those things I didn't intend to cause you pain, I ask your forgiveness."

"For all those words that were said out of forgetfulness or fear. Out of my closedness, out of my confusion. I ask your forgiveness."

Don't allow any resentment you hold for yourself to block your reception of that forgiveness. Let your heart soften to it. Allow yourself to be forgiven.

Let yourself be freed.

Let that unworthiness come up, that anger at yourself—let it all fall away. Let it all go.

Open to the possibility of forgiveness.

"I ask your forgiveness for whatever I may have done in the past that caused you pain. By the way I acted or spoke or thought, I ask your forgiveness."

It is so painful to hold yourself out of your heart.

Bring yourself into your heart. Say "I forgive you," to you. Don't reject yourself.

Using your own first name, in your heart say, "I forgive you." Open to that. Let it be. Make room in your heart for yourself.

"I forgive you."

All those resentments, let them fall away.

Open to the self-forgiveness. Let yourself have some space.

Let go of that bitterness, that hardness, that judgment of yourself.

Say, "I forgive you" to you.

Let some glimmering of loving-kindness be directed toward yourself. Allow your heart to open to you. Let that light, that care for yourself, grow.

Self-forgiveness.

Watch how thoughts of unworthiness and fears of being self-indulgent try to block the possibility of once and for all letting go of that hardening.

See the freedom in self-forgiveness. How can you hold to that pain even a moment longer?

Feel that place of love and enter into it.

Allow yourself the compassion, the care, of self-forgiveness. Let yourself float gently in the open heart of understanding, of forgiveness, and peace.

Feel how hard it is for us to love ourselves. Feel the pain in the hearts of all those caught in confusion. Forgive them. Forgive yourself. Let go gently of the pain that hides the immensity of your love.

● ● ●

What usually blocks forgiveness is pride and resentment. When resentment arises, we usually dive right into it. We lose our space. We identify with it and, instead of recognizing resentment as simply the frustration of old desires and old holdings, we close. But resentment can be used as an object of investigation. Allowing that state of mind to be there without judgment or fear allows the heart to open and we find ourselves not loving out of separateness and duality, but simply "in love" with another. Sharing the space of love. Sharing being. Beyond the mind's models and fears, we sink deeply into the heart of things.

In the years that I taught a meditation class, I discovered that even those who had considerable meditation experience found it quite fruitful to include the self-forgiveness meditation in their practice. To cultivate those qualities that went beyond the mind's narrow concepts and images. Simply opening to how things are. Those who practice this meditation, even fifteen minutes a day, found, in a relatively short time, that there was more room in their hearts for themselves and all others.

Indeed, some who have worked with this meditation have, in the beginning, found a very real warmth and openness. To others it seemed mechanical and dry. In the beginning of this practice, many wonder if indeed there is any forgiveness in their heart. Sometimes it takes a while to nurture this much neglected quality. The mind may interpose all sorts of "rational" blockages to the heart's openness, insisting that self-forgiveness is simply indulgent: the merciless mind. When we observe our unfinished business with ourselves, the painful encrustations of the heart, we come to sense the pain that is present in every heart. And forgiveness turns to compassion. When we have compassion, pain dissolves into love. All that seems so separate merges into the One. All are ourselves. No unfinished business.

8
GRIEF

When I was seven my best friend died. I was born with a systolic heart murmur, a leaky valve, which caused me to tire easily and did not allow me to participate in sports or the heavy play that joined most of my peers. Eric had leukemia. When we met we instantly tuned into each other. Our play together had a joy I had never known, a camaraderie and equality I had not experienced. He was my first real friend. I can remember sitting on the floor of his bedroom surrounded by toy soldiers and Lincoln Log fortresses, happier than I had ever been. The room was filled with light. My heart was wide open; we loved each other. We could hardly wait to get together after school. Then one day he wasn't in class. After school I ran the two blocks to his home only to be met at the door by his weary mother, who told me Eric was too ill to play. He died two weeks later. I was torn apart, bewildered, disbelieving, angry. It couldn't be so! I had at last a close friend but where had he gone? Who could I turn to? No one understood.

My grief and confusion were an embarrassment to my teachers and parents. I couldn't believe he was gone. In disbelief, going once again to Eric's house, slouched on the lawn waiting for Eric to come out and play, his mother peeked from behind closed curtains and then disappeared. I went up on the porch and she met me at the door. Dismayed by my great sadness she told me that I shouldn't be so sad—"Eric didn't die, he just moved away"—and I should go home. For weeks I was lonelier than I had ever been. I felt I couldn't trust anyone or anything, not even life.

As the years passed the valve in my heart healed and I found other friends and loves. I even apparently forgot Eric. Until almost thirty years later, assisting for the first time in a "Death and Dying Workshop," listening to the closing comments of parents who had gone through considerable grief work, thinking to myself how lucky I was to have never lost a loved one, when Eric's room, aglow with our friendship, flashed into my mind. I was seven years old again. I had lost the source of my greatest joy.

As a child I could often feel the pain of others in my heart. It made me angry to be alive in such an anguished world. I couldn't stay open to the suffering I saw around me, or to the pain within. It took years to allow my heart its vulnerability. The grief had torn me open but I hadn't known what to do with the pain.

Now, as I think back to that time, tears still come and I feel Eric still in my seven-year-old heart. And though I somehow still miss him, I sense that his death was a kind of initiation for me. What I felt seems never to have quite left. Each dying friend I am with reminds me to let my heart be torn open, that love never dies. We are here to discover the truth and to use it in the service of love. No one I have ever met has given more meaning to my life than Eric.

● ● ●

I've been with many people whose grief has been beyond bearing. And in some ways it has been the best thing that ever happened to them. For they come to plumb the depths of their being. When we experience grief, we are not just experiencing the loss of our son or daughter, our husband or wife, our parent or loved one. We are dropped into the very pit of despair and longing. We are touching the reservoir of loss itself. We experience the long-held fear and doubt and grief that has always been there. It is not an experience that most would choose, though the confrontation with this area of deep holding seems to be an initiation often encountered along the fierce journey toward freedom, spoken of in the biographies of many saints and sages.

We push away the unpleasant, and there are probably few experiences that are more unpleasant than grief. But there you are in grief and your whole awareness is dropped into the reservoir of loss, where all the holdings, longings, and fears are painfully present. Some people speak of grief as though they were walking beneath a great ocean. Some experience it as an incredible opportunity to get in touch with places they would probably never have access to otherwise. I see people start to bring some acceptance and light and softness into a mind that is on fire, some openness to the grief and loss that they have held for so long.

Some years ago a woman told me of her daughter's death while the family was vacationing on the Oregon coast. Her six-year-old daughter and ten-year-old son had been floating on a log just offshore, bobbing in the water, yelling and playing as the waves rolled over them and they tried to hold on. A wave would come and they would ride the log, squealing and laughing. A lot of joyful chaos. A wave came along and rolled the log over, but as the children scrambled to hold on, an unusually large second wave hit, and the six-year-old girl was dragged out to sea before anyone could get to her. They couldn't find her body anywhere.

A few days later, the coroner called her down to the morgue to identify the body of a child that had that morning been retrieved from the ocean. As the woman came into the coroner's office, he said he wanted her to know that what she was about to see was the partially eaten remains of a child. A shark had gotten to the body after it had drowned. As they pulled back the sheet, she went through the most profound pain she had ever experienced. She also went through the most profound experience of love. Looking at the partially eaten remains of her daughter, there was simply no way she could hold the experience. She was blown out of her mind. She went beyond herself. And she touched something that was essential in her being. That moment confronted her with all the places she was separate from other beings. And, most painfully, from herself. There was no place to hide. There was nothing she could do that would make it go away. She just had to be there, in the presence of the moment. Indeed, I don't think she could have met an enlightened being that would have transmitted more to her than that moment did.

The potency of that grief was so intense she had to let go, to surrender. All the places she hid were illuminated in a blinding flash. A year later, she told me it was the most profound experience of her life and that, "It opened me. It turned my life around. My priority became to touch and understand and open to the hearts of others."

If we can say that grace is a sense of connectedness, that it is the experience of our underlying nature, then we may see how what is often called tragedy holds the seeds of grace. We see that what brings us to grace is not always pleasant, though it seems always to take us to something essential in ourselves.

There is a story of the great Tibetan teacher Marpa, who lived on a farm with his family a thousand years ago in Tibet. On the farm, there also lived many monks who came to study with this great teacher. One day Marpa's oldest son was killed. Marpa was grieving deeply when one of the monks came to him and said, "I don't understand. You teach us that all is an illusion. Yet you are crying. If all is an illusion, then why do you grieve so deeply?" Marpa replied, "Indeed, everything is an illusion. And the death of a child is the greatest of these illusions."

He honored the moment, allowing himself the heart's capacity to hold the paradox that though things may not be as they appear; nonetheless, the pain of separation from a dearly loved one is among the greatest of a lifetime. He acknowledged the natural transcendence beyond the body, awareness continuing its journey, but also honored the deep feelings of loss on the level at which they occur, excluding nothing, opening to the dynamism of the universe offered at this time of intense loss and potential oneness.

This is perhaps the most difficult of the balancing acts we come to learn: to trust the pain as well as the light, to allow the grief to penetrate as it will while keeping open to the perfection of the universe.

When we speak of loving someone, what we mean is that that person acts as a mirror for the place within us which is love. That being becomes our contact with ourself. When that mirror is shattered, the grief that we feel is the loss of contact with that place within us which is love. Thinking of that person as other than ourself, we mourn our loss, we reexperience our sense of separateness and isolation that originally motivated us to look outside of ourselves for that essential unity we call love.

Examining the loss of our reflected love we come back in contact with ourselves, with love itself, in the formless connection that was always present between us. In touching love, we touch the other. In touching what was shared, the grief burns its way to the center of the heart.

As we have said, "love" usually means the emotion, the state of mind that looks outside of itself to find itself. The emotional love of that businesslike way of relating that keeps totaling the accounts, that continues to make sure that another is not getting the best of us. It is a very tentative way of relating. It is the self-interest out of which a friend of twenty years can be "written off" because he no longer reinforces our image of ourselves. We notice we love no one who does not pay tribute to our idea of who we are. But it is our essential love that we experience when the grieving mind sinks into the ever-present heart. Grief of the loss of the mirror. Grief for the lost reflection of the place within where all love originates.

Recently we spent some time with a couple whose eleven-year-old daughter had been abducted and murdered. It was every parent's worse nightmare. There was no way they could control the universe. There was no way they could make it go away. Their pain was so extraordinary that they simply could not hold onto it any more, and their hearts were torn open.

Soon after the death, they wrote a letter to Ram Dass:

"We go on, though we have no stomach for it. We try our best to be there for our two remaining children and that is also sometimes hard. We constantly search our own hearts and those of many friends and relatives who have opened to us, for deeper understanding and new meaning.

"I see Rachel as a soul who was actively engaged in her work while on earth. Her last three years in particular showed me the flowering of a shining being—caring, loving, and reaching out to the members of her family and many friends and relatives, young and old. She was always giving little 'love' somethings to everyone. To make you smile, to help you feel good, to show she cared. She had learned somehow to bear her defeats and frustrations and not be intimidated or slowed by them. The petals were opening and reaching for the sun. She was not a clone of her parents. She was who she was. She was the best of us and the strongest of us. The wake of Rachel's death leaves the many beings who knew her and a surprising number who didn't torn open to this 'teaching.'"

When Ram Dass received this letter, he responded:

"Rachel finished her work on earth and left the stage in a manner that leaves those of us left behind with a cry of agony in our hearts as the fragile thread of our faith is dealt with so violently. Is anyone strong enough to stay conscious through such teaching as you are receiving? Probably very few, and even they would have only a whisper of equanimity and spacious peace amidst the screaming trumpets of their rage, grief, horror, and desolation.

"I can't assuage your pain with any words, nor should I. For your pain is Rachel's legacy to you. Not that she or I would inflict such pain by choice, but there it is. And it must burn its purifying way to completion . . . For something in you dies when you bear the unbearable. And it is only in that dark night of the soul that you are prepared to see as God sees and to love as God loves.

"Now is the time to let your grief find expression—no false strength. Now is the time to sit quietly and speak to Rachel and thank her for being with you these few years and encourage her to go on with her work, knowing that you will grow in compassion and wisdom from this experience.

"In my heart I know that you and she will meet again and again and recognize the many ways in which you have known each other. And when you meet, you will, in a flash, know what now it is not given you to know. Why this had to be the way it was.

"Our rational minds can never 'understand' what has happened. But your hearts, if you can keep them open to God, will find their own intuitive way.

"Rachel came through you to do her work on earth [which includes her manner of death]. Now her soul is free and the love that you can share with her is invulnerable to the winds of changing time and space."

As our friends opened to their grief, they opened to their love. They experienced Rachel at a level which they seldom touched before. Less and less, as they opened, were they so caught in the forms which always separate parent from child, loved one from loved one. Instead, the grief which spins and burns the mind begins quietly and gently to sink into the heart.

In grief it is often seen that at first the pain of separation is in the mind—thoughts of the departed, fantasies, conversations, and memories. The relationship, still in form, conflagrates the mind. The relationship is experienced as mother for child, as husband for wife, as body for body. But eventually the grief opens into the heart, and the individual is not so much experienced as a separate body but is the essential connection that joined them in the first place. Then just the love remains. The abyss of "I" and "other" that once separated them melts away and they become one, beyond the form, beyond the ideas and models of who each might have been. The forms are seen through and just the love is felt. Then grief, the tearing open of the heart, leaves the heart vulnerable and exposed. And the deep lesson of compassion, for which we were born, becomes evident.

During a workshop a few years ago, a professor of parapsychology at a southwestern university mentioned that he had done fifteen hundred hypnotic life-regressions. One of the other participants said he would be willing to be regressed to feel what that process might be like. The fellow to be regressed was a big, burly white-water rafter from Oregon, about six-foot-five, two hundred and forty pounds, with a huge red beard. A very gentle sort. As he timidly lay down on the large couch, many of the people from the workshop gathered round.

The regressionist seemed quite skillful and quickly hypnotized his subject, taking him back through earlier childhood memories. His sixth birthday party. His first day at school. Infancy. And then past this lifetime into what appeared to be a previous life. Taking the fellow to twelve years old in this earlier life, he asked how things were going, at which the white-water rafter became very scared and said, "I'm lost. We're all lost. What should we do? I'm frightened!"

The regressionist reassured the fellow that everything was going to be O.K.; to relax, to let go. Going backward, taking him out of this painful moment, and into yet an earlier life in which it appeared that at twelve he was very happily living with his father in what was the northern forests of Germany. His father was a woodcutter and he was his helper and great admirer. Telling about how his life is at thirteen, fourteen, and fifteen in the great forests, stacking wood and occasionally going to town with his father to trade for essentials. The regressionist, after a bit, asked him to continue in his native tongue. A linguist from a Texas university attending the workshop told us he was speaking an antiquated German-Dutch dialect. She was able to translate much of what he was saying. He was very happy, living and working with his father, learning the skills of a woodcutter. At eighteen, with great alarm, he told of an accident, of a tree falling on his father and his father being killed. He began to sob. His grief shook the couch on which he was lying. His face was red, his eyes swollen, tears flowed down his cheeks and soaked his beard. His body was shaken by convulsions of grief. "Oh, Pappa is dead; my pappa, my pappa!" This eighteen-year-old boy was clearly experiencing a great loss. The regressionist continued to move forward through that lifetime. At twenty he had taken over his father's business. Still, at any reference to his father, considerable grief was displayed. Twenty-two, twenty-three. He had settled into the life he had shared with his father. A woodcutter who occasionally went to town to sell his wares and trade for those goods he needed. At twenty-seven, the fellow met a woman in a nearby village where he was delivering wood. He was talking about his new friend with much interest, and began courting her over the next years. He was obviously very shy. After the fellow told about rather formal meetings with her over the next three years, the regressionist asked, "Have you kissed her yet?" And he blushed and said, "Oh no! No!"

At thirty-two years old, they got married. A few years of happy married life ensued and then his wife died. The grief that came forth was immense. Again, shaking the couch, his beard dripping with tears. The regressionist gently brought him back. The fellow sat up, his eyes puffy, and looked about with absolutely no recollection of what he had just shared, at the commiseration of his fellow workshoppers surrounding him in a hushed circle of condolence. All of us were struck by the immense unnamed grief that this fellow was carrying with him.

Everyone in the room was moved by the potency of the unrecognized grief he carried from lifetime to lifetime, each of us acknowledging the grief that we all seem to carry. The grief we are born with, that unnamed heaviness in the heart that sometimes makes us wonder, even as children, "What are we here for? Why does it hurt sometimes just to be alive?" How many people, imagining the pain in their hearts to be the result of traumas originating in this lifetime, seek out psychiatric help to try to uncover what are essentially unrecoverable events? How many are left with an unnamed sadness for existence itself?

How much of what we call grief is the experience of previous loss? And how do we allow such grief not to be a motivator for our life? How do we get in touch with that deep pain, that place of loss that creates a fear of life itself, our doubt in ourselves about our ability to deeply experience the world because we so fear loss and change?

Guided Meditation on Grief

[To be read slowly to a friend or silently to oneself.]

Standing comfortably or in a relaxed sitting position, explore with your thumbs that very sensitive spot between the breasts on the sternum where the pressure seems most noticeable.

Let your attention come to the heart center, the center of the chest. Just feel it there, right at the sternum, just under that bone. You might feel some heaviness there. Something dense that seems to be blocking the spaciousness beneath.

For some there's a very noticeable ache there. A pain born of the losses and fears of a lifetime.

Don't think it, feel it. Is there a sadness at life?

Don't create it, just open to what's felt. A nameless ache that may have been there for as long as you can remember.

If you're a parent, it's the place that knows that someday either you will witness your child's death or they will witness yours. Inevitable loss.

It's the ache for the thousands of beings starving to death at this very moment. Of the mothers who hold their starving babies to a withered breast.

Reflect on the holdings of the heart. The encrustations and armoring that seem to guard the feelings lodged there.

Begin to press into that sensitive spot, feeling the discomfort, the pain there. Regulate the intensity of the sensation by the pressure of the thumbs pushed gently but firmly into that touch point.

Feel how the heart's pain pushes back against the thumbs that gently probe the inward suffering.

Feel the pain in the heart. Breathe into it.

Let the thumbs push into that sensitive area. But beware of any tendency to use that pain as punishment.

Let the thumbs push into the armoring that guards the feelings of loss and grief there. Focus the attention like a single point of light in the center of the pain.

Go deeper.

Don't try to protect the heart.

Maintaining a steady pressure at the center of the chest, feel the suffering held there. All the loss held, all the fears, the insecurity, the self-doubt.

Surrender into the feelings. Let it all come through.

Allow the pain to enter into your heart. Allow it to meet whatever pushes back. Allow the heart to be completely vulnerable.

Let the achingness open. Don't be afraid of it. Don't push it away. Open into the deepest grief locked there.

The isolation. The complete lack of control over death, or life. The fear of the unknown. The ache of the loss of love.

There is so much grief in all of us. Open to it. Don't judge it. Just experience it as it is.

The inevitable loss of everyone you love. The impotent anger of being tossed into a universe of such incredible suffering.

The death of your mate, your parents, your children.

Just let yourself experience that. Nothing to add to it, nothing to push away. Just see what's there, what we carry with us all the time.

Keep the pressure of the thumbs steady.

Bring it into a soft awareness that melts the holding. Let yourself be fully born even in the midst of the pain of it all.

Let go into the pain. Breathe into it. Allow the long held grief to melt.

Let your heart open into this moment.

Allow awareness to penetrate into the very center of your being. Use the pain as though it were a tunnel and move down that tunnel into the center of your heart, into a universe of warmth and caring.

Feel the heart expanding into space. The pain just floating there. Fear and loss suspended in compassionate space. Breathe into the center of the heart pain. Let go of it. Let the heart open past its longing and grief.

Now take your hands away and fold them in your lap. Feel the sensitivity remaining at the center of your chest as though it were a vent into your heart, draw each breath into that warmth and love.

Breathe in and out of the heart.

Breathe gently into your heart.

●   ●   ●

In this meditation the touch point is revealed which can be used to open the heart. Breathing in and out of the heart center as though it had a vent directly into it is a very useful practice for coming in touch with the compassion within. Breathing in with each breath, the extraordinary perfection of things; breathing out with each breath, those things that block the heart from experiencing its perfection. Staying with the sensations in the heart center, feeling the heart melt.

Some people work with deep meditation practices to penetrate into the mind and experience aspects of themselves quite beyond who they thought they were, beyond their limited personality. their name, beyond even this incarnation. And they uncover unrecognized holdings, primal fears and terrors. But this is the path for relatively few, though I see many people arrive at this same understanding in a moment of grief, when they are so deep in their feelings that they see it isn't even the loss of their child, no matter how immense, or the loss of any loved one. It is the place of loss itself. They are touching themselves more deeply than they had ever imagined possible.

Entering into this deep darkness is like going into a cave that has been dark for a million years. Yet the light from a single match illuminates the cave and dispels the ancient darkness. Some while in such grief begin painfully to lift their head and look about, seeing the pain they've always carried. It is in this experience, which so magnifies our old ways of separateness, that a new healing begins to occur. We begin to sense all beings as within ourselves. We break our identification with the seeming solidity of separate bodies and separate minds. And we merge into the one heart that beats in us all. After some time, the experience of grief seems to create in many a greater sensitivity to life because the potential for deep healing is so deeply touched. It is difficult in the midst of such anguish to begin to explore a reality so painful. And yet it is the very opening to this level of being, to these hidden fears of loss and desires for security, that brings us to see the possibility of freedom.

Grief can have a quality of profound healing because we are forced to a depth of feeling that is usually below the threshold of awareness. Though many of our motivations come from this level of fear, of loss, yet we don't know where these volitions originate. We simply find ourselves lost in action, in anger or fear, pushing away others, grasping at what we imagined to be our safety, constantly guarding our heart.

This tearing open of the heart leaves us exposed to that which has caused us and our loved ones the pain of imagined separateness so often before. This experience of discovery that grief leads us to is, for some, like going below ground level to look at the roots of a tree whose branches and twigs, leaves and flowers were all you thought was meaningful. It is the tree of life, of your life. The foliage is like the personality, the outward manifestation of being, a by-product of being born you have always imagined to be you. You notice how the leaves appear, the flowers unfolding, and are proud or frightened, depending on how much their shape fits your model of how it should look to the world around. But you have always been "above ground level" in the conscious mind. You have never seen the roots from which all this growth originates. You have carefully pruned and trimmed the tree to eliminate the painful, the magnify the pleasant. Life has become

like an ornamental shrub. The living truth buried beneath layer
upon layer of longing for things to be otherwise. But in grief
there is no hiding. There is no choice or control and you are
forced beneath ground level to the very roots out of which your
life experience has arisen. You enter the dark holdings and the
clamorings of the heart and find yourself torn open to the truth.
Then this tree of personality seems not such a wondrous display of
who you imagined yourself to be. The grief forces you into the
pain you would never examine voluntarily. You find yourself
immersed in the darkness of millennium, and you behold the
very roots and tendrils, even the root hairs, from which this tree
of personality has been nurtured. You start to see the roots of
various desires and judgments and feelings and doubts. You begin
to see the possibility of freedom, of relating to the whole of being.
Not just the flowers and leaves, but to the source from which they
arise. You enter below what is usually accessible to awareness and
see the immensity of this process of growth and being. You see
what has conditioned the arising of so many traits and preferences,
so many ways of acting in the world. Ways now recognized as
inappropriate for the communication of love and the opening to
wisdom.

There is in grief a pitfall for many who think of themselves as
spiritual. A tendency to push away deep feelings, thinking that
they are "unspiritual." "If I were really spiritual, I wouldn't be so
frightened or angry or upset." And on the other hand there are
those who regard only their emotions as real. They say, "All this
transcendental stuff is a way of trying to suppress my feelings."
But in grief one cannot push away hell in order to attain heaven
any more than one can grasp heaven in one's teeth by embracing
hell. It is not either/or—it is both/and. Which brings to mind a
photograph of the silent Indian teacher Hari Dass standing with
his chalk board on which is written, "We must do all."

There is a story of a Zen monk mourning beside the grave of
his recently dead teacher. One of the other monks comes up to
him and says, "You are supposed to be a monk, why are you crying?" The grieving monk turns and says sternly, "I am crying because I am sad."

When understanding comes, when we see the root out of which

experience arises, there is room for everything. There's room for the joy of our original nature, without grasping or holding to it, without hiding behind it as an idea that allows us to suppress feelings. There's room, too, for sadness. But it is unusual for us to give room to such sadness, for feelings that are so unpleasant. We imagine we must suppress them, hide them, keep a stiff upper lip. Some in grief have told me that they are confused about how to allow for such immense emotions. They feel they must manifest their sadness in some socially acceptable way. We have long-conditioned ways of being in grief. We are confused by the immensity of our feelings.

But we are all in grief. All have experienced loss. Even if your loved ones are still alive, there is a place within of disappointment and loss because we live in a world where everything changes. Most display the old scars and rope burns of having one object of desire after another pulled beyond their grasp.

Whatever you want, the more you want it, the more there is a kind of grief, a sickness, a hollowness in the pit of the stomach. Whether it is the desire to see a loved one again, or to stay alive, or to die, or to be successful, or for some new shiny bauble, the very nature of such longing has a quality of grief about it.

There is no security in this world of change. There is no unchanging ground on which to place our seemingly solid feet. Nothing remains the same. There is only the constant flow of changing events, of shadows flickering on the wall. And it is in the holding to such temporal things that suffering originates.

Grief comes from trying to protect anything from being what it is. From trying to stop change. Even for those whose priority is the truth, there may be experienced the great pain of loss as the tendrils of their connection with a loved one are cut, leaving them bereft of their heart's contact with themselves. Each experiences his humanness to the degree he can open to his joy and sorrow.

It is perhaps in grief that we discover the force that carried us once again into incarnation, the reason we incarnated in the first place. It is in the tearing open of the heart that we discover how guarded our lives have become, how small a cage we have traded off for safe ground. We see how our work is to be more loving, to live more fully in an often confusing world.

A world of constant change and infinite insecurity. Where no thought stays but for a moment, where states of mind are constantly in flux and often in opposition. Where nothing that begins does not end. We see that all we love will be pulled beyond even our most tenacious grasping by the ongoing flow of time. We mourn the absence of peace, of some contact with the unchanging, with the essential. We mourn the loss of our original nature. But as we begin to focus on the spaciousness out of which each changing form originates, we begin to see beyond thought. That just behind the ever-changing momentum of the illusory mind, there is a stillness which witnesses all that passes with a sense of equilibrium and compassionate nonattachment.

It is from this stillness that we come to watch the constant change and changefulness of the mind. We see the whole world reflected there. And we notice that everything ends. Every thought ends. Every feeling ends. Each taste, each moment of hearing, each seeing ends. It has never been otherwise. Every experience, every relationship ends. Moment to moment, change unfolds. A moment of hearing followed by a moment of seeing, by a moment of tasting, by thought, by a memory, which dissolves into yet another imagining, which melts into yet another sensation arising in the body. Our experience of life is the experience of change. We see that every state of mind changes. The breath you're breathing right now will end. Birth and decay are the ongoing manifestations of creation. Everything that has a beginning has an end. Nothing stays the same. In this flow of change, there is no real or solid place on which a lasting foothold can be taken. There is nothing which can absolutely be said to be who we are in this incessant unfolding.

Once someone asked a well-known Thai meditation master, "In this world where everything changes, where nothing remains the same, where loss and grief are inherent in our very coming into existence, how can there be any happiness? How can we find security when we see that we can't count on anything being the way we want it to be?" The teacher, looking compassionately at this fellow, held up a drinking glass which had been given to him earlier in the morning and said, "You see this goblet? For me, this glass is already broken. I enjoy it, I drink out of it. It holds my water admirably, sometimes even reflecting the sun in beautiful patterns. If I should tap it, it has a lovely ring to it. But when I put this glass on a shelf and the wind knocks it over or my elbow brushes it off the table and it falls to the ground and shatters, I say, 'Of course.' But when I understand that this glass is already broken, every moment with it is precious. Every moment is just as it is and nothing need be otherwise."

When we recognize that, just as that glass, our body is already broken, that indeed we are already dead, then life becomes precious and we open to it just as it is, in the moment it is occurring. When we understand that all our loved ones are already dead—our children, our mates, our friends—how precious they become. How little fear can interpose, how little doubt can estrange us. When you live your life as though you're already dead, life takes on new meaning. Each moment becomes a whole lifetime, a universe unto itself.

When we realize we are already dead, our priorities change, our heart opens, our mind begins to clear of the fog of old holdings and pretendings. We watch all life in transit and what matters becomes instantly apparent: The transmission of love, the letting go of obstacles to understanding, the relinquishment of our grasping, of our hiding from ourselves. Seeing the mercilessness of our self-strangulation, we begin to come gently into the light we share with all beings. Taking each teaching, each loss, each gain, each fear, each joy as it arises and experiencing it fully, life becomes workable. We are no longer "a victim of life." And then every experience, even the loss of our dearest one, becomes another opportunity for awakening.

If our only spiritual practice were to live as though we were already dead, relating to all we meet, to all we do, as though it were our final moments in the world, what time would there be for old games or falsehoods or posturing? If we lived our life as though we were already dead, as though our children were already dead, how much time would there be for self-protection and the re-creation of ancient mirages? Only love would be appropriate, only the truth.

9
DYING CHILDREN

There is a story from ancient China of the emperor of a great dynasty who wished to celebrate the hundred-year rule of his clan. Hearing of one of the great Zen master-poets, he sent couriers to bring him to the court. When the Zen poet arrived, the emperor requested that he write a poem to commemorate and celebrate and bless the dynasty in its long and powerful rule.

Some weeks later, the Zen master returned to the palace. Taking out a parchment he read: "Grandfather dies, father dies, child dies."

The emperor, upon hearing this poem, became enraged and threatened to cut off the poet's head. The poet bowed to the emperor and said, "Master, this is not a curse on your house, as you presume. But rather the greatest of blessings. For what greater blessing could we have in life than that the oldest die first, and that each may live a long and fruitful life? What is a greater curse to a family than the death of a child?"

Today, as in all times, the death of a child is perhaps the greatest of tragedies. But now, in the technologized West as in no other time this is the experience of the minority, rather than the majority, of parents. A hundred years ago in this country and still in many less technological, so called "Third World" societies, infant mortality and the consuming fevers of childhood caused most families to experience the loss of one or more children. It was a common practice to build a large family with many offspring to carry on the work of the farm or artisan craft, because it was an accepted given that a number of children would never reach maturity. Wandering through any 18th or 19th century cemetery, the number of tombstones marking the graves of children is striking. Though these times may be unique so far in medical history, the loss of a child is certainly no less painful now than it ever has been. Though fewer may grieve the loss of a child, the heart's experience of loss, the deep grief and mourning, is no different from what it has been from the very beginnings of time.

There is a story from the Buddhist tradition of Krishna Gotami, whose only son died. In her grief, she carried her dead child to the neighbors asking for medicine to cure her son. People thought she had lost her senses. So Krishna Gotami went to the great teaching master known as the Buddha and cried out, "Lord, give me the medicine that will cure my boy." Buddha answered, "I will help you, but first I want a handful of mustard seed." When the mother in her joy promised to procure it, Buddha added, "But the mustard seed must be taken from a house where no one has lost a child, a husband, a parent or a friend. Each mustard seed must be procured from a house which has not known death." Krishna Gotami now went from house to house in the village, and the people pitied her and said, "Here is a mustard seed. Take it." But when she asked, "Did a son or daughter, a father or mother, die in your family?" they answered her, "Alas, the living are few; but the dead are many. Do not remind us of our deepest grief." There was no house but that some beloved had died in it.

After some time Krishna Gotami returned weary and hopeless, and sat at the edge of the roadside, watching the lights of the city as they flickered up and were extinguished once again. At last, the darkness of the night reigned everywhere and she sat contemplating the ever-changing fate of humanity.

On her return, Buddha, seeing the understanding that had arisen during the night, said, "The life of mortals in this world is troubled and brief and combined with pain. For there is not any means by which those who have been born can avoid dying." Allowing the pain to be as it was, Krishna Gotami buried her son in the forest. Returning to the Buddha, she took refuge in his teaching and began to tread the heartful path of liberation.

A few years ago, I was invited to visit Presbyterian Medical Center's Children's Hospital in New York City. The two floors I spent time on were the children's wards for cancer and cystic fibrosis. These diseases often have a long degenerative process, so that the child might come into the hospital at first diagnosis and be there a few months before returning home, coming again to the hospital for occasional chemotherapy and diagnostic testing on and off for years. Often these children, returning for a last-ditch effort against their disease, died on these wards.

I shared a few days with a girl who, when I met her, was just a couple of weeks away from her twelfth birthday. She was dying of leukemia. Her mother was very attentive and stayed in the room most of the time. The young girl had been in and out of the hospital for three or four years, and it now seemed that she was getting close to the end of her life. She had some physical pain, but more evident was her confusion. As it turned out, she and I had an instant rapport and soon found ourselves talking about the degeneration of her body, as it seemed it might soon fall away. I asked her, "What do you think is going to happen?" She said, "I guess I'm going to die." I asked her, "What do you think is going to happen after you die?"

Now, as I entered into this communication with her, I did not come with any knowing, any understanding that I was attempting to superimpose. I was there, willing even to be wrong, just sharing with her whatever seemed appropriate in the moment. She said, "Well, I guess I'm going to die and go to heaven. And I'm going to be with Jesus." I asked her, "What does that mean?" She said, "Jesus is fair in heaven, but he's not so fair on earth."

To me, that was a signal that she was mimicking her parents' confusion. The child was confused about what or who Jesus was, though this was the unknown quantity into which she must leap upon leaving her body. How could anyone be trusted who was fair in one instance, but not in another? It meant she thought that

Jesus was essentially unfair, even quixotic in his judgment. In essence, she believed she was going to a place that was not altogether just.

We began to share an extraordinary investigation together, neither of us knowing the outcome. Both of us were willing to open to this moment of truth we were sharing. Not in a self-conscious way, but immersed in the loving feelings of the moment. I asked her, "Why do you think that Jesus is not fair in one place and yet is in another?" She replied, "I'm so sick and I haven't done anything wrong. Why should I be sick? Why should I be dying?"

Trusting the intuition that allows us to sense the heart of another, we began talking about how it was for her in her daily life at home. She said, "I'm in school for maybe a couple of weeks at a time. Then I'm away, because I'm too weak or because I have to go to the hospital. But I'm trying to keep up with my studies." I asked her how her relationship was with the other children in the school. And she said, "Well, I've got a friend in school who has a withered arm. And I'm really the only one there who is kind to her, who hangs out with her. The other children are so busy with themselves that they call her names and sort of pick on her in the schoolyard. They seem so angry at everything that's different. I think they're really scared." When I asked her if she was the same way, she said, "No." When I asked her why not, she said, "Well, I have been in such pain and have been so weak at times that I somehow can feel what it must be like for her. To have life be so hard and to be so pushed away like that."

It was clear how much her heart had opened from the experience of these years of cancer. And I said to her, "Look how much more compassionate, how much more open, how much more caring you are than your schoolmates. Isn't that all because of your sickness, which you say Jesus gave to you? So this openheartedness, this kindness and love you feel for people that has come out of your illness, is it a tragedy? Or is it somehow, in some remarkable way, a gift of love, a gift of caring that sensitizes you as others seem not to be?" She said, "No, I wouldn't trade this feeling for anything." And then a big smile lit her face and tears rolled from her eyes, and she looked up at me and said, "Jesus is fair on earth. Jesus is fair in heaven."

She had resolved her confusion and fear by entering into them. Not by mimicking another's feelings, but by trusting her own process of learning and maturation, which had obviously gone so far beyond her contemporaries' feelings for other beings. She was able to feel Jesus, this unknown, within her as compassion. She had a context for her illness that she didn't have before. It somehow became workable for her. And a few weeks later on the day before she was to be twelve, sharing imaginary birthday cake with her in the morning before I left New York City, she looked up at me with weary, peaceful eyes and said, "Thank you." She died that afternoon.

Another child I was asked to see was a two-and-a-half-year-old boy dying of leukemia. Besides being very weakened from the illness, he displayed several side effects of the treatment, including a severely fissured anus, blood clots in various places on his body, and a shunt to aid the induction of the chemotherapy he was undergoing. His body clearly reflected the degenerative state of his illness. As I walked up to the metal crib in which Tony lay, he looked up at me and the two other people who accompanied me with eyes that seemed wide open to every possibility. His eyes stayed with each face for a few moments before moving on to share with the next. There was nothing cursory in his glance. He was completely present. Looking into his eyes was like looking into the night sky. He was so open to the moment, to death. He was so extraordinarily there for what was happening.

Although, clearly, Tony's body could hardly hold his life-force, he did not withdraw, but instead moved toward this unknown spaciousness that he so willingly shared with all who came near. His acceptance of death was somehow transmitted to his mother, who later took me aside and asked me what she should do. She was confused because, although the most precious thing in her life was clearly moving beyond her touch, somehow in her heart there was an incredible okayness about it. She feared there was something the matter with her. Her husband, a career military man, insisted that his boy was not going to die. He found it very difficult to visit, to see his son so close to death, to experience the peace in that room.

Tony's mother and I spent some time together sitting in another room, talking about how it was for her, feeling such openness and yet such confusion. She spoke of a warmness in the sharing with her son. And she said that somehow she could understand, could feel—not intellectually, but in her heart of hearts—that there was a contract between her and Tony that was bringing each to a fulfillment for which they had been born, but she said she couldn't imagine how this was so. And I said, "Well, can you imagine, can you just fantasize for a moment that there are these two unborn beings, floating between births, with love and great concern for each other's well-being? One of these beings turns to the other and says, 'You know, there's so much to be learned in a lifetime, I wonder if we couldn't help each other. Imagine if one of us were born a woman and, at thirty-one, had this beautiful, incredibly shining child. Every mother's dream of angelic perfection and loving-kindness. Then, let's say after sharing two years of life, the child is found to have some serious illness that evicts him from the body. And these two beings are forced to share the loss of this powerful contact. They share it in love, not holding on to the body, but remaining in each other's heart to complete the experience.'

"These two beings, between births, sit down and say, 'Well, that sounds fruitful. Let's do it. One of us can be the two-year-old and die surrounded by love, and the other can be the mother, so confronted with all that has kept her separate that she completely surrenders her knowing and just remains in her heart, in the very essence of the contact she has with her son, as she watches his body deteriorate beyond her control. And it takes her to the direct experience of what's real. Her heart opens more fully than ever before.'

"So, one being turns to the other and says, 'Well, I'll be the mother.' 'No, no,' says the other, 'You did that another time. I'll be the mother.' 'No, no, I'll be the little boy.' 'No, no.' And so they flip for it. And one comes in and thirty years later the other one comes through and they play it out." Tony's mother said that somehow she could feel the truth of this possibility. Her body could shake with tears at the loss of her son and yet her heart could remain open to whatever possibility might arise. And so, they made their choice and now they find themselves playing out

the end game of this extraordinary contract to bring each other to
deeper awareness and compassion.

A few weeks later, Tony left his body and his mother told me
that somehow she knew beyond reason, beyond anything that
anyone could tell her, that it was all right for him to do so. The
work they had to do was completed with the grace and love with
which it may originally have been intended. After the death,
Tony's father was grieving greatly, with much anger and guilt and
confusion; he felt that he could never resolve it in the way his
wife had. Then a few days later, at the funeral, he had a most unexpected experience. For a moment his eyes shone with understanding and he turned to his wife and said, "I guess I know what
you mean. Somehow I know it's all right for Tony to have died. I
know he is O.K. and doing exactly what he needs to do for himself."

The growth and closeness that they shared was unparalleled by
any other moment in their lives. And though they grieved the loss
of their son, they also experienced great joy and fullness. An
opening into the oneness that death cannot shatter, that cannot be
separated, that does not depend upon a body for the communication of love and the sharing of the very essence that we
are.

A third child that I was asked to visit was a sixteen-year-old
girl who was suffering considerable pain from her cancer. When I
went in to speak with her, she seemed very happy that she would
be returning home later that day. "My dad's coming to pick me
up for the weekend. I won't have to stay in this place for the next
few days." We spoke about what we might be able to do with her
pain and began working with the pain meditation. As we began
softening around the pain and letting the sensation start to float
free, she began to get a little more space around it so that she
could experience the sensation without resistance and fear. Her
whole body seemed to relax and soften, and the light in her became all the more evident. After about fifteen minutes of the
guided meditation, we sat together in soft silence. A few minutes
later, when we were talking about her ability to apply the technique, a nurse came in and said, "Your father's here, but he's
downstairs talking to Dr. Brown." And Charlene, like most

children who have been in and out of hospitals, was very savvy about hospital affairs and knew immediately that something was amiss. She said, "I'm not going home, am I? I'm going to have to stay here this weekend!" The nurse nodded yes and left the room as Charlene began to cry.

I turned to her and said, "Right now, instead of it being physical pain, why don't you try opening around the mental pain of this experience." And she began to open around the disappointment, to release the fist that held it in her mind. She began to soften and open in the same way that she had with her physical pain, and the light returned to her face. She said it was incredible for her; she had never imagined being able to open around disappointment, and that strangely enough, it was somehow more gratifying to be able to soften, to open around this knot of pain in her heart than it would have been to get her original wish. For now she felt that her disappointment, her pain, her cancer, even the degeneration of her body, was somehow workable for her. "I have a tool now," she said. She had some leverage, a way of meeting her experience with some softness, letting go of resistance, using even disappointment and pain as a means of staying open in the midst of a whirlpool of uncontrollable unknowns.

I'm told that she died a few weeks later in softness and acceptance.

I have learned from the dying children I have worked with that children tend to die with greater softness and ease than adults. Perhaps because they have not so involved themselves with attempting to control the universe, there is not so much tension in their minds. They are more open to how things are. They don't have a solid concept about life or death, and so are less attached to name or fame, to reputation, even to their body. Perhaps many aren't afraid of death because they have just come from there. I have noticed that usually the younger the child the less the fear of death. The fear that I do see is often the reflection of the dread that their parents feel.

What children know about death usually comes from their immediate environment. Their fear of death may often be their parents' fear.

There are indeed classic psychological demarcations about how

"the average child" presumably deals with death. It is said that up
to the first year or two, a child really has no concept of death.
Death doesn't exist. It's just another word floating in the air. Between two and four, there seems to develop the idea that death is
impermanent. "Gramdma's dead; when will Grandma be visiting
again?" "My dog is dead"—but they still put food out for Spot.
Death is impermanent. Each comes and returns. As children mature, however, entering school age, they are pretty much in the
world, walking and talking, exchanging ideas, learning and becoming socialized beings. They have already learned where they
must relinquish their naturalness in order to become an acceptable part of the environment. They are already becoming acculturated. They reflect the cultural fear that they have begun to ab-
sorb from the family. In those early school years, you often see a
child relating to death as though it were approaching from outside. The Grim Reaper. Death is going to come and take you
away. As children mature yet more, in the elementary school
years, they have a tendency to become a very solid part of the
world. And then death is often seen as obliteration, as though
your lights got put out, a permanent absolute that sweeps you
away. This feeling develops yet more deeply and can be seen in a
greater fear of death in many teen-agers. What's interesting is, the
older a child gets, the less comfortable he or she is with death. In
a very real way, the older the child becomes, the further he or she
grows from the truth. The child's original belief that death does
not exist, that it's just another moment in life, is closer to the
truth. It's almost as though the longer the child spends in the
body, the more he or she thinks the body is the only reality and
that the loss of the body is the loss of experience itself. It seems
that the younger the child, the greater the contact with the
deathless and therefore the less the fear of change.

Because children seem to have a greater faith and a deeper
contact with the deathless, death does not seem to be such a
problem. It seems that dying children's greatest problem is the
pain they feel they are causing their parents. A child may feel
guilty for creating such discomfort. As adults we sometimes forget, in the self-centeredness of our relationships that the concern
for a loved one's well-being goes both ways. We forget how at-

tached our children are to us, how very protective they can be of our well-being. Though they may argue or even do what we ask them not to, they are in essence very concerned for their parents' happiness. I've seen children dying with considerable acceptance (though of course they didn't want the physical discomfort); their greatest distraction was their confusion about causing their parents such distress. I've seen children hold on to their body and struggle to stay alive, not so much for themselves but to decrease the anguish their parents feel.

A friend of ours, now in her mid-thirties, was on a children's critical care ward when she was ten to undergo open-heart surgery. She told me, "All the kids knew what shape they were in. But they were very light. Not much fear. Pretty joyful. Except when their parents visited, with great heaviness and fear. That got them down for a while sometimes. They all knew they were going to die. I even remember one boy who came in with what we thought was just a broken leg who seemed perfectly healthy. It seemed like no big deal. But he told us he was going to die, and two weeks later he did."

The youngest seriously ill child I've spent time with was fifteen months old. She was dying of a neuroblastoma, a cancer which had originated in the womb. A genetically programmed time bomb that would soon after birth begin to grow and eventually cause the child to be evicted from the form it had so recently inhabited. For the past eight months, Sarah had been undergoing treatments in the hospital. I noticed that while I was with her she was quite calm, lying fairly still in her crib; she seemed almost introspective. But soon after her parents entered the room, Sarah would become agitated and petulant, reflecting their discomfort. The parents, seeing this restlessness, would retreat to the hospital cafeteria with yet greater pain in their hearts. "Oh, my child is so upset with what's happening." Because they never saw their child when they weren't around, they saw only the child's reflection of their feelings. They never saw how O.K. it was with the child.

Spending some time with the parents afterward, one could feel the contention and anger between them. The husband had left work for some weeks to be with his daughter, but since it seemed that her illness might continue for some time, he felt he had to return to work. His wife was nearly hysterical at the prospect of being "left alone with poor Sarah." Resentment and tension were building. She felt that he was calloused in wanting to return to work. He felt she didn't understand how deep his pain really was and how much he needed to surround himself with something familiar. Their daughter was dying, and so was their relationship.

As we continued to share, they began to see that somehow, though what Sarah was going through might be painful for all of them, it was not unnatural. It was a given that they could not wish away. The option existed of either withdrawing in fear and anger, thereby increasing the pain of this experience for all involved, or entering fully into it with love and support and a deep sharing of their grief that went beyond the separateness that such heavy emotions can often create. They could see that somehow this wasn't happening just to them, but was part of Sarah's unfolding as much as their own. That there was a level of sharing that was available to them, of which they had never taken advantage. He said, "You know, I pray that she will be all right and that my wife and I be given some understanding of what this is all about, but my prayer is never answered." As he spoke, I felt that perhaps if his wife could have gotten down on her knees beside him when he was praying, his prayer would, in that moment, have been answered.

The percentage of divorce among couples with an only child who dies is extremely high. Perhaps because they don't share the grief, don't open to the impossibility of that moment, and somehow allow each other to enter into their heart and feel that child within them. Parents need to encourage each other to open to their pain, to acknowledge it, to allow their heart to be torn open and remain vulnerable and sensitive to the truth. The death of a child presents an opportunity for the deepest kind of sharing and commitment to understanding and caring and love.

As it turned out, Sarah's parents had come to the end of their tether and were willing to try anything, even opening to their fear and projections. And Sarah quieted down considerably with seemingly less discomfort in the weeks that followed. The love that her parents were able to share with her allowed her to come into balance, to die with noticeable contentment in her face.

Remembering that attachment goes both ways, and that children also wish to protect their loved ones, does not mean that the parents should hide emotions so as not to upset children who are ill, but rather to let go of all the boundaries of separatism, to share openly and lovingly the pain, and work together to recognize the givens of the moment. The bridge between the known and the unknown is always love.

A nurse friend was working with a six-year-old boy who had been in a full coma for six months. He had been disconnected from the extensive life-support systems that maintained his bodily functions, but did not die. Instead, he remained unmoving, wasting away to nineteen pounds, an inert bundle of flesh, unable to be alive, unable to die. By this time, his parents found it too painful to see him and had stopped visiting. No one could understand why Mark held on or what he held to.

One day, this nurse spent her whole shift with Mark. Although there was no visible response, as she spoke softly to him, she felt that somehow he could hear what she was saying. It was not rational, but she trusted the heart of the moment. As she was about to massage him with some skin cream, she decided instead to put the cream on his hands. And then, taking his hands, she began slowly to massage his body, talking to him all the time. "Look at this body. Doesn't seem like it can carry you much longer. You may not be able to hang out in it much longer. Why hold on to it? Why not just let it go?" She played music that she felt would be soothing to him, relating to him the images that Elisabeth often uses about the cocoon and the butterfly: that his comatose body was like a cocoon, a chrysalis, and that soon he would leave it behind, becoming the butterfly that he always was, and just go on. As my friend worked with Mark, she felt, beyond verbalization, that somehow there was communication. As the day went by, she sang to him and stroked him and spoke to him about the okayness of letting go. And an understanding intuitively arose that perhaps the problem was not that he needed permission to die, for his parents had said to him on many occasions that it was O.K. to let go, but his concern for his parents' well-being. His attachment was so strong that he needed to know, not only that he

would be O.K. when he died, but that they would be all right as
well.

After the shift was over, the nurse called the parents and asked
them to meet with her in the garden behind the hospital. Spending
some time with them, she related her feelings of the day.

Two hours later, she received a call from Mark's mother. She
said, "We went up to the room and put on the music you left
there, and the nurse in charge put Mark in my arms. I sat there
rocking him, this lifeless form, back and forth in my arms. And I
said to him, 'You know, honey, you'll be O.K. if you die—and so
will we. We'll be all right, if you just let go and die.'" And, at
that moment, he sighed and died in her arms.

We need to remember how compassionate children can be and
reassure them that we, the big tough guys, the adults who know
everything, also have pain, but that we can work with it and, like
them, are learning more of love and life through what is being
shared.

I have a friend named Wavy Gravy who often volunteers as a
clown for dying children in the hospitals in San Francisco. He's
been doing it for some time now. He told me that when he is with
a dying child he says something like, "You know, look at this
body. You can see that it's really not much use. It's not strong
enough to ride a bicycle. It can't play ball. It can't go out and
skip rope. In fact, you can't even go to school. When your body
falls away, you'll be just fine. And you'll probably see a light. If
the light goes left, go left. If the light goes right, go right. That's
all there is to it."

The children aren't so involved in the melodrama he says. The
children aren't so lost in concepts of death. And when the children cry, he gently picks the tears from their cheeks and puts
them to his lips. If you want to work with dying children, it
would be useful to be able to eat their tears. To love them within
the full circumstance of their pain and the confusion of those
around them. For, as he says, the real pain around most children's deaths is not the children's pain, but the parents'. "There is
so little you can do except share your acceptance of the child's
death, so that you don't reinforce the fear and pain of the parents."

The death of a child is a fire in the mind. The mind burns with alternatives that never come to pass, with fantasies of remarkable recuperations, with dreams of adult accomplishments. If we let this fire burn compassionately within us the grief of the mind, the fantasies, the burning of the spirit, begin slowly to melt away and the child comes more into our heart. Our anguish can be used to open more fully, to enter as completely as we can into this final sharing. And then, as Rabindranath Tagore wrote in the final lines of his poem "The End," "Dear Auntie will come with presents and will ask, 'Where is our baby, sister?' And, Mother, you will tell her softly, 'He is in the pupils of my eyes. He is in my bones and in my soul.' "

QUESTION: I can hear how being with a dying child could be very heart opening, but what do you have to say about sudden infant death syndrome?

ANSWER: Some parents have months or years with an ill child. They have an opportunity to open to their loss. But ten thousand infants each year are discovered dead in their cribs with no apparent cause. Those who came crib-side to see the still form of their child are often crushed by the irrational guilt and fear the mind produces when it senses that things are altogether beyond its control. It is a time that calls for great kindness to themselves. And I am reminded of the poem *On a Child Who Lived One Minute,* by X. J. Kennedy, which ends with the lines: "Still I marvel that, making light of mountainloads of logic, so much could stay a moment in so little."

10
WORKING
WITH PAIN

A few years ago a friend requested we meet with a young woman who was dying in a great deal of pain. She had a tumor wrapped around her spine. Her legs hurt much of the time because of the pressure on the sciatic nerve. Her back felt as though it were on fire.

In the first minutes of our meeting, it was clear that this woman had worked hard in her confrontation with cancer and opening to the possibility of her death. Indeed, in the three years since her cancer diagnosis, she had become a very skillful counselor and caregiver and had been with several people at the time of their death.

She told me of the various pain meditations and techniques she had learned from the healers and holistic clinics she had attended. She knew several methods of dispersing pain from the various Eastern and American Indian traditions as well as more recent holistic visualizations and meditations. Techniques for placing the awareness elsewhere so that pain would not be experienced.

She had become so adept at the use of these techniques that her therapists and counselors had asked her to participate in helping teach at their workshops. She had been invited to participate in healing festivals by some of the most respected healers of the Native American tradition. She said, though, that now that her body was in such agony, most of what she had learned was of very little help. The pain was so intense she could hardly concentrate. She said she had worked with the pain for more than two years, but now it had grown to a point where she just prayed for some release.

With considerable difficulty, she lay down on the couch as I sat on the coffee table next to her. And we began working with a guided meditation to investigate pain, which has been used with many people in similar predicaments. It is an attempt to begin to soften around pain, to open to the intensity of the experience, beyond the concepts of pain and the conditioned fearful responses, the confusion that so often amplifies the experience of intense discomfort.

Directing her attention to the sensations arising in her back and legs, she began to soften around the pain, began to allow the pain —perhaps for the first time—to just be there, so she could uncover what its real nature actually might be. To notice the resistance that seemed almost to form a fist around the pain, and slowly to loosen the fingers that closed around the pain. Bringing her awareness to the mass of sensations in her legs and back, she started to soften the flesh, the tissues, the muscles, the ligaments, all about the pain, allowing the resistance to soften and stretch, encouraging the opening at almost the cellular level. Not trying to change the pain, but letting it float free, letting it just be there in space, not even trying to get rid of it. Just opening to the pain as it was, see Pain Meditation I.

When pain arises in the body, it is very common to close around it. But our resistance and fear, our dread of the unpleasant, magnify pain. It is like closing your hand around a burning ember. The tighter you squeeze, the deeper you are seared.

We have seen that much of what is called pain is actually resistance, a mental tightening reflected and experienced in the body.

As she began softening around the pain, allowing it to float free in the body, she then began to soften around the ideas and fears in

the mind. Thoughts of "pain," "tumor," "cancer," which intensified the resistance and magnified the scope of pain. The concepts and models that turn reality into an emergency.

Without the least force, doing no violence to the mind or body,
she began to let such thoughts and fear-producing images dissolve, giving them space, allowing them to be gently let go of.
Reminding the body to be allowing and soft, she was no longer at
war with her pain. Not reinforcing the compulsive resistance
whose goal is the elimination of the unpleasant. She began to
enter into the sensations, to investigate what indeed this thing
called pain might actually be. It was a process which, she noted
later, was quite different from any way she had previously related
to her pain. Taking her attention and directing it into the pain,
she began to explore the moment-to-moment truth of her experience. As she said later, "I was in pain for years but before going
into it and examining it I would have been hard put to describe
what pain is." She began to investigate: What is the texture of
this sensation? Is it hot? Or cold? Does it stay in one place? Is it
moving? Does it vibrate? What color is it? What is its shape?
Does it have tendrils? What actually is the experience that mind so
quickly calcifies with labels of pain and emergency?

To cultivate the relaxation and sensitivity that allow this soft
awareness and spaciousness to develop see Pain Meditation II.

She entered the sensations arising in her back and legs with an
acceptance and openness she had not previously encouraged. She
began to explore that which her whole life had encouraged her
to escape from. She penetrated the moment-to-moment intensity
of sensation. Later, she related back to this moment of moving
into, instead of pulling back from, her pain and said, "There was
a spaciousness, a gentleness involved in this investigation that I
never associated with my condition." The direct experience of her
pain was quite different from what she had imagined. She said
that indeed most of what she had called pain was actually resistance. Yes, there was pressure and intensity. But the word "pain"
didn't quite suit the experience. She gained considerable satisfaction from entering into that which she had always attempted to
elude.

As she began to soften, moments of resistance would tighten around the pain and cause it to be amplified, creating a knot of tension all about it. Her aversion to the pain had become a hell-realm for her, reinforcing and intensifying each day's discomfort. The more she resisted, the fiercer the pain became. The more frightened the mind, the more she tried to hide, but the only place to hide was in hell. Now though as she opened into it, she found the space to see what was actually happening.

She said she could almost see the waves of resistance that came to meet this new openness ripple along the nerve to magnify the pain. Letting go of resistance allowed a softness, an ease that made room for the pain and allowed it to float free as she had never imagined possible.

She said it was ironic, because it was the first time in these years she had directly experienced that which was so much a part of her life. In opening and entering into the sensation, she noticed that actually the pain didn't stay in one place or even maintain one shape. That it was amoeba-like, vibrating and constantly changing. It was not the burning hot laser beam she had imagined. Not some solid knot of pain. But rather a mass of multiple changing sensations. Sometimes experienced as heat, sometimes as a tingling or pressure. And that in letting go of resistance, much restlessness seemed to dissolve in the mind. Concentrating on the moment-to-moment change of sensations allowed her to become one with her experience. And it brought a quietness to the mind because pain is such a clear object of investigation. She said it was like looking into a bright sun that she had at first wanted to pull back from, but that as she penetrated into the instant-to-instant experience her eyes became accustomed to the brilliance and could almost see the particles of light that made up the blazing orb. See Pain Meditation III.

She said she felt that all the techniques she had acquired for ridding herself of pain were, by their very nature, subtly cultivating the resistance that so amplified her suffering. That until she looked directly into the experience of her pain, those methods whose goal was the removal of pain subtly reinforced her desire to withdraw, her resistance. She had for a moment become one with that which she had always so desperately sought to stay apart from. The pushing away of pain had, she said, subtly intensified her desire for control and her fear of death.

Using her reaction to pain as a mirror for her resistance to life, she saw how much holding there was in the mind, how much fear of life and death. Once she had some insight into the nature of pain and resistance, pain was no longer the enemy and she was able to employ other methods to alleviate discomfort. No longer trying to pry her awareness away from pain she was able to trust her pain, to open around it and to direct her awareness toward some sense of peace.

Much of our pain is reinforced by those around us who wish us not to be in pain. Indeed, many of those who want to help—doctors, nurses, loved ones, therapists—because of their own fear of pain project resistance with such comments as, "Oh, you poor baby!" Or a wincing around the eyes that reinforces the pain of those they are treating. Those who have little room for their own pain, who find pain in no way acceptable, seldom encourage another to enter directly into their experience, to soften the resistance and holding that so intensifies suffering. Pain for most is treated like a tragedy. Few recognize the grace of deeper investigation. As one person said after opening to and exploring their pain, "It isn't just the pain in my spine or my head or my bones, it's all the pains in my life that I have pulled back from that have imprisoned me. Watching this pain in my body makes me see how little of the pain in my life, in my mind, I've given any space to."

Many who have worked with these exercises have said that it wasn't just the pain in their body that they hadn't understood, it was also the fear, the boredom, the restlessness, the self-doubt, the anger which they had always pulled back from, which they had never allowed themselves to enter into. That they had never fully met themselves in life or dealt with death because they had always been encouraged to withdraw from anything that was unpleasant. The unpleasant had always acted as their jailer.

Many have told us that their opening to pain has allowed them to begin to open to what has made life difficult. Has allowed them to begin to understand what anger is, what fear is, what life itself might be. Life begins to open when we begin to recognize the enormity of our opposition. As painful as the body can become, the mind's fearfulness is so much more discomforting. Many begin to make friends with their pain, to meet it as softly as possible, to investigate it as it is. Not just the pain in the body but the suffering in the mind. To look beneath the anger and discover the frustration, the blocked and unfilled desires at things not being as we wished. Investigating this frustration we find beneath it a great sadness and yet letting go deeper the most immense love is discovered. Starting to examine all these states of mind which have imprisoned us in the past becomes a fascinating meeting with ourselves. To penetrate into each state of mind, into each sensation in the body, and to experience it fully so that they no longer have some strange mystique but are seen simply as clouds constantly changing in density and form yet always floating in the spaciousness of being.

Many who have spent their whole life withdrawing from pain come to see that by withdrawing they have never gone beyond their pain. That their whole life has been a juggling act, always trying to keep one ball in the air, never quite grounded in life. They begin to cut the bonds of fear that the investigation of their reaction to physical pain has made them aware of. They move fully into life and, at the moment of their death, leave the body behind without resistance or struggle, in an openheartedness and love that become a legacy of wisdom.

Ironically, we have found that those people we have worked with who have been in the greatest pain are those who tended to go deepest into an exploration of what has kept them bound to fear and resistance. In pain, they have seen how shallow their philosophies or imaginings have been. They come right to their edge in the investigation of life they were never prodded to undertake before. Their pain acted like a fierce and loving teacher that reminded them again and again to go beyond their holding, to investigate deeper, to let this moment be as it is and observe what arises in the fullness of the next.

Then it is not the death of one who wishes at any cost to be rid of pain. It is an opening to how life has been blocked. A clear reception of life that allows one to go beyond death. These are the people who go naked into the truth.

Many we have worked with who were not in pain had less of a tendency to investigate, had less motivation to examine and begin to let go of their suffering. Because things weren't "so bad after all," they imagined they could somehow hide from death in the same way they had hidden from life.

Perhaps the first and most common reaction that locks us into pain is the unending questioning, "Where does it come from?" Those who dwell in the mind's incessant cross-examining of pain have a tendency to stay resistant in a kind of dread that causes pain to linger in the very marrow of their experience. The questioning, self-protective mind screams out, "When will the pain leave!" This, too, is an amplification of that subtle tendency to be elsewhere. It is not easy to let go of such long-conditioned, long-relied-on self-protectiveness. But it is the direct experience of pain these questions cause that encourages us at last to come in peace to ourselves, to open our heart to our experience. Then the question becomes, "Whom did pain come to? Whom will it leave?"

The fatigue that arises out of conflict and resistance to pain decreases our ability to stay present. To perhaps find in the midst of what seems so unacceptable the seeds of freedom, of possible liberation from clinging to the mind and body as being all we are. By withdrawing from pain, we never go deeper, we never ask, "Who dies?"

When the pressure on the spinal nerve is so intense that we can hardly keep still for a moment, we begin to see how that which has encouraged us to "be in control of our life" causes suffering. That the goal of controlling pain, with the idea that pain is the enemy, actually intensifies our suffering, causes the fist to close more tightly. While cultivating the capacity to allow pain to float free in the body and mind offers the possibility of insight and even peace in the midst of that which has always seemed a raging inferno. Control is suffering. Control is the bars that lock us in our cage of identification with our suffering as being all we are.

Many who have been in pain for some time have said that, at the onslaught of their pain, they felt that what was of value in their life had come to an end. All they could think of was, "When will it go away?" Life seemed a tangle of knots and threads, like looking at the windings and loose ends on the back of a tapestry.

Their whole life was a confusion seen from the context of this unacceptable pain. But, as they began to soften and open into pain, as they began to use it as a reminder to go beyond pain; then it was as though the tapestry turned itself around and at last they could see the whole picture. Pain for many seems like a very unworkable situation. But there is no situation that is unworkable. Openness and investigation bring us a deeper understanding of who is in pain, of the essential spaciousness of our original nature. See Pain Meditation IV.

But often, in pain, it is difficult to concentrate the mind, to focus on meditation or even a simple conversation. The technique of counting the breaths has been useful for many in this situation. To count the exhalations up to ten and then begin again. If the specific count is forgotten, to begin again at one. So that it is inhale, "one"; inhale, "two"; etc., to the count of ten. Then beginning again with the number one on the next exhalation. This concentrating on the breath tends to stabilize the mind and quiet the anxiety that may arise from discomfort. (See Paul's experience, in the "Approaching Death" chapter.)

When pain becomes workable, there are no more enemies. There is only an investigation of the unknown. Life once more becomes worthwhile.

It is that willingness to work with what is given—that deep surrender which is not defeat but victory—that allows us to let go of "the experiencer" as a victim, that begins to make room for pain without some separate "sufferer" who is scrambling to be elsewhere. It allows a melting into the One.

The examination of the resistance to pain is an examination of the resistance to life. A resistance that has always been there, that has filtered every perception through its liking and disliking, like a shimmering veil through which every moment of our experience must pass before it can enter fully into our heart. And we discover what may be beyond our idea of ourselves as the tormented victim, the loser. The holding to preferences and judgments, the addiction to old desires, causes more pain than even the burning in our bones. The exploration of pain becomes a passageway back into life.

Working with a woman who said she was suffering from a lot

of pain, I suggested that she begin with a pain meditation which involved moving awareness through the body, sweeping slowly from the crown of the head through the facial muscles, down through the neck and shoulders into the chest, down each arm into the fingers; then through the chest and torso and through the buttocks, and down each leg, until the whole body had been experienced and examined in clear awareness. Going into each area of pain to examine at each point whether indeed that sensation was pain or fear.

She went into the experience with complaints of considerable pain in various parts of her body. But, as she began examining one part of her body after another, she said she saw that most of what she had called pain was actually fear, a yearning for her condition to change. She said, "You know, the way I react to the pain in my body is a reflection in miniature of my whole life."

It is at this point that I would like to underscore the need to begin with great gentleness in this new relationship to pain. One must take one soft step after another, recognizing the mind's addiction to control, its fearful lunges and parries. Our opening to pain is accomplished by an opening of the heart otherwise it will just become another endurance course that creates more of "someone doing something." It is a letting go of what causes suffering, not another false conquering, not some empty heroic gesture. As C. S. Lewis states in his introduction to his book *The Problem of Pain,* "When pain is to be borne, a little courage helps more than much knowledge, a little human sympathy more than much courage, and the least tincture of the love of God more than all."

Opening beyond the aversion that calcifies the heart brings the recognition of how isolated and tense life becomes when avoidance is the predominant strategy. The soft recognition of our long-conditioned withdrawal from what is considered unsatisfactory reminds us of the easiness of mind that is available when we begin to let go, to let things be as they are. The examination of pain breeds compassion and deepens our understanding of how merciless we often are with ourselves. We see that there is nothing to fear in fear. That it is just a state of mind whose magnetic and seductive quality has drawn us away from the spaciousness of awareness again and again, has caused identification with our suffering. The only way out is in. Fear, like all states of resistance, is reinforced by our identification, by our attempt to protect the imagined self, by a sense of emergency.

Fear has the capacity to close the mind, to motivate us compulsively. But fear also has the capacity to remind us that we have come to our edge, are approaching unexplored territory. Its very tightness helps us to realize that the appropriate response is to let go softly, to acknowledge it, to enter into it, to become one with it so as to go beyond to whatever truth may present itself.

Rose came into the hospital in great pain, antagonistic and confused. Her whole life had been lived in a very ambitious businesslike manner, very self-interested. Distrustful that people were "just out for all they could get" and that anyone who was not "was just a failure trying to hide behind some bleeding heart bullshit." The nurses said that she was a very difficult patient, "a real pain in the ass," as one nurse put it. Because of her competitive, resentful lifestyle, she found herself dying with no one visiting. Even her family, her grown sons and daughters, estranged by her consistent judgmentalness and nastiness, refused to come and see her. She was alone and in considerable pain with nowhere to turn. As the days went by, she found that her resistance only caused her illness to become more and more of a hell. Lying in pain day after day was almost too much for her to bear. Until one day, seeing how uncaring she had been of others' pain, something in her heart began to dissolve. Slowly, she began to melt, to become kinder to those who offered aid. Until, at last, the pain of a lifetime of separation and fear tore her heart open. And waves of compassion for the suffering of others began to engulf her. She said, "It's not just my pain. It's the pain of the universe." After Rose had been in the hospital for some time, one of the nurses told me of bringing her a picture of Jesus in the form of the Good Shepherd, standing surrounded by loving animals and little children. And as she was handed the picture, tears began to fall from Rose's eyes and she said, "Oh, Jesus, forgive them; have mercy on them." She saw that her pain was the pain of all. And that in some indecipherable way she lay in the midst of a merciful universe. Her heart had opened because her pain had burned through her resistance to life.

Pain has the ability to open us to love in a way that we never imagined possible. We have never been so vulnerable, so defenseless, as when we are in pain. And it was the falling away of those barriers, the melting away of the knot in her heart, that allowed Rose to touch the existence she shared with all that lived and breathed.

When we open compassionately to our pain we feel the hearts of all around us. All our resistance to having to be taken care of, all our desire for control can no longer be sustained. And we are left torn open to the tenderness of our unknowing. Brought into the immense strength and spaciousness of our ability to accept and go beyond. Not out of aversion, but out of a respect for life and a new wonder perhaps never before experienced. It is this willingness to play the edge of our pain that allows us a greater expansiveness, a deeper experience of who we really are. The resistance to pain obstructs the clear seeing of our true nature. Opening to our suffering we open to all.

I have a friend, a chemotherapy nurse in a children's cancer ward, whose job it is to pry for any available vein in an often emaciated arm to give infusions of chemicals that sometimes last as long as twelve hours and which are often quite discomforting to the child. He is probably the greatest pain-giver the children meet in their stay in the hospital. Because he has worked so much with his own pain, his heart is very open. He works with his responsibilities in the hospital as "a laying on of hands with love and acceptance." There is little in him that causes him to withdraw, that reinforces the painfulness of the experience for the children. He is a warm, open space which encourages the children to trust whatever they feel. And it is he who the children most often ask for at the time they are dying. Although he is the main pain-giver, he is also the main love-giver.

It seems ironic that despite our conditioning to elude pain, to hate that which brings discomfort, our real work may be to bring love to our pain. To allow it a new openness and acceptance that have not been encouraged in the past. Not to hold it or to push against it. But simply to let it be in self-awareness and compassion. Rejecting no part of ourselves. But to relate to all the changes with love and kindness, acknowledging how difficult it is to open when so much of what we have learned is to be closed

Many may ask, "But how can I love my pain? Isn't that some kind of idealistic foppery? Can one really love pain? It's easy to say, but how do you really do it?"

Again conditioning interposes itself, says it can't be done, that we are victims of circumstance, contracts life to some model, to the self-imprisonment of how things are supposed to be.

It is important to recognize that there are various levels and intensities of pain. That all pains may not be able to be opened to with the same ease or perhaps even opened to at all. If we have waited until "the great pain" to open, it is quite possible that we will not have the spaciousness for deeper examination, because there has been so little preparation for such openness. But if we begin to play the edge of lesser pains, disappointments, fears, the wobblings of the mind, the contractions of the heart, in a gentle, day-to-day meeting and expansion, it prepares us for what comes later. It is the daily opening to the little pains that prepares us for the great pain. Playing the edge of our pain should be done with great compassion. Though it takes a certain steadfastness to maintain our concentration on, and openness to, pain, we should be aware of that quality of endurance that subtly creeps in to create some sense of a separate self with its accompanying resistance to life.

One cannot play another's edge any more than one can do another's work for him. Working with someone in pain we recognize that the only work we have to do is on ourselves. We don't push someone else's edge. We only prod our own. It is not our work to insist another play the edge of their pain or, through our confusion, recommend they not use analgesics or pain-killers. It is our work only to understand our own suffering and, therefore, be available at deeper levels to those we serve.

Because we live in a society programmed to escape pain, a society that consumes literally tons of aspirin daily, many are conditioned to elude suffering at any cost. When the physician prescribes powerful analgesics, most take them unquestioningly.

Though, if you are working with someone in pain and are listening closely enough to yourself, you may sense at some moment
the timeliness of gently offering alternatives that may be available. This offering should not be accompanied by even the subtlest
suggestion that if those in pain use these techniques they will be
"doing the right thing," that if they accept your advice they are
good and that if they don't they are weak. This is an openhanded
offering made with a sense of its appropriateness for you, perhaps
even relating how it has worked in your life, without righteousness or judgment.

A friend asked if I would visit her mother, who was dying of
cancer, because she felt she would soon leave her body and that
our meeting might be beneficial. As I entered the room, her
mother's clear eyes met mine with a warm smile and a sense of
quietude. Obviously I had come not for the mother's needs, but
for the fears of the daughters, who crowded around the open
doorway to find some acceptance in themselves of their mother's
death. Talking about having just returned from the hospital for
what the doctors had said would probably be the last time, she
seemed to have little identification with her body, playfully
curling the few strands of gray hair that remained in the wake of
her chemotherapy. She was quite accepting of the considerable
wearing away of her body. There seemed to be little she needed
from me.

Just as I was about to leave I asked if there was anything that
seemed to be obstructing this openness that she so obviously felt.
She said that everything was pretty O.K., except that sometimes
she felt a bit groundless and muddled and didn't know why. This,
of course, could have been the effect of nutritional changes, of
weight loss, of the toxicity in her system, or any number of the
side effects of her condition. But I also sensed that it might be the
effect of the powerful pain-killers her daughters had mentioned
the doctor had given her. She said she didn't have a lot of pain,
but that the doctors had said, "This is a difficult enough time for
you. At least you don't have to be in pain," and had given her a
relatively high dose of a powerful pain-killer to be taken regularly. We spoke some about how she felt after taking her pain
medication and I mentioned that, if she wished, she might play

with decreasing the amount of medication to see if indeed there might be a certain edge she could come to where she wasn't trading off clarity for pain control. Some point at which she was not increasing pain appreciably but was able to maintain a clear awareness of the process. A very delicate balance, but one that she could examine and participate in as she felt appropriate.

As I offered this alternative, I watched closely for any quality in myself that wished her to be in any state other than the way she was, any desire that might in some subtle way motivate me to be "selling" her something that I imagined was best for her. The suggestion arose without the intonation that she "should" do anything at all. Simply an alternative available to her, within her own ability to choose as she saw fit.

Her daughter told me that the next day her mother decreased her medication and within a few hours found she was clearer, yet had no more pain. And that a few days later, she died her own death, with much clarity, surrounded by her loving family, able to say good-by directly and lovingly. She died the death of a whole person, taking responsibility for her life with love for herself and all around her.

Those who wish to work in such a manner with their own pain and with the pain of others will never imply that another has any obligation to them to die or relate to his or her pain in any manner other than that person's own natural way. There is indeed the difficulty, even the real danger, that those who work with dying patients may be making another die their death for them. There is no need to make someone else be who you wish you were, as we so often do with our children and loved ones, frustrated that they are not becoming who we wish we were. Instead, we make room for even our pain and resistance, without self-judgment, we open to ourselves, the universe.

When we begin to play the edge of our pain, we are cultivating a willingness not to compulsively react to life—to start moving toward it, to have a compassion and self-understanding that opens gently into each moment, entering life more fully. Seeing clearly the conditioning that urges us to withdraw, we understand that in a very real sense nothing is coming from outside of us. That it is the pain and confusion of the long holdings of the heart and mind. That such situations as physical pain and the inability to control our destiny cause frustration to arise like slag in the molten mind.

A few years ago, I woke one night with a stabbing pain from a kidney stone. Spending the night alternating between meditating and relaxing in a warm tub, attempting to practice what I preach, opening and softening around the pain, I could see all too clearly the conditioned resistance to tighten, to try to save myself from discomfort. The next morning, going to the doctor to find out more about this condition, I delayed taking the offered pain-killers. During the next hours of tests and X rays and much jostling, the pain became more intense. At this point I accepted what I was told would be a "mild analgesic" to diminish the pain. "Just take the top off it," I said kiddingly to the doctor. I should have known when I saw the wheel chair brought into the office that I was about to get more than I bargained for. A few minutes later, in a deep opiate stupor, my chin was slumped on my chest as they wheeled me into the waiting room to be notified of what they found in further examination of the X rays.

Through the haze I could hear two nurses whom I knew say one to another as they passed the door, "Look at Stephen. Even in such pain he is still meditating." I was not meditating. I was bent.

Every few minutes a technician or nurse would float through my stupor exhibiting their fear of pain. One said, "You know, the pain of a kidney stone is the closest a man can come to experiencing the pain of childbirth." Not too skillful! Another said, "Oh, this must be awful for you. Are you sure you don't want more pain medication?" They were transmitting their fear of pain, their fear of life.

The doctor, returning a bit later, suggested that I go see a specialist because, he said, "Where the kidney stone is lodged could become quite a problem. It's a big one. God, you must be in pain!"

So off we went to the kidney specialist, carrying our X rays under our arm, the world drenched in an opiate suspension. Bouncing along in the car on the way to the kidney specialist, fatigued from hours of pain and an intensification of the kidney's activity because of all the bouncing about, I heard myself say,

"Jesus, please take this pain away." And in the next instant the message arrived, "Take it away? I just gave it to you."

I remembered once again to be present. Although the long conditioned resistance to pain was still evident, I gave the sensations more space. I stopped pushing against the flow. My identification with myself as a victim, as someone in suffering, lessened. And the pain once again floated free.

Entering the doctor's office, he took the X rays and put them on the frosted-glass viewer beside his desk. Turning to us, he picked up a brass letter opener from his desk and pointed to the shadow in the X ray that denoted the kidney stone. "We should operate now. We can go in right through here," he said, angling the letter opener across the gray shadow that defined the side of my body. And I had the distinct feeling that he was going to lay me down right there on the desk and operate with the letter opener in his hand. He became quite excited. "Oh, it's in a wonderful place. It's wonderful to operate on it when it's right there." I felt the shadow of Dr. Mengele floating above us and said with some trepidation, "No thanks, no thanks; I don't think surgery is the way I care to work with this one." And he said, "But if it gets stuck down there, you'll be sorry." I thanked him for his time and quickly retreated.

Returning home, I found it difficult to concentrate because of the presence of the Demerol in my system. But as it began to wear off, I could once again focus my mind and begin to soften around the pain and open into it. I could see that, in a sense, the dosage they had given me to kill my pain was in a way prolonging it by not allowing me to work with it. As the pain-killer wore off, I was able once more to just hang out with the pain until my mind's ability to concentrate re-established itself. As the fog cleared I was able to focus on the kidney stone in the ureter and, using visualization meditations, within two hours had moved it through and out in the most joyous clink I have ever heard as it struck the inside of the toilet bowl.

I saw that the amount of analgesic which had been given to me to alleviate my pain had, ironically, continued my discomfort. That attachment to the cause of my suffering increased as I wished it to leave. It was an interesting one. I learned a lot from that kidney stone. I appreciated that grace. It gave rise to many of the meditations we have since developed.

I saw during those hours of pain that the degree to which I thought of myself as a suffering body was the degree to which the pain intensified. But that as I gave it space and opened, started to feel the space in which all the pain was floating, instead of simply focusing on the pain, that the experience changed.

I was reminded of the experiment done at the Springgrove Clinic in Maryland, working with cancer patients, considering cordotomies, nerve blocks, and other radical remedies to deal with the intensity of their pain. Many of the people who joined in this experiment had for months been so contracted in pain, or their consciousness so dulled by massive dosages of pain-killers, that they had been unable to leave their bed, to go to work, to have sexual relations, or any meaningful communication with their family. With proper preparation and considerable care, the researchers offered these patients an opportunity to use mild dosages of psychedelics such as LSD to see if the experience that ensued would have any effect on the intensity of their pain.

Those who had an experience which took them beyond themselves, a transpersonal experience if you will, as being one with nature, another tree in the forest, or a sense of being some part of the universal energy, whether in a picturesque cosmic melting into the brow of Buddha or a nestling into the open heart of Jesus, seemed afterward to have a very different relationship to their pain. Their experience of themselves as being something more than they imagined broke their identification with their models, including the model that all that they were was their body, that all that they were was their pain. They had a more spacious relationship to themselves. Some who had previously been incapacitated had no pain for months afterward. Others, no longer considering cordotomies, were able to treat their pain with simple aspirin and became quite active once again. All who shared in this experiment did not have the same experience. Those who did not experience some expanded sense of themselves had little change in their pain afterward. But for those who did it was perhaps not that the pain had gone away but that the container, the space within which that sensation was experienced, had greatly increased. There was more room for whatever was felt. They saw there was more to them than the solid body or the limited mind. They had expanded their edge. Because they were beginning to relate to the pain, instead of from it, pain was not the whole of their experience. They began to sense the spaciousness within which it was all floating, see Pain Meditations IV and V.

As the experience of being expands, the experience of pain changes. When some sense of our spaciousness is directly experienced, we start tuning in to "who" it might be that is in pain. We start to see that what changes one thought into the next is precisely the same energy which moves the stars across the sky. We see the context in which we are happening. Not so lost, so imploded by our pains and dramas, opening to some universal process we sense we are. The experience at Springgrove parallels what a pediatric surgeon told us about his experience with his patients' pain. He said that he could probably operate on a newborn using almost no anesthetic, "They have so little identification with their body, so little resistance to pain that it is as if the sensations have more space to float in." He said it wasn't that they didn't feel the sensations but they didn't close around them so quickly. "The pain threshold seems to tighten as the child gets older. The longer he is in the body, the less the area of acceptability, the more the identification with that body. As children get older the same stimuli require more pain reliever. For instance, a one-year-old can get what might be hypothetically called a number-three stimulus and it doesn't bother them too much. A rub on the belly and a few soft words might be sufficient to alleviate the tension. But by the time that child is two or three an aspirin might be required. And by the time they are five or six or seven, that stimulus becomes yet more bothersome. By the time they are ten, there is yet more resistance and it necessitates stronger pain relief. By adolescence the pain has become an emergency and necessitates opiates and the like."

We have been so conditioned to relate to ourselves as the body, so much fear of pain has been absorbed from our environment, that when pain arises it takes up the whole of one's awareness and pain becomes all there is, no space, an emergency to be relieved as soon as possible.

The real end of suffering is not the deadening of nerve sensations, but rather the experience of the underlying reality in which all things flow in context and all things are workable.

A woman, dying in the hospital with a great deal of pain, remarked that many of the nurses came rigidly into the room, fluffed her pillow, remarked at how good she looked that day, offered to comb her hair and put lipstick on her, and left the room without the least ability to help or even be present in any really meaningful way. Others, she said, came gently into her space, open to her situation, and very present. "Those open to their pain were open to mine. Those hiding could only posture and wait for the first opportunity to escape."

As with the meditation that encourages the expansiveness of being where every sound, every sensation, every feeling, every image is seen changing moment to moment in the vastness of awareness, simply bubbles arising and passing away, we come to see that nothing happens outside of us. All floats like clouds in the sky of awareness.

For some people as they undertake this meditation there is a kind of queasiness, a signal of how tightly we have held to our dense idea of who we imagine we are. How much we have clung to our pain! How little openness we have cultivated. As this denseness begins to dissolve, as all is experienced within the vastness of being, there may be a momentary grasping as though to catch oneself from falling. This is not unlike our fear of death, the fear of letting go of control. We fear that if we should take the next step we will drop off into space and that nothing will stay our fall. Not realizing that this space is our original nature, our only real security.

It is the direct experience of who we are that cuts the root of pain. It is by entering into the vastness of being that we go beyond identification with the body and mind. We don't find ourselves so contracted about experience. Indeed, we see that it is the loss of contact with our natural spaciousness that is at the root of much of our suffering. When we start to honor our original nature, no longer is a resistance to life encouraged, a desire to keep a stiff upper lip, an unbreakableness. Instead we touch on the strength of the open heart which has room for it all. Letting go of the control that attempts to suppress life, we open to the possibility of freedom from our greatest suffering: the isolation and self-protectedness of some separate "I."

"Who is in pain?" becomes an echo in space. We sense there is not even some "who" but only an is-ness; nothing separate. And that the nature of such is-ness is love.

Guided Pain Meditations

[Each of these five meditations may be read very slowly to a friend or silently to oneself.]

PAIN MEDITATION I

[Opening around pain]

Sit or lie down in a position you find comfortable. Allow yourself to settle into this position so that the whole body feels fully present where it sits or lies.

Bring your attention to the area of sensation that has been uncomfortable.

Let your attention come wholly to that area. Let the awareness be present, moment to moment, to receive the sensations generated there.

Allow the discomfort to be felt.

Moment to moment new sensations seem to arise.

Does the flesh cramp against the pain? Feel how the body tends to grasp it in a fist, tries to close it off.

Begin to allow the body to open all around that sensation.

Feel the tension and resistance that comes to wall off the sensation.

Don't push away the pain. Just let it be there. Feel how the body tries to isolate it. Tries to close it off. Picture that fist. Feel how the body is clenched in resistance.

Feel how the body holds each new sensation.

Begin gradually to open that closedness around sensation. The least resistance can be so painful. Open. Soften. All around the sensation. Allow the fist, moment to moment, to open. To give space to the sensation.

Let go of the pain. Why hold on a moment longer?

Like grasping a burning ember, the flesh of the closed fist is seared in its holding. Open. Soften all around the sensation. Let the fist of resistance begin to loosen. To open.

The palm of that fist softening. The fingers beginning to loosen their grip. Opening. All around the sensation.

The fist loosening. Gradually opening. Moment to moment, letting go of the pain. Release the fear that surrounds it.

Notice any fear that has accumulated around the pain. Allow the fear to melt. Let tension dissolve, so that the sensations can softly radiate out as they will. Don't try to capture the pain. Let it float free. No longer held in the grasp of resistance. Softening. Opening all around the sensation.

The fist opening. The fingers, one by one, loosening their grip.

The sensation no longer encapsulated in resistance. Opening.

Let the pain soften. Let the pain be. Let go of the resistance that tries to smother the experience. Allow each sensation to come fully into consciousness. No holding. No pushing away. The pain beginning to float free in the body.

All grasping relinquished. Just awareness and sensation meeting moment to moment. Received gently by the softening flesh.

The fist opened into a soft, spacious palm. The fingers loose. The fist dissolved back into the soft, open flesh. No tension. No holding.

Let the body be soft and open. Let the sensation float free. Easy. Gently.

Softening, opening all around the pain.

Just sensation. Floating free in the soft, open body.

● ● ●

PAIN MEDITATION II

[Deep relaxation, filling the body with silence]

Take a few deep breaths and settle into a comfortable position. Bring the attention to the top of the head.

Let the mind quiet to receive the multiple sensations arising there.

What is experienced—tingling? warmth? fullness? hardness? Allow whatever arises to come fully into awareness. Allow it to be received by a soft, open mind.

As sensations become noticeable, observe that sense of soft presence wherever the awareness is focused. Begin slowly to direct the awareness down through the body.

Feel the sensations in the muscles and tissues of the face. Let awareness and warmth soften each part of the body they enter into.

Direct the attention, this feeling of presence, through the whole face. Let all tension be released from behind the ears.

Soften the muscles around the eyes. Let the holding melt. Notice how you may be "trying" to see and let the eyes be soft.

All around the jaw. Let the tension leak away. Let the face be completely soft and relaxed.

Let the attention continue into the throat and neck. Feeling the muscles and flesh. Moment to moment, sensations arising in soft openness.

As each sensation is received, that area releases its tension. Each sensation softening. Opening that area.

The shoulders. The bones and ligaments. The muscles and flesh. Softening.

Nothing to hold. Nothing to support. Just let the shoulders be soft and easy. Completely relaxed. Letting go of tension, of any holding whatsoever.

Let the attention move slowly down each arm. Feel the current in each hand pouring out each finger, releasing all the tension in the shoulders, arms, wrists, fingers.

Feel the abdomen and chest. The torso. Feel the sensations from within. Softening each organ as awareness enters it. The stomach softening. The lungs, breathing free and easy. All by themselves. Let go of any holding in the torso, in the chest.

Just let the breath breathe itself. In open, warm awareness. Nothing to hold to. Nothing to push away. Just awareness, receiving sensation. Moment to moment. In warm silence.

Feel the back. Let the attention move slowly down the spine. Relaxing vertebra by vertebra. All the tension, all the holding, softening, melting away. Just sensation, moment to moment, releasing any tension, any resistance, any holding in the muscles, in the flesh. Softening.

Let the awareness continue to move slowly through the body. The small of the back. The buttocks. Completely relaxed.

Let the awareness come to the anus. If there is any tension, soften. Let go of any tightness. Completely relax the pelvis.

Feel the thighs. Any holding? Let the flesh and muscles melt into the body. Each moment of sensation releasing another instant of tension. Softening. Deepening.

The knees. Any feeling of stiffness? Let go.

The lower legs. The ankles.

Let the awareness enter fully into each part of the body as it moves slowly from head to toe.

Feel the soles of your feet. The tingling. The vibrating. Let each moment soften the body.

Bring the awareness from toe to toe. First, the large toe on each foot. Then, the next. And the next. And the next. Feel the current draining from each toe. The whole body soft and open.

Beginning from the toes, the soles of the feet, the ankles, begin to fill the body with a soft stillness.

Through the calves of the legs. The knees. Let the body be filled with silence. With a vast quietude. Each muscle releasing its tension. Even the bones seemingly to soften, in silence, in space.

Through the hips. A deep stillness. Openness.

Through the stomach. A quietude that permeates every organ.

The chest. Softly breathing as it will. Silence filling the lungs. The heart cradled in a great stillness.

The spine filled with a deep quiet. With a deep sense of peace and relaxation. Sensations coming and going floating in the stillness.

In the arms and shoulders. In the elbows and hands. Silence filling the body. Quieting the mind.

In the neck. In the chin. In the throat. Silence. Stillness. Openness. Let the silence slowly fill the area behind the face. So that the whole face—eyes, mouth, ears—is just sensations floating in the stillness.

Let the stillness fill the body to the very crown of the head.

The body silent. Yielding. Still.

Now let the awareness flow through the body, bringing warmth and patience to each cell; let it soak into each strand of muscle, each layer of flesh. In the ligaments, in the tissues, let the body melt into stillness and warmth.

Let the whole body fill with silence. A deep, spacious softening.

Let the silence engulf you.

Sit gently in the stillness.

●   ●   ●

PAIN MEDITATION III

[Exploring pain]

Sit or lie down in some position as comfortable as possible. Take a few deep soft breaths as you let your body settle into its position.

Bring your awareness into the body. Gradually, let the awareness come to the area of sensation in the body.

Let the body soften all around these sensations. The whole area, soft and open.

Let the tissues soften. Let the flesh soften, so that nothing holds on to the pain. Ligaments soften. Muscles soften.

Don't push the pain away. Just let it be there. Allow the body to soften all about it. To open.

Let it just be as it is.

Don't hold it. Don't resist. Just open softness.

Let the pain float free in the body. Let the sensation be felt in the vastness of awareness.

Gently, allow the whole body to become like open space. No holding. No tension.

Let go all aound the pain. Almost at the cellular level, let the flesh soften. Let it become pliant and open. No contraction. No pushing it away. Let the whole body be soft. Even the bones. The tissue.

Soft and open. All about the area of sensation.

Let go of any tension in the breath. Let the body just breathe by itself. Let the body be an open space in which sensation is received without the least interference.

And, in the mind, where ideas and thoughts of pain cause tightness, gently let go. If you notice thoughts of "tumor," of "cancer," creating fear, soften all about such thoughts. Let go of fear. Let it float free in the mind. Just notice any ideas of pain, desires to escape, fears of being trapped. Don't close around them.

Let these thoughts arise and pass away by themselves. Soften all about them. Old thoughts creating old resistance.

Let go of resistance in the body, in the mind. Let each experience float in the soft, open body. In the vast spaciousness of the mind.

Notice if fear looks for a way out. "When will this pain end?"

"Where did it come from?" "How can I get rid of it?" Such thoughts intensify pain. Cause contraction in the body and the mind.

Allow the moment to be received fully. Let the mind be soft and open and yielding. Whatever thought arises. Let it come and let it go. No need to protect yourself. No need to hide. Just the soft, open mind, without the least interference.

Let the body become like an ocean. Each sensation floating gently to the surface.

Let the body be open and fluid and soft. The hardness melting away. The rigidity dissolving in the vast open sea of awareness. Feel the waves of sensation in the ocean of the body. Feel the still depths. Softening. Opening.

Now, gently direct your attention toward the pain. Without tightening. Without even trying to make it go away. Allow the attention to enter directly into sensation. Investigate this thing called pain.

What is the truth of this experience? What is pain?

If the mind is unsteady in its approach to the sensation, focus on the moment-to-moment flow of sensation in that area. Allow your attention to enter directly into the very center of sensation. Experience it directly. Pain is not the enemy.

For just this moment explore its reality. What is its texture? As you enter deeply into the moment-to-moment change in sensation, at the very center of the area of discomfort, what is the weave, the fabric of this sensation?

Let the body and mind stay soft and open. Allow the truth of this moment to reveal itself in a mind that is not holding or fearful.

What is the "feel" of this sensation? Is it hot? Is it cold? Allow the mind to penetrate into the moment-to-moment flow of sensation.

Does it stay in one place?

Does it move?

Is it round and hard?

Is it flat and soft? Does it have tendrils that move through the body?

Let the attention merge with the sensation. Become one with it. In the very midst of the ever-changing flow, allow awareness to explore the moment-to-moment changes. Penetrate each particle of sensation. Receive each sensation as it arises. Like carefully listening to a melody, note by note. Don't push ahead of yourself. Don't hold back. Just enter fully into the moment. Tune to the instant-to-instant flow of sensation.

Is it solid? Or constantly changing?

Does it stay in one place? Or is it amoeba-like, constantly altering its boundaries? Varying in intensity from one area to another, from one moment to the next.

Let the mind become one with the sensation. Soft. Open. Entering directly. Notice any tension in the mind or body. Soften.

Investigate. What is this sensation? Is it a solid mass? Or constantly moving?

Is it experienced as a knot? As a pressure? As a tingling? A vibrating? What color is it?

Is it heavy or light?

Moment-to-moment change. Sensation arising and passing away. Instant to instant. Enter that flow. Letting go of all resistance. Letting go of any idea of what is being done. Discover the truth for yourself. The sensation just floating in the vastness of awareness. Changing. Moment to moment.

Is it a single point of sensation? Or multiple tinglings that vary from point to point?

Is it weighty and hot? Or light and cool?

Without the least force, enter directly into the moment-to-moment experience of sensation. Opening. Softening. The resistance of the mind and body melting away.

Investigate with a soft, open mind. Examine the experience with an open heart. With an open body. With an open mind.

Gently, gradually, open into the very center of sensation. The mind steady and awake in its very midst. Experiencing it as it is. In the vast spaciousness of the mind. Not holding. Not even thinking. Just receiving this moment. The direct experience of what is. Unfolding. Instant to instant.

Now gently bring your attention back to the even flow of the breath and allow your eyes to open as they wish.

● ● ●

PAIN MEDITATION IV

[Exploring awareness beyond the body]

Sit or lie in some position as comfortable as possible. Let your body settle into its position. Let the whole body be relaxed and soft.

Let it just melt into the chair. Let it just sink into the bed you're lying on. No attempt to support the body. No holding.

Bring your attention into the body. Feel the denseness, the seeming solidness of its mass.

Explore the sensations arising in the body. Feel the hardness of the bones. The substance of flesh and ligament and muscle. Feel the body's density. Its weightiness.

Let the awareness move, slowly, from the top of the head through the body to the feet and the tip of the toes.

Wherever awareness is focused, sensation is received.

Begin, gradually, to allow awareness to come to the edge of the body.

Feel the skin touching the air. Feel the scalp, the top of the shoulders, the hair on the forearms. The point of touch where the buttocks meets its supporting cushion. Feel the feet touching the floor.

Allow the attention to come right to the point of touch. Let awareness examine the edge of the body.

Is the edge of the body the edge of awareness? Feel how awareness extends beyond the skin. Let awareness go beyond this feeling edge. Feel outside the body. Explore the space that touches the skin.

Feel how awareness seems to exist beyond the edge of the body. Feel an inch out into the room. Feel one foot beyond. Feel how the attention radiates outward. Investigate what lies beyond the skin and flesh. The air that surrounds you. Feel how the awareness expands beyond the body.

Let the awareness gradually fill the room.

Feel the walls of the room around you. Like a second body. Expand beyond these walls. Let the mind open into space. Expanding. Stopping nowhere.

Awareness has no edge. Allow your awareness to be the space in which the moon and the stars float. No edges anywhere. Limitless awareness. Expanding into vast space.

Your body is the center of the universe. Your awareness extends out limitlessly into the vastness. Expanding. Soft. Open. Endless.

Moment to moment, awareness extends out in all directions. Let your awareness radiate out into the vastness. Expanding. Explore the awareness beyond the body. Vast open space. The whole planet floating in the vast spaciousness of awareness.

Expanding outward. The clouds floating within you. The stars. The moon. All the planets. The whole universe floating in the vast spaciousness of mind. Extending everywhere. Expanding to the very edge of the cosmos. And beyond. Vast. Open. Space. Awareness itself.

Go beyond. Beyond, beyond. Let awareness expand into infinity. Open. Endless. Space.

Feel how your body floats in the spaciousness of awareness.

Let your attention come back to the breath.

Each sensation floating in the vastness.

Each breath drifts through the body. Each sensation received in limitless awareness.

Feel the eyes as they begin to open. Look about you.

Move when you feel like moving.

● ● ●

PAIN MEDITATION V

[Letting it all float free]

Bring your attention to the area of discomfort.

Begin to soften all around that area. Let the pain just be there. Open around it. Let all the resistance melt away. Let the skin, the flesh, the muscles begin to soften all around the pain.

Let the fist that grasps pain begin slowly to open. Releasing tension, rigidity around sensations. Let the muscles soften, relaxing. No tightness anywhere.

Let the pain just be there. Not holding it. Not pushing it away.

Soften the ligaments. The flesh. Let the sensations float free in the body. Without force. Without tension. Open all around the sensation. Gently. Pushing away nothing. Let all resistance melt from the body.

And in the mind. That same softening. That same nonholding. Letting go of thoughts. Opening into the spaciousness of awareness.

Whatever thought arises, let it float free. Whatever sensation arises, let it float free. Thoughts of pain, floating in the vastness of the mind.

Soften all around the thought. Experience the space in which it floats. Fear. Doubt. Softening. Floating free.

Each mind-moment, like a bubble, floating in the vast spaciousness of awareness. Whatever arises in the body, in the mind. Doubt. Confusion. Expectation. Fear. Just let it pass through. It's there one moment, dissolved the next.

Notice the ever-changing flow of thoughts and sensations. Constantly arising and disappearing into the vastness of awareness.

Sensations float in the body. Changing. Moment to moment. Thoughts float in the mind. Constantly in change. Constantly unfolding.

The whole body soft. Open. Relaxed. Not holding. Not pulling back.

Let sensations arise into this openness. A soft, nonclinging space that just allows things to be as they are. No interference. Sensations arising. Thoughts arising. No resistance. No reaching out for them. No pushing them away. No tightening. Just soft, open space. Each moment experienced in vast awareness.

The sound of my voice arising and dissolving in the open space of awareness. Hearing happening all by itself. Nothing to do. Just sound changing, instant to instant, within your vastness.

Feel the spaciousness of being that expands outward in every direction, encompassing each sound and sight. A moment of hearing followed by a moment of seeing. By a moment of thought. All floating in the vast space of mind. The sound of my voice. A car passing in the street. An airplane crossing overhead. All occurring within the endless spaciousness of awareness.

Let the mind become like a vast sky. Each experience like a cloud floating, constantly changing, folding in upon itself, dissolving in the vastness. Feel how awareness exists everywhere at once. Boundaryless.

The edgeless space of being. No longer held to the outline of the body. To the space of the room. Awareness constantly expanding into unlimited space.

Let awareness become like the sky. Which holds nothing. Which creates nothing. Which allows all things to pass. Without the least clinging or interference. Observe sound. Sight. Memory. Feeling. Arising and dissolving in the open sky of awareness.

Notice that all sound is happening within this spaciousness. All thought. All feeling. Floating within endless awareness. No edges anywhere. All that occurs, occurs within your vastness. The limitless spaciousness of awareness.

Body soft. Mind, open and clear.

Let the edges of the body, of the mind, melt into the vastness. The body. Sensations. Feelings. Floating in vast space. Each moment of changing sensation floating free in pure awareness. A moment of memory. A moment of fear. A moment of joy. Ever-changing clouds in the open sky. Each thought, each sensation floating free in edgeless awareness.

In this vastness the mind and body are just thought bubbles floating in open, endless space.

Awareness itself. Containing everything, holding nothing.

The whole mind dissolved into vast openness.

The body, sensations, floating, dissolving into space.

Dissolving.

Dissolving.

Just space. Just peace.

11
APPROACHING
DEATH

Some years ago at our first conscious living/dying retreat, in the introductory circle, a handsome gray-haired woman, unself-consciously wearing a colorful T-shirt which revealed that both breasts had been removed, introduced herself saying, "Two years ago I was gifted with cancer." She was the first person to tell me that she wouldn't exchange the clarity and depth she felt for a healthy body. The light in her eyes indicated how precious had been her confrontation with death and the power of the teaching it offered.

Few meet their perfect spiritual teacher or find a technique completely suitable to their needs. Few discover a vehicle for their liberation: a being or a teaching that they are so attuned to that it acts as a mirror of their holdings held up before them. Yet for some of the terminally ill patients we have worked with, their illness has become just that. They have discovered the hard-found perfect teacher which brings them to themselves. And experience the same difficulties and grace which might be expected from any such teaching which uncovers the holdings and fears that block us from the experience of our original nature.

No longer making their sickness a disability, they have found a teaching which they sensed would not have been forthcoming in any other way. They honor their predicament with a strength and clarity which displays the depth of their insight.

To open to our original nature, to the truth of being, we must stop postponing death. To take death within allows us to go beyond death, beyond what we imagine dies. To come to that vastness of being that many speak of as the deathless. Using death as a way of confronting ourselves with the places we hide, the places we disallow the heart.

How many, right now, could let themselves die? All of us could die, but could we die fully, just expanding beyond ourselves, not trying to change it. Not trying to make our death something else, not making it the famous last words of a grade B movie, but just "Ahh," melting out of the body, not holding anywhere.

We are each in a process of awakening. Becoming fully born so that we may die each moment past our fear and isolation. The illusion of separateness dies to reveal the deathlessness of our essential nature.

During a workshop in California, in the midst of a discourse, the room was shaken by an earthquake. Having been sharing about death for the past few days, one might imagine that the group would be as prepared to let go as they ever would be. But as I looked into the startled faces of some of the hundred people sitting there, the fear and holding, the difficulty with death, was clearly evident. When the waves of gulps and sighs subsided, I asked the group, "What if that moment had been the last of your life? What if that was it? Whatever thought was in your mind right then, that was your last thought. That thought, 'Oh my gracious!' That was it, you are all dead. No refunds. All the work done to open until that time was all the work of a lifetime. To whatever degree you had the truth in your heart, able to let go of your name, your idea of yourself, your family, that would be the degree of love and wisdom that would accompany you into whatever came next."

How many people driving home one evening see the flash of lights in their rearview mirror, hear the screech of brakes, feel the impact of steel on steel and think, "Oh, shit!" as the darkness descends. How many people die with "Oh, shit!" on their lips instead of the name of God? How many people have cultivated "Oh, shit!" as their death chant?

The Tibetan Buddhists living with the recognition that each moment could be the last emphasized the use of death as a means of awakening. Many monks drink from skull caps, the top portion of skulls taken from the cremation grounds. Many use prayer beads carved of human bone to constantly reawaken to death. Because they recognize we could all be dead a moment from now and then there would be no more words, no more resolution to do better tomorrow. Life becomes immense when we start recognizing that there is no assurance that we will live out this day. Our fantasies and presumptions that we will live forever confuse us as we enter death. In reality, all the time we have is right now. The past and the future are dreams. Only this moment is real. If we come newborn to each moment, we will experience life directly, not dream it. Born each moment, we let ourselves die to the mind's habitual commentary, its judging and merciless self-protection.

There aren't many moments in our life when we are fully awake. That may be why we find death so difficult: because we keep dreaming our lives, we dream our death.

Many have told me how illness has awakened them from the dream. How their models have been seen as a limitation rather than as a goal. How though the body has gotten weaker, their spirit has gotten stronger. Some have said that the degeneration of their body has taught them that they are not that. They wear the body lightly. Their voices are soft and full of love.

The following are excerpts from a journal kept by Paul, whom I met in spring just after he took to his bed following a "couple of years running battle with Hodgkin's disease." Each entry reflects the ups and downs of his ability to work with the intensity of this situation. He is a good example that in any kind of growth there are peaks and plateaus. That sometimes we can open to it and sometimes we can't but that it is our willingness which allows us to expand. Paul was a thirty-one-year-old audio engineer who had led an active and interesting life. His main difficulty was an extreme restlessness that arose from seeing one model after another of himself as a "man," as a "person who could take care of himself," as an "up and comer," torn away by the intensity of grow-

ing disability and the clear approach of death. He said his restlessness made him feel like "jumping out of my skin." We
suggested he work with balancing the restlessness by the technique of counting breaths. Counting each exhale up until ten,
then beginning again. If one loses count, and can't recall if it's
breath six or seven, one begins again at one. He worked with this
practice for twenty minutes a few times a day or whenever he felt
an energy imbalance. As his mind quieted his heart began to
open.

As he worked more and more with the givens of his predicament, his insight grew and he said, "The melodrama's not too
different but the stage is a hell of a lot bigger." As his resistance
began to melt he was surprised at his new-found peace. "Acceptance is magic," he smiled one day incredulously. Indeed, a few
days before he died, looking about him as one person irrigated his
catheter tube, and another emptied his bedpan, while a third
made carrot juice in the kitchen, he remarked, "You know, this
all looks a bit like a Marx brothers movie!"

◉   ◉   ◉

Some excerpts from Paul's journals over the last months of his
life—

It's important to learn that you never really need to jump for a
pain pill. So instead of taking it without thinking, try moving
around, refocusing your awareness. Remember: relief won't be
instant anyway, even if that pill works. So give your own head a
chance first!

Sometimes, it's amazing how little it really takes to be able to
accept "unacceptable" discomfort.

In general,

> *Don't* use pain pills against "discomforts." The latter are
> dealt with much better by meditation.

I AM NOT MY DISCOMFITURE!

And this too shall pass.

(1) Acknowledgment—*naming*

> Ah! fear . . .
>
> Ah! restlessness . . .
>
> > (passing soon, states of mind)
> > it's just conditioned response

(2) Opening—letting go
        not holding on
        Whatever seemed so solid before
        is really just a cloud passing by

* * *

It's pretty scary to have periods when you don't remember
where you're at, etc., even though we actually have these periods
hundreds of times in one day. But when you're bedridden you
have time to notice them much more.

It's interesting how I instinctively fight it with writing in this
book or otherwise "keeping occupied."

* * *

This constant restlessness is driving me crazy. I have sensations
in the back and stomach that keep me "bothered" and make it
hard to relax. Well, maybe it's better than the dizziness I had
previously.

I think my best move now is to practice

TOTAL LOVING ACCEPTANCE—

* * *

The afternoon slowly trundles along like a 3rd class Spanish
passenger train. I have to accept the boredom, the apparent
meaninglessness, which is actually a great teacher.

* * *

Phoned my parents. The security of the known. Well, why not?
Why not treat myself to a little security after all the strange stuff
I've been going through? It's starting to be fun again, watching
my mind try to close around ideas.

IT'S BEAUTIFUL!

TO SEE THIS THING POSITIVELY, AS AN
ADVENTURE, AS A LEARNING EXPERIENCE.

* * *

I feel very enthusiastic, like an apprentice monk.

The greatest challenge is that we must go through this alone. It
would be much easier with a companion.

As the sunlight gets dimmer, the end of day is apparent, and I
start to feel that aloneness. It might be very helpful and comfort-
ing to find someone who can stay overnight, who could provide

simple human contact, help bridge that separation that sometimes comes.

Meanwhile, I can stay aware of the tricks my mind plays as it gets fooled by one carrot after another.

* * *

Seem to be going through very strong crises about sleep and surrender. I'm confused, but I try to keep my heart open and find a way out.

I seem to be fearing being trapped. I just lie here in bed, resting my exhausted body, fighting for its ego sense, its sense of self.

What illusions! But they sure seem real!

It's just so strange to be so afraid in the body, and yet be able to endure it with calm patience, waiting. As if "I" don't want to panic so I let my body do it instead, and "I" just watch.

* * *

When you got your sense of humor, you got everything. Humor leads to love. So keep on laffing.

Just work with what you have at any moment. Because that's all you're getting. It's all relative. What makes you think no one else is trapped? We're all trapped. You're just lucky enough to be reminded more often.

* * *

Time passes slowly when you're suffering. It would be O.K. if I didn't feel so lousy. The only way out is through and it's hell in here. The best defense seems to be to stay still and to focus on writing. Perhaps I can forget or lose myself temporarily, that way. But I need a more permanent forgetting. A decision not to be that person I thought I was. Not to be the bored, tormented sufferer. To be someone just hanging out, nobody special.

Already after 5 minutes my bedsores are hurting. Bad . . .

* * *

Again, woken up from a sleep of exhaustion . . . I felt somewhat rested, but I immediately started to feel the gut fear, too. It's so strange because I am able to stand back and to see the fear, and intellectualize about it; but I feel trapped or forced into *feeling* the fear in my body, whatever I do.

You see, it's confusing because I would like to think that I don't have anything to fear. I thought I was "too advanced" to fear and yet here I am and here this fear is. (Well . . . here we all are.)

For a while I sensed love and beauty in my predicament. I am uncertain, *completely* uncertain, about tomorrow or even one hour from now. I am afraid of pain, especially excruciating pain that won't let go. I am afraid of the feelings of unreality I get. I am afraid of waking up with amnesia. I am afraid of never being able to completely wake up. I am afraid of total helplessness. I am afraid of my next bowel movement. I am afraid of what will happen to me. I am afraid because I don't know what will happen. I am afraid of hospital trips, operations, medicine. I am afraid because I am no longer in control of my life. I am now powerless and unable to do anything except trying to love, to keep my heart open.

* * *

Who would have ever thought that eating and sleeping would become such adventures. I feel love for life.

Because life will always be an adventure, no matter how tortuous!

I really believed, yesterday, that that state of restlessness would last forever. And now how laughable that seems.

I'm grateful for this opportunity, but I mustn't blow it.

The best thing for me now is to

CULTIVATE A CALM AWARENESS AND ACCEPTANCE OF THE SHOW. IT'S NOT AS BAD AS YOU THINK! (In fact, it's only as bad as you think.)

● ● ●

During his last weeks, as Paul's body became more emaciated, our work together became the shared recognition that who he was was clearly not this body which was obviously slowly dispossessing him. Each time I would say to him that he was not his body, I could feel the words penetrate to a certain depth and then come up against some denseness, some bit of conditioning, some fear or doubt that couldn't let go.

After a week of rapid deterioration and deeper silent meditations, one morning as I gently rolled Paul onto his side to wash his back, I was once again struck by the frailty and deterioration of his body and said to him, "Paul, just look at how this old body is falling away, just see how you are not this body. How could you imagine for a moment that you are this worn-out old thing?" But this time I felt no resistance, I could sense the words go right through and Paul just went with them; no resistance, letting go into empty space. A friend cradling Paul's head in her arms said, "I think he's left." His restlessness and fear fell away with his identification with the body. His long teaching from cancer had opened him to life, to death. [See Appendix I.]

QUESTION: You speak about those who are terminally ill approaching death; what about those who find themselves in old age?

ANSWER: A dear friend in her late seventies told me that each morning she looks into her mirror and can't believe the old face that peers back at her. "I never liked old people and now I am one." She speaks of how things have changed. Of friends who are no longer around. She worries about who will take care of her if she should become ill. She is concerned that she might at some point have to go to a nursing home, which she despises. "There are pills for sickness but no pill for old age. My whole life has changed. I sleep differently, I eat differently. I even go to the bathroom differently; everything has slowed down. Nothing is the way I thought it would be. Whoever would have thought!"

For most in old age there is the feeling that the body has outlasted them. Few outgrow the body. Many want to get out of it before it dies. The mind's image of the body changes more slowly than the body. The body goes to ash while still a strong flame burns in the heart. Many are unable to walk with any ease though they still carry the image of athletic youth in the underdream.

"My batteries are running down." The energy of the life-force is no longer found in body exteriors; muscles become soft, the skin spots, the eyelids droop. For those who think of themselves as the body it is hell. But I hear others say that all that has happened is that their life-force has withdrawn into their heart and that it is in their heart that happiness has at last been found. "Like the sap going back to the roots in fall and winter."

For some the world is so rapidly changing that they feel out of tune, misfits, foreigners in a culture they had once participated in. Watching television much of the time to fill vacant space, they are confronted with the "cult of youth," where 80 per cent of the television actors are between twenty-five and forty though only 20 per cent of the public is between those ages. It seems like a strange land where one is punished for being old. Some feel like a victim.

In India the first twenty years of life is considered the time of being a student, of maturation. In the second twenty years you are a householder supporting your family. For the third twenty years you are perfecting your spiritual practice while watching your children mature and providing for your parents' well-being. By sixty it is presumed that most of your responsibilities to family and society have been fulfilled, and many spend the rest of their lives as "sanyasin," as free-roaming renunciates. It is a time of pilgrimage, quiet contemplation, and devout song.

Many societies honor their elderly for the wisdom accumulated during a long life. Our society does not approach old age with that reverence but rather with revulsion, so it becomes necessary for each to give themselves the respect they deserve. It is in the last years that many touch on a sense of being but few trust themselves sufficiently to let go fully into it, to let themselves be who they suspect they really might be. Though many come to learn the real meaning of service: volunteering in hospitals, visiting people in nursing homes, sharing as big brothers and sisters, baby-sitting, in remedial reading groups, in grief counseling, they shine with wisdom and compassion.

It doesn't seem to matter whether one has lived twenty years or seventy years, at its end that life seems to have been exhausted in a single moment. The past is irretrievably gone but the sense of being is ever present. Indeed, if one asks someone right at the edge of death if they feel any less alive at that moment than they have at any other time in their life, they will say no. Those who follow life to where it resides in the heart live life fully.

In the workshops we have been conducting around the country in the past few years, we have met many people in their late sixties and seventies and some in their eighties who wished to turn inward. Who sensed some deeper experience to life than the transitory holdings and losses of the past. They trust the youthful heart that seeks to go beyond the body's increasing limitation. Looking out across a room of meditators, here and there an older, deeply wrinkled face will smooth as the breath slows and the eyes quiet behind closed lids. The love that radiates from them is vintage love.

The old who live in their body are bent under the strain. The old who live in their hearts are aglow.

Friend, hope for the truth while you are alive.
Jump into experience while you are alive!
Think . . . and think . . . while you are alive.
What you call "salvation" belongs to the time before
    death.

If you don't break your ropes while you're alive,
do you think
ghosts will do it after?

The idea that the soul will join with the ecstatic
just because the body is rotten—
that is all fantasy.
What is found now is found then.
If you find nothing now,
you will simply end up with an apartment in the City
    of Death.
If you make love with the divine now, in the next life
    you will have the face of satisfied desire.

So plunge into the truth, find out who the Teacher is,
    Believe in the Great Sound!

Kabir says this: When the Guest is being searched for,
    it is the intensity of the longing for the Guest that
    does all the work.
Look at me, and you will see a slave of that intensity.

                                        Kabir, via Bly

12
WORKING WITH
THE DYING

The other day, I received a phone call from a old friend saying that her brother had just returned from a general checkup where it was discovered that he had tumors in his lungs. A biopsy was in process. What should she do? How could she help a loved one who it seemed might be about to go through a very difficult time?

The answer to that question is, of course—you relate to one who is ill the same way you relate to any being. With openness. With an honoring of the truth we all share. Work to dissolve the separateness that keeps one lost in duality. Become one with the other. No help, just being. See the conditioned illusion of separateness. Break that ancient clinging. Allow both of you to die. Go beyond the imaginings of separate bodies and separate minds. Come to the common ground of being.

You are with one who is dying in the same way you are with yourself. Open, honest, and caring. You are simply there, listening with a heart that is willing to hold the joy or pain of another with equal capacity and compassion. With a mind that does not separate death from life, that does not live in concepts and shadows, but in the direct experience of the unfolding.

If it hurts, it hurts. If it makes you happy, it makes you happy.

Not trying to change things. Not trying to make something or someone other than it is. Just hear the truth that the moment has to offer.

Some years ago, teaching a week-long retreat with Ram Dass, I met Elisabeth Kübler-Ross. Ram Dass had invited Elisabeth to participate earlier that year. Elisabeth and I spent a few minutes together at the retreat, but at the time I didn't have the slightest idea that we would ever meet again. However, a few months later, it became quite clear that there was work for Elisabeth and me to do together. I got in touch with her and she said, "Let's do it." In 1976, I started teaching meditation at her retreats. I thought I was just going to share techniques for being open with others and ourselves. But the universe, in its infinite wisdom and mercy, didn't let me get away with that.

At the first retreat in Texas, thinking how lucky I was to be able to "do my thing" in such a loving environment, one day Elisabeth turned to me and said, "Let's go into town to visit this friend of mine in the hospital." She spoke of a woman dying of leukemia a few miles away in Houston. "I think we should go in and visit her. She might be someone who would benefit from spending some time with you." I thought it a wonderful opportunity to see Elisabeth in action. I had never been at the bedside of someone dying. I thought, "I'm going to have a front-row seat to watch Elisabeth's delicate intuitive work."

On the way to the hospital, Elisabeth told me that this woman was at the time sort of a superstar on the ward. She had undergone a bone marrow transplant, which was still quite an experimental process at the time. She had lived twenty-one days, considerably longer than most receiving this new procedure.

As we walked down the corridor toward Dorothy's room, I thought, "Elisabeth knows what to say, but what am I going to do?" I could feel the tension in the pit of my stomach. As we entered the room, Elisabeth pulled a chair next to the bed and said softly, "Why don't you sit here." She went over to a chair in the corner and sat down. As I sat stiffly next to the bed, with all my fear and need to be someone doing something, I was unable to elude or deny my feelings of self-doubt and unworthiness. The conditional opening of my heart was painfully clear: I could see how much my openness was dependent upon whether it was a "safe environment." I saw I was only open when I was comfortable. And I wasn't comfortable. I was not fully present, sitting in that chair wondering who I was and what I was to do.

At that moment, I felt as though I was closer to death than this wan twenty-eight-year-old woman lying so pale next to me.

Quieting my mind as best I could, we began the meditation that centers on opening the heart by breathing in and out of the heart center, letting go of what blocks the spaciousness beyond, opening to the underlying reality. Breathing out those things that block our awareness, Dorothy and I came into a clearer space together. Breathing in the light and wisdom of the universe, allowing the mind to soften, to become translucent so as to see through to what lies beneath. As we meditated together, I could see how much the holding of fear and "someoneness" kept me separate, made it difficult for me to open my heart fully to this other being. As we meditated, I suspect there was more clearing going on in my mind and heart than in Dorothy's. I needed the meditation at that moment more than she.

Perhaps sensing my discomfort, Dorothy was extremely compassionate. Here, sitting next to her, was this person who had come to help. But who was so full of his own holdings that he wasn't quite there. My shoulders felt as though they were tensed up around my ears. The tension in my upper body was very noticeable. It was obvious how uneasy I was outside my cage.

Teaching in the environment of the workshop, I had my own territory. It was easy for me "to know," to be the wise man of the group. It was simple just to play out a role. But being there for this other person, I found myself distracted by confusion and doubt. Though I knew that when you feel separate you reinforce another's separateness, you reinforce their suffering, there was surprisingly little I could do about it at the time. All I could do was enter into the meditation as fully as I suggested she should. As I could see my holdings melting away, I could see how much arose to block my heart.

I could see how my attempt to maintain my "specialness" reinforced a separateness between us, which reinforces the fear of death. Because it is evident that the one thing that's seemingly

going to fall away when one dies is our ability to hold on to who
we think we are. Our body, our name, our personality, our preferences. I saw what a rich opportunity it was for me to die right
then, to let go of all that blocked my reception and participation
in being. To die out of my specialness.

As we left the room, I recognized what an incredible opportunity it had been to see my mind. I was confronted with a fiercely
polished mirror that would in no way tell me "I was the fairest
one of all." Being in that room amplified my mind so that I could
not escape the truth of my posturing and holding. I could not
hold to who I thought I was. There was no place to hide. I could
see where I was blocking, how my mind was creating the universe
in my own image and likeness.

It was obvious why I had come to the retreat. I hadn't come to
teach. I had come to learn. To discover the power of the opportunity to work with people as a means of working on myself.

In the years since, it has become increasingly clear with each
being I open to, whether it is someone who is dying or a taxi cab
driver or a cashier in a restaurant, that the more I open to that
being, letting go of what blocks the heart's contact, the more I
open to my own being, the more we share the essence.

A year later I met a Dominican nun by the name of Sister Pa-
trice Burns, who asked me to work with her on the oncology
ward of a San Francisco hospital. In many of the rooms we
would enter there would be a patient whose life it seemed had
come full circle in its final moments. You could see the effects of
a lifetime focused in those last days. All that was scattered had
become focused as though through a magnifying glass and burned
through all else. Each room was like the final pages of a long
novel.

Coming into each room was like entering into the center of a
karmic whirlpool. (Karma is not punishment. It is an aspect of
the merciful nature of the universe to offer teachings that we have
somehow misunderstood in the past, to allow us to learn from experiences that we have not paid close enough attention to previously.) People whose life had been one of faith and brotherly
love were surrounded by kindness and compassion. Those who

had lived in competition and fear were surrounded by restlessness and confusion.

Going from room to room was like entering one mind after another. The attitudes, preferences, and preconceptions of a lifetime were personified in the scenario of these final days. Each person's lifestyle predicting their deathstyle. In one room was a woman considerably deteriorated from cancer with her diamond rings taped to withered fingers. Pictures of her children in their graduation gowns: "He's a lawyer. She's a nuclear physicist." Her lipstick painting full lips over a thin mouth. A wig hiding the baldness resulting from chemotherapy. She had been "a pillar of society," an outstanding example of someone so busy "doing well" that she could hardly give herself room to breathe, much less to die. When her children visited, she would straighten her wig and add another layer of cosmetics. When asked why she didn't share what she was feeling she said, "Oh, I'd never let them see me that way." She was still keeping a stiff upper lip, giving herself very little heart. The pretense in the room kept her in bondage to death.

In another room was soft-spoken John, who had been working for twenty-five years in a Greyhound depot. One day a few months short of retirement, he became dizzy and collapsed. His dear friend and coworker had helped him to the hospital. The doctors soon found a large brain tumor. John's friend, sitting by the bed, said he would quit his job and take John to his farm in Oregon. He said they could just hang out and go fishing. John had given so much love, so much comradeship to the people around him, that this was the predominant energy around his bed. You could feel the supportiveness, the givingness of the people who came to visit. Five days after diagnosis, John died, surrounded by a deep love and concern for his well-being that did not hold him back, but wished him well on his voyage.

In another room was sixty-one-year-old Alonzo, dying of stomach cancer. All his life he had tried to do what was "right for the family." Twenty years before, he had fallen in love with a divorcée named Marilyn. But because of the intricacies of his Catholic and Italian environment, he wasn't allowed to marry her,

though he maintained a relationship with her until her death a
year before. His father and sister and brothers never really acknowledged her existence, for twenty years they had referred to
her as "that woman." He had given up much of his life to "protect my family." Now, with his ninety-one-year-old father sitting
by his bed saying, "My boy can't die; my boy's not going to die,"
he was still trying to be the good son. He was trying to protect his
father from death. "It's O.K. I'm not going to die." But he was
dying. His brother and sister, standing next to the bed, were arguing about breaking his will so that none of his money would go to
Marilyn's thirty-year-old married daughter, whom he cared for
so much. He lay there, listening to all this, not saying a word, trying not to die so as not to cause his family distress. Seeing the
thickness of the karmic mesh all about him, I would sit in the
corner watching this extraordinary melodrama. People arguing
and denying his death. I found that, as I was sitting there, I
started silently to talk to him through my heart. In my heart, I
would speak with him with all the love I felt, thinking, "You
know, Alonzo, it's all right that you're dying. You're not doing
anything wrong. Here you are in this extraordinary predicament
where you cannot admit to the loved ones around you what you
need or what you want. You're protecting them to the end. But
it's O.K. to die. It's fine. It's the appropriate thing at the appropriate moment. Open to yourself. Be compassionate to this confused Alonzo, lying in his sickbed. Let go of the pain of not being
able to protect everyone from everything. This is your moment.
Trust yourself. Trust death. You need protect no one. Only let go
of what keeps you stuck. Open to your being, the immensity of
your underlying nature. Let go of all this now. Let yourself die.
Let yourself die out of being Alonzo. Let yourself die out of
being a son. Let yourself die out of being someone whose goods
are being quibbled over. Let yourself go into the open heart of
Jesus. There's nothing to fear. It's all O.K." And, through the
forest of people around the bed, Alonzo's angel-blue eyes met
mine, twinkling acknowledgment of this wordless heart contact.
None of those words could have been spoken aloud in the room.
There would have been a shriek from his family heard all the way
down the hall. But Alonzo would, every once in a while, catch

my eye with a profound acknowledgment that everything was O.K. What was communicated was not the words, but the feeling in my heart. Somehow, it seems, many who are seriously ill are sensitive to such a deep touching.

Every once in a while, he'd turn to his sister and say, "You know, there's something different about when he's [pointing to me] in the room." Because that was the only time when there was any acceptance in the room of what he was going through. Later, he acknowledged that he had felt some sense of openness to his predicament when I was sitting there "so quietly in the corner."

Indeed, we began to discover that the technique of talking through the heart was so useful that even those tossing restlessly in their sleep quieted down when someone next to them began sending love and understanding silently through their heart. Even those in comas seemed to soften. Not that the person picked up the words. But rather the attitude, the love and care generated an acceptance of the moment so spacious that the person had room to be who he needed to be.

As we experienced the skillfulness of this heart-speech, many of the nurses on the floor began to try it. Those who used it said it changed their relationship to many of their patients and their often painful job in general. They had a tool to open to another and perhaps transmit that openness.

As we began to share the technique of speaking silently through the heart, many nurses came forward to say how wonderful it was to hear someone speak of a technique that they had intuitively been employing for some time. It is important before using such subtle techniques to examine your motivation. Are you trying to change someone's consciousness to what you imagine is "best for them"? Or are you just there with another sending love and a sense of the okayness of things. One does not take from another what is not given. You do not steal money or food from another, nor do you steal their states of mind. To attempt to steal "denial" from another is an act of righteousness and separatism.

We heard a story of a nurse who, having seen the videotapes of the workshops in which I was talking about this method of communication, decided to "try it out" on a particularly recalcitrant patient who did not want to talk about his illness, to see if she could "break him through his denial." A few times a day for ten or fifteen minutes she would sit silently next to this fellow and in her heart tell him how he "should be" working with his predicament. "Don't get so hung up in your fear, stop denying your death," she would say to him silently. "There is nothing to be afraid of, denial won't get you free."

For a week she continued to sit with "her patient," who, she felt, she was helping by telling him what she thought he should do. Returning to duty after a weekend she was met by the head nurse, who told her that her prize patient no longer wanted her to visit. "Why?" she asked in considerable confusion. "Because," answered the head nurse, "he said you talk too much."

When you speak from the heart you send love, not your needs or desires for people to be any other way than they are.

It's not just a technique for people who are dying. That would make dying more special than it is. It's just another way of touching, of opening your heart so other people can open theirs. It often works as well across the breakfast table as it does in the emergency room.

Because of this trust between us, one day Alonzo asked what it might be like to die. As we spoke about leaving the body behind and going on into the light of the Christ he loved so much, our hearts touched in great love and timelessness. Leaving the room that day, the mind was dense with pride. "I really broke through," it thought.

The next day, heading toward his room, I was imagining how pleased Alonzo was going to be to see me. But as I entered the room, he took one look at me and turned away with an "Oh no." My heart went clump! Yesterday he was so open about death. But today he wasn't buying any of it. My presence only represented death to him. Yesterday, I was the welcome savior and had to work on the painful pride that arose. Today, I am persona non grata and my work is to keep my heart open when rejected. My work is not to change him. My work is to open beyond my holdings. To watch my expectations, desires, and projections. To let my models fall away, one after the other. Instead of closing, to let myself die out of who I thought I was. Dying into the preciousness of the moment, the truth of being once again presents itself. There is no longer someone dying or someone helping. There is just this moment of clarity and love.

The idea of "dying," the idea of "sickness," the idea of "helping" are no longer substituted for the living presence and there are just two beings becoming one. Each using the other as a mirror to uncover their holding and fears so that they can get on with it. Because we need all the help we can get.

There's one person in the bed sharing their dying. But there are ten people around the bed dying also, losing some important part of themselves. To the degree that life has been an investigation of truth, the truth will be present at the end of that life. Their death is a sharing of the spirit. But if the accumulation of material goods has been the predominant drive, those around the bed will be seeing the dying as only the body, just more material goods, lost in the crossing. Their death is frightening and confusing, and they are lost from view.

Who are you in the minds of those closest to you? What "meaning" will your absence have? Are you precious for what you do or what you are? How can you make your death a gift of love?

It became clear to me in the hospital, as I'd go from room to room, that it might take days or weeks for a patient to develop the kind of trust and confidence in what we were sharing for them to open to an exploration of what was happening. But some don't have weeks or many days of life left. Though I'd notice that often there would be a sister-in-law or niece or granddaughter or father-in-law at the bedside whose relationship with the patient was very strong and clear. Often, it was not a primary, but rather a secondary relative. Not a husband or wife, brother or son, but someone who was one step away, who had a different investment in the patient and who had the deep heart contact that's necessary for the truth to be shared without posturing or holding. Spending time together in the waiting room there would often open a sharing about their loved one's dying and how they might serve to make it easier. Their deep heart contact with the patient made them want to know if there was anything they could do to help. These loved ones needed no long introduction or testing to establish deep rapport with the patient. They had access to the heart and could ask what needed to be done before their loved one could let go. They could share the exploration of what it might be to die and what might come after death.

So we would sit, often for an hour or two, sharing about the okayness of death, and I would encourage them not to let their fear of death block their loving communication. Reminding them that, because they had the person's ear as I might never have, they really didn't need me but could themselves be the major support and transition guide to the degree they could open beyond their fears and trust the heartfulness of the moment. Answering their questions and sharing with them the experiences of other people in similar situations overcoming similar obstacles, I would encourage them to be vulnerable to the moment, to trust the love they felt and to use it as a bridge between the known and the unknown, so that their loved one might travel openheartedly through transition. We would share how to use techniques for decreasing pain, finishing business, and deepening awareness, without creating attachment to the patient being other than he was. I would suggest books that might be read aloud to their loved one. "Do whatever seems appropriate. Don't hold your heart back. Trust it. It's a very precious moment." Often, they would go back into the room and experience remarkable communications that might have taken someone working with that patient, an outsider, months to touch. Because when you trust someone, he or she can encourage you to trust yourself and can allow you to hear yourself. There's much tension released just by letting it out in words. Sharing dreams, fulfilled and unfulfilled, allows us to confront our predicament. I have seen patients take a giant step toward letting go after such intimate and honest sharing with a special loved one.

One of the simplest and most profound techniques for sharing consciousness with patients or loved ones was told to me by Richard Boerstler from his experiences with the Clear Light Society of Boston. It is a method many have found to be remarkably useful.

After asking the patient if they would like to share a little experiment, one suggests that there is nothing they need to do but relax and breathe comfortably. Sitting next to them, you tell them you are going to breathe with them. Watch the rise and fall of their abdomen so as to tune in to their breath rhythm. Tune into that rise and fall and adjust your respiration rate to theirs, breathe their breath. After a few mutual breaths have been established, as the patient breathes out, you allow an "Ahhhh" to escape with your simultaneous exhalation. Each time the patient breathes out you sigh a deep and audible "Ahhhh." Each exhalation is accompanied by your "Ahhhh." The patient need do nothing, though he can join in if he wishes. (How often do we care enough for others to even wholly pay attention to what they say, let alone take on their breathing pattern?) Often something quite unexpected occurs. The two beings meet in a oneness that is so deep and so simple it is surprising. This meditation may be maintained for twenty minutes to an hour as one wishes, sharing the "Ahhhh," melting together into the vastness. "Ahhhh" is the great sound of letting go.

The relaxation that results dissolves tension and pain into a sense of oneness. After sharing this experience a few times, the patient then has a means of centering his own consciousness for himself. He may, at four in the morning, when all seems desolate, when the pain seems greatest and sleep impossible, find that as he breathes out his "Ahhhh" with each exhalation, level upon level of tension melts away and there is more space in which to experience his predicament.

What is shared goes beyond any philosophical or ideological construct. It opens the way for deeper communications to come. The patient need do nothing but be as he is and allow himself to enter into what is given. Often the two become one merging in the care and silence of the heart.

When you are working with seriously ill patients, it is important to remember that it is not "you" who has to do anything. All you have to do is get out of the way so that the appropriate response to the moment can manifest itself. You don't have to save anyone except you. Working with the dying is work on yourself.

One of the pitfalls of this work if you think in terms of "helping" is the tendency to project your death upon another. But no one can die your death for you. You would like to die with angelic heralds and a score of trumpets guiding the way, following your breath right out of the body. But that's your fantasy.

You can't make another die your death for you. You'll live that one out as you can, as you do in the moment. As you deal with your dying now, that's what you'll bring with you as you approach that moment.

But this is somebody else's melodrama. You're not there to save them. You're there to be an open space in which they can do whatever they need without your coloring to the least degree their unfolding.

When you meet the pain of another with fear, it is often called pity. When you're motivated by pity, you're motivated by a dense self-interest. When you're motivated by pity, you're acting on the aversion you have to experiencing someone else's predicament. You want to alleviate their discomfort as a means of alleviating your own. Pity creates more fear and separation. When love touches the pain of another, it is called compassion. Compassion is just space. Whatever that other person is experiencing, you have room for it in your heart. It becomes work on yourself—to let go, to stay open, to feel that being within you. When somebody is in incredible pain, though you can't do anything to alleviate it, you don't withdraw. When people say, "Help me," you stay soft, your hand in theirs, sharing their pain without closing around it. To have room in your heart for whatever pain arises, not differentiating between "I" and "other," is compassion.

As death comes out of the closet in this country there begins to be established a new hospitableness toward dying. This hospice movement is a manifestation of the desire for people to die without pain and with as much psychological support as possible. To finish business. To die with dignity. Many of these support groups allow a person to die in the warmth and care of their own home. Others have created caring, homelike environments in which one may die peacefully. But even in this new openness to death there may be some confusion. Hospice workers, like any of us, are a product of their conditioning, and there can often be transmitted the fears of life and the grasping at the body which makes death so difficult. Many who work in hospices don't recognize the trap of being "a helper"; the separatism which sometimes comes when you use another to reinforce your self-image, to make yourself feel that you are living up to who you are supposed to be.

In many hospices the predominant goal is the alleviation of distress, the palliative care of the patient. There is little encouragement to cut through identification with the body as being who we really are or the mind as being the whole reality. Hospices can have a tendency to overlook dying as a means of spiritual awakening. Though many hospice workers' hearts are opened greatly by confrontation with the impermanence of this body, few use this as an opportunity to touch the deepest aspects of themselves, to explore their inherent wisdom and joy. Most still consider death only a tragedy, an emergency, a loss. There is seldom the recognition of the deeper unfolding, of the need of the body to die so that the next life experience may arise. Few hospices encourage their workers to make their work with the dying work on themselves. Few recognize the ripeness of certain patients and ask "Who is dying?" Few encourage the investigation that allows that person the direct experience of being a passenger in the body. Few teach the patient how to keep the heart open in the midst of this hellishness. There is no fault in this and "no blame," it is just another example of how the unexamined mind may allow its hidden fears and confusions to be transmitted to others no matter how unintentionally.

Even in so supportive an environment few are encouraged to die out of their specialness, to enter into the very essence of their sharing, the oneness of being itself. Yet it is the experience of this oneness, the touching of the deathless, that cuts through the fear of loss. Experiencing that one is part of the whole kills death.

A woman dying in considerable pain in the hospital said, "I can tell, as they come in the room, which people have opened to their own suffering. Because they are the ones who can open to mine. And the people who haven't opened to their own suffering, who haven't opened to their pain, who aren't using all this as a way of going deeper are just tight. They're nervous. They're not particularly helpful. If I am in pain, they grimace. They make the pain the enemy."

While spending time with some nurses on a children's cancer ward, a few said, "The longer I'm here, the harder it gets." Working with children through years of treatment, going to their birthday parties, sharing their triumphs and confusions, a very close

bond occurs. Then they see these children die, and their wish for
it to be otherwise burns through them. They're trying to push
away death.

We started talking about the moment when you see how much
pain there is in the world. How you can either hide or move
gently into it. Resistance to the pain about us causes the heart to
wither. Allowing that pain to enter into us tears our heart open
and leaves us exposed to the truth. Clearly, if you try to resist
death, you resist life. Nurse after nurse on this ward had burned
out. For them, it was a hell realm. They spoke of how difficult it
was to keep their heart open in hell. How difficult it is to be clear
when all about you is other than you long for it to be. We shared
how to use the resistance, when it arises in the mind, as a reminder to tune into the heart. Start to soften around the resistance, as you would any other pain. Relate to the resistance, not
from it. Let go of the resistance in our hearts so that we won't be
acting from pity, but can be there fully for those we care for, in
love instead of fear. These nurses, on the edge for so long, were
looking so deeply for understanding, that many almost instantly
integrated what we were sharing. Several saw that what they had
thought of as an "untenable situation" could indeed open them in
just the way they sought.

A couple of months later, two of the nurses who had been
about to quit decided instead to go further into the fire by joining
the staff of the Sloan-Kettering Hospital, where there is much em-
phasis on researching advanced technical, mechanical, and chemi-
cal methods of keeping the most seriously ill children alive. They
willingly entered hell as a way of self-discovery and service. On
these wards, the parents are often holding on for all they are
worth to children whose breath is melting away. The pain in the
corridors can be palpable. To keep your heart open in such an
environment would indeed take all most of us have. To be there
in love for another, you must go beyond death. These nurses were
able to use their work as a means of self-purification.

Burn-out occurs when we give from the little self, the small
mind. We give from who we think we are. We become "helpers."
Because the little mind, the little personality, doesn't have much
room, we don't have space enough for the suffering of others. We

feel isolated and struggle to keep from being submerged in our separate suffering.

It's like trying to give water to somebody dying of thirst. You can either wring the fluid from your cells to give them something to drink, thereby becoming dry and wizened in the process. Or you can go to the well, the great source of sustenance, and carry buckets of clear water to those who need it, finding there's plenty to drink for yourself. Those who give from themselves burn out. Those who give from the source are nourished in the giving. Approaching the well, they enter intuition, sensing the subtleties of another, responding from the heart, not the mind.

You act from a sense of appropriateness, not from a knowing. Letting go of what stays the flow, one experiences the harmonic between beings. When our precious individuality drops away, just being is shared.

It's the care you have that allows healing. Yet the problem for many who work in hospitals, the fear of becoming "involved," is the fear of becoming involved with ourselves, of directly participating in our life. It is the difficulty of opening ourselves to another's predicament so fully that we can feel it in our mind and body and yet stay open to the heart of the matter. Noticing the tendency to pull away, we instead enter the fire that burns through our holding.

We perhaps forget the root out of which the word "care" arises —it is the same root as for our word "culture." To care is to become one with another, to join with a person in the greater "culture" of mankind, of life itself. For, in truth, there is no "other." There is just being, experienced from different focal points. When you are fully present, you see there is no such thing as "another person." There are just two perceptions of the one existence. There is "your" unfolding and there's "mine." Our work is to come together in truth. To become the perfect environment for each other's recognition that there is no other, but just the One to be shared.

13

A LETTER FROM
A FRIEND

Dear Friends,

"I have been working in a hospital as a nurse's aide for a while now and see what a difficult place a hospital is for one to let go into death. For most people the presence of death is never even acknowledged and those dying are constantly encouraged to hold on to life, to get well, to ignore the fact that they are dying and never, under any circumstances, talk about it. In short, to run and hide from death in every way possible. It's a funny movie. The loved ones "comfort" the dying by pretending that dying is not happening and the dying comfort the loved ones in the same way. No one dares bring it up. Everyone hides his head in fear and trembling.

"This great freedom terrifies most people and what they share with each other is simply fear. They believe that death is something different from and opposed to life and do not perceive or embrace their own death daily so that they might know the freedom of it.

"I have noticed (different from believe) that all people have a break in their specific selves, in their egos or personalities; an openness, God living within, a knowledge of truth, a place where they are already free—and if you sit in truth and offer love (unconditional love), they will relax their grip and let go.

"Very few people that I work with can respond on a verbal level to any concepts (no matter how right on) about dying. To *tell* them this is it, be here now, let go, melt into the one or rest in Jesus, is only to bring on confusion or an intellectual discussion. Somehow you must go with them into a space called love, openness, freedom, God. Invite them in by simply being in it yourself, a loving open being, watching and acknowledging their perfection (not judging their movie at all). Only open hands, open heart, and peace. Often I just sit by someone's bed. I wait open, in love without conditions. Open to this being, open to God to sing to His child through me, in willingness to help, to do what's needed, a state of Yes. And I listen, listen with my heart to hear whatever God is whispering in this moment, in this time, in this being, in this experience.

"Each time I look at death it is a completely new experience. I know *nothing* about it. I can only be open and in that openness, perhaps, make it easier for the dying one to be open, to embrace this most direct approach of God. Death, what a teacher!

"For the most part my work at the hospital is to relieve suffering. Even those who are nearing death are often caught in the trap of suffering and struggle hard against it. It is amazing to me to see how much relief simple compassion can bring to someone in intense physical pain (say, terminal cancer).

"There was an old man named Mr. Pine who I loved as dearly as any lover. He was dying of terminal cancer and I was his nurse for a time. He would get this pain in the right side of his back and after taking pill after pill to drug it away, he would finally tell me and I would massage his back for him and sing to him the 23rd Psalm, his favorite (a song which always turned him into a baby and helped him let go into trust of God). I say massage, but what happens is that the medium of touch reaches into the light of which he is made. And in knowing that this is what he is (and communicating it with my hands), the pain disappears and peace takes its place. Well, something like that anyway. It just happens.

"May I share some specific stories with you? Mrs. Goodall; God gave her a perfect name for her part in this play. An old black

lady, dying of cancer, who'd done God's loving work all her life.
Streams of visitors came to her bedside and they all went away
comforted, cheered, and loved by this shining light. She lay there
in great physical pain for months only giving love. If you but
straightened her covers, she'd give you a warm "I surely do thank
you" like you just brightened her whole day. This one was ready
for death (as ready for death as she had been for life—embracing
it with the same openness). We shared a very deep love for each
other, had an opportunity to talk about our love of God (Christ)
and to speak of death a little. When her last hours came, she
could not move at all without great pain. I was sent in to change
her bedding and dressings. She appeared to be in a coma, eyes
glassy. But I remembered what she once told me: 'You think I'm
lyin' here sleepin', but I'm lyin' here prayin' for ya.' I knew this
being to be aware. She was sharp as a tack and present no matter
what her body was doing.

"I set about my duties with gentleness. There is a way of loving
touch which heals rather than hurts a body in pain, and with
hands offered to God and full of His love I tended her body. I
saw, lying broken in the bed, the body of Christ. It was not someone like Christ, one who reminded me of Him because of the
suffering. This body was/is Christ. I was blasted against the wall
by the light which radiated from her/Him. In this state of awe at
the sight of God, I dressed her wounds and sang to her. I don't
know what song it was because it simply sang itself out of the
light. I think it was about resting in Jesus. Mrs. Goodall was too
weak to speak but she managed to raise one arm and put it
around my shoulder. My heart wept with the goodness of this
lady, that with her dying breath she reached to share love. As in
living, so in dying. Mrs. Goodall went out in a blaze of glory.
And if angels ever sing for anyone, they sang when this lady went
home to her master. Death for her was the loving embrace of
Christ.

"Mrs. Thayler wasn't ready. True, she had cancer but it would
have been a few more months. The doctor suggested an operation
to remove a block in her colon caused by the cancer so she could
eat without throwing up all the time and eliminate into a little bag
so she'd be more comfortable.

"I had only a little time with her. Enough to share love but not yet to share a space called God. She returned from the operating room and it was clear she was dying. She lay in agony for hours, every breath a groan. Her pain drove everyone away. Doctors and nurses couldn't stand to come into the room, so I had an opportunity to sit for long periods of time with her undisturbed. I sat open, waiting for anything that needed to come through. Nothing came. Only groans. I sat, willing to do anything to help her soul fly free. And Mrs. Thayler struggled on into death. I thought, 'What am I doing here? What kind of presumption is it of me to sit with this one in her agony of death? I know nothing.' Well, knowing nothing is my usual state, so I sat on. She struggled and I felt her struggle. I came away troubled, my body full of her groaning agony.

"It wasn't until the next day that understanding came. I came to my friend to talk about this struggle I still felt in my body and lay down with my head in his lap. I couldn't tell the difference between Mrs. Thayler and me. Her body, my body, the same. My body began to groan like hers and as I let her, my, our, groaning come; finally it came clear. Exactly the same as when I see a bird singing in the trees. Perfect praise of God. The bird's life, the bird's song, a statement of the perfection of God. And Mrs. Thayler's life, her death agony, a song in praise of God. A perfect song, a perfect statement of God. The groans were labor pains, only she was giving birth to her soul out of her mouth, letting it fly free from her body; and the death agony—labor pains. I couldn't see how it was because I wanted her to be out of what appeared to be struggle.

"Mrs. Karas was ready. So ready she pursued death. Old, feeble, she decided to stop eating. She was in the hospital about six months ago (when she first stopped eating) for weight loss. She weighed 68 pounds. The doctor said, "Ain't nothing wrong with her except the bitch won't eat," and sent her home. But I had a chance to get to know her a little, a tiny little bird, who lit up the room with her smile, a minister's wife, hated to dirty the bed, quite firm in her resolve to stop eating. It worked. Six months later she's on her deathbed, 24-hour family watch in the hospital, but sometimes they take a break and I get to slip in and sit with her. She looks like she's practicing dying. She goes out for a couple of hours. Comes back for five minutes to ask in a whisper for water or to be moved, goes out again. Real peaceful, very little pain. She goes out for the last time and splits. I come onto my shift about twenty minutes after her death and walk into the room and rub my eyes like a drunk looking at pink elephants. It's like an acid trip. Mrs. Karas isn't there any more. She's been blown to all the corners of the universe. Her eyes go back into eternity. Her mouth an endless black hole. Everything rushing out into freedom. No walls. No specific personality. Her whole being an explosion into infinity. I step to the next bed, thinking it must just be me. I am in some weird space. Maybe somebody slipped acid into my postum. The old lady next to her was busy being very specifically Mrs. Ruth, a perfectly defined concise little package of personality and body. Precisely Mrs. Ruth, doing things a Mrs. Ruth's way, wrinkling her nose, clutching her handkerchief, mumbling. Back to Mrs. Karas (whom I had observed as a specific before her death) and the acid trip is still swinging out into infinity. Some freedom this thing called death. I stay with her, just hanging out with the rushing explosion that we once called Mrs. Karas, until they take the body to the morgue.

"Granny: No bother to anyone when she first came to the nursing home. Did everything for herself, spent most of her time in her room alone, couldn't call you for anything. 'Don't want to trouble nobody.' Then she became very ill, her heart mostly, could just barely walk and was very unsteady. She fell and broke a hip and now needed help with all basic functions: getting up, getting dressed, going to the bathroom, combing her hair. And with her illness came fear. Her body gave her a lot of pain, she had trouble getting her breath, she 'just couldn't seem to get well.' Wanted someone to just sit with her all the time, complained if a nurse didn't come immediately every time she called. To most of the nurses she was becoming quite a pest. Every fifteen or twenty minutes Granny is yelling 'Nurse!' She held a lot of anger at people for not doing something to relieve her suffering. 'Couldn't the doctor do something?' 'Can't the nurse give me something more?' 'Can't you do something?' 'Why don't they do something?'

"Well it isn't too hard to see what's up. Granny is struggling against her death. So she says sort of into the air, 'Do you think I'll ever get better?' And I'd answer her, 'Your body is very sick, the doctor has done all he can.' 'Why doesn't the doctor come?' 'Because he can't do anything.' It's totally unethical by hospital standards to tell this lady, 'Granny, you're dying.' But she needs to know. Everyone is supporting the illusion that she'll get better and it's multiplying her suffering ten-fold. So she gets the idea after a few more questions and answers, a few more trips into her room. We speak about 'the Lord' (her name) and I direct her to Him for comfort and strength rather than looking for it from the doctor. So she stops fighting and sort of sighs like 'Oh, what a relief, I finally know what's up, there's nothing to be done.'

"All day long I'm answering her calls, doing all the physical stuff that needs to be done with loving-kindness and some kisses and cuddles thrown in, and she says, 'I'm glad they assigned you to me' and I say 'They didn't. I'm here because I like you.' And she says 'I love you because you're good and kind and I can feel the love of Jesus in you.' And I tell her I love her, and her love for me, and mine for her, is Jesus and we're sharing Him. And she gets all peaced out and says she feels the presence of the Lord and I know she does because we just moved up into this open space and there is no separateness between us any more and her soul is shining clean before me and mine before her and we understand each other deep without need for words at all. So we pray together and the words don't matter; we're just hanging out and I'm on my knees beside her bed and she's holding my hands to her heart and we're floating in light. So her family walks in and the first thing they say is 'What's wrong?' Comical. I tell them everything is perfect, we're just praying and they can see the peace Granny is in and they say 'God bless you' and 'thank you' and I float out of the room. Granny says, 'You've done me more good than any doctor.' And I know she got what she's been calling for for two weeks and I also know this is the county hospital and those are her relatives and nobody else is going to confirm this reality. They'll assure her she's getting better, talk about the grandchildren, ask if she's had a BM today. She needs someone to confirm the fact that she is dying and to pray with her, be with her, so that she may turn her face toward God. How can she embrace death when no one will even admit she's dying?

"For a while I hung out only with people who were 'on the path,' who at least wanted to want God. I was director of an ashram for three years until I found out I didn't know anything, then hung out for the next three in India and the U.S. Walking out of this 'holy' life into the solid granite non-reality of the hospital turned out to be pretty much the same after all; just my own mind free in some places, sticky in others. The hospital has been in truth a perfect teacher. What with no support for the reality of God coming from the environment, my own truth needs to be solid, not based on externals. I need to live it and be it. No words or beliefs can work here. Nothing but the real thing, nothing but pure unconditional love has any reality at all. People always open to it, turn to it like flowers in the sun. You can't fake it with an old deaf lady too senile to know where the bathroom is.

"One wonderful thing about working with beings in real old bodies is most of them don't have the slightest idea who you are. Leaving you quite free to be their mother, daughter, minister, nurse, as needed. But they dive right into the love. They're never too old or too far gone to miss it. Moths to a flame. They know light. The more darkness surrounds them, the quicker they move toward it. I work with the old ones a lot out of choice. (There's a nursing home connected with the hospital.) They have let go of their role in life more than people in the regular hospital.

"Well, if there's any place for me in whatever you're doing with dying people, I'd like to serve and learn in this way. Could be someone is needed to schlep bedpans."

In God's love,

Marge Koenig

14
WHO DIES?

"It is because you believe you are born that you fear death. Who is it that was born? Who is it that dies? Look within. What was your face before you were born? Who you are, in reality, was never born and never dies. Let go of who you think you are and become who you have always been."

Believing we were born, we imagine ourselves this body. Expecting to die, we identify with this body as who we are. When we are asleep, though the body lays inert, yet the mind continues. The dream of life continues without the body.

"When I die, I shall no longer exist." This is the "I" of the mind. The mind that dreams life. We fear we shall awaken from this dream, that the mind shall no longer be able to maintain this fantasy.

To the degree we identify with the body as "me," or "mine," we fear death. The body dies, of that we are certain. Decay becomes noticeable soon after death. But does the energy which animated that empty form decay as well?

When "I" calls itself the body, it suspects impermanence. When "I" identifies with the mind, it fears dissolution. Though the examined mind is seen constantly to be dissolving and re-emerging. Constantly dying and being reborn, moment to moment.

When we think of ourselves as the body, as the mind, we are confused, for we see that nothing is permanent in either of these. All is constantly changing. When you think of "I" as the mind, is it this thought or the next that is "I"? Or is it both thoughts, though they may conflict? Who is the "I" that is sad, that is happy? Or is it the mind's incessant unfolding? Thoughts think themselves.

Sitting in a comfortable chair, absorbed in a book, a friend walks into the room and offers a glass of water. But because awareness is focused in seeing, we say, "I didn't hear you. I was reading." Who is this "I" that reads but does not hear? When our attention comes once again to our ear, to hearing, we say, "Oh yes, I heard what you said that time." Wherever awareness is, consciousness arises. When awareness is focused in the eye, in seeing, when we are absorbed in what we are perceiving through the eyes, the awareness that allows consciousness of an object does not touch the hearing, though all the potentials for hearing are present: a sound, and the ear's capacity to hear. Without awareness coming to hearing, there is no hearing consciousness. There is no experience without awareness present. Is it awareness itself that we refer to when we say "I"?

Awareness is like a beam of light that shines endlessly into space. We only perceive that light when it is reflected off some object and consciousness is produced. When the light of awareness touches an object of thought, a moment of hearing, of tasting, of seeing, the light from that object is reflected in perception, just as the reflected light of the sun allows the moon to be seen by night. Awareness is the light by which we see the world. It is the Evershining that illuminates thought and feeling. The more focused the awareness, the brighter the light, the more clearly we can see. It is here that we uncover the illusion of our identification with consciousness as "I."

We mistake the clear light of pure awareness for the shadows that it casts in consciousness. Pure awareness, pure is-ness, has no personal identification—it is the essence of being itself, identical to the unconditional love that embraces all things equally. When this is-ness produces consciousness there arises the universal sense of "I am." We mistake the reflected is-ness of "I am" for the object of awareness and say, "I am this thought." We are already two steps removed from the truth of pure being. Awareness allows consciousness to come about. It is the light by which our experience is perceived. Consciousness gives rise to the sense of presence, the "I am of being." Attachment to and identification with the objects that float in consciousness give rise to the small self which imagines its contents to be all it is. In many spiritual practices the word "ignorance" denotes not stupidity or a lack of intelligence, but rather the misidentification with the contents of consciousness as being who we are.

Few can tell the difference between awareness and the object of awareness. Most often we mistake thoughts, feelings, perceptions, and even consciousness itself for some "I," and forget our true nature by which all is seen. We forget that we are the light itself and imagine that we are the densities that reflect the light back to us.

Awareness touches a sensation in the knee and we say, "I am this body," instead of recognizing that awareness has reflected sensation. Even what we call the body is just a mass of sensation, an image in the mind. It's sort of like one of those connect-the-dot pictures. There are simply moments of sensation, instants of experience, which the mind puts together, draws an outline about, and imagines to be some solid reality. At first as we investigate "who am I," we examine the thoughts and feelings that have led us to believe that we are the body and mind. The body you call "me" when you are four years old, is that the same "me" as the forty-year-old body? Is it the same body, the same personal "I"? But the sense of being, behind it, can be seen to be unchanged. Somehow being remains the same, a "presence" that is not affected by the vessel's permutation. And in the mind, is that "I" of this moment the same as the "I" of a year ago? States of mind change, but the awareness by which they are seen remains unmoved.

Examining "Who am I?" is like beginning to go to the movies just to see how the movie is made. As we first sit down in the dark theater we find that we are relating to the objects of the melodrama, the motion on the screen. We pay attention to the story line, which we notice is like the contents of the mind, allowing it to unfold as it will without judgment or the least interference. As we focus our attention on the process, we begin to see that the frames that constitute the film are like separate thoughts; then we begin to recognize the process by which the images are produced, and it breaks our enthrallment with the story line. We notice that all the activity is just a projection on a blank screen. That all these figures dancing before us are an illusion produced by light passing through various densities on the film. We see that the film is like our conditioning, a repetitious imprint of images gone by. We see that the whole melodrama is a passing show of motion and change.

In the second stage of this process, we begin to focus on the screen, on consciousness itself. The objects of consciousness, the forms on the screen, no longer draw us into identification with them as being real. Instead, the reality becomes the space in which consciousness presents itself. Focusing on the screen, we recognize the flashing images to be just momentary illusions of no real substance, containing only the meaning we give to them.

In the last stage, we come to recognize that this shadow play arises only because of the presence of a constant source of light. And we begin to focus awareness on itself. We experience the spacious sense of "I am" as the screen of consciousness. However, awareness does not experience itself as some "thing," as a separateness, so there is no sense of I, only undifferentiated being.

When the conditioned tendency to identify awareness with its various objects falls away, it reveals the edgelessness of being, the light itself, unfiltered and unqualified by conditions and false identification. We examine the endless reels of our conditioning, projecting the images we find on the screen of consciousness. And when we peer into the theater to see who is watching the film, we find the theater is just another image on the screen.

We discover that all we imagined ourselves to be—all our becoming, our memory, all the contents of mind—is just old film running off. The projectionist has died. "Who am I?" can't be answered. We cannot know the truth. We can only be it. Constantly living life in the past tense, rummaging through consciousness to decide who and what we are, the truth is obscured. The truth cannot be discovered in the contents of the mind. Only the untruth of false identification can be uncovered. Going beyond the false, the true is revealed.

What was your face before you were born? When you examine the sense of presence, of simply being, does it seem to have a beginning or end? Or does it have a quality of constant presence, of just being, dependent upon nothing, self-existing? What can affect it? Though consciousness is constantly perceiving change in the body and mind, it does not mistake these changes for the light by which change is perceived.

Follow "I am" to its root. Experience consciousness itself. Don't identify with the reflection. Let "Who am I?" become unanswerable, beyond definition. Become that space out of which all things originate and into which all things recede.

Albert Einstein was quoted as saying, "A human being is a part of a whole, called by us "universe," a part limited in time and space. He experiences himself, his thoughts and feelings, as something separate from the rest—a kind of optical delusion of consciousness. This delusion is a kind of prison for us, restricting us to our personal desires and to affection for a few persons nearest to us. Our task must be to free ourselves from this prison by widening our circle of compassion to embrace all living creatures and the whole of nature in its beauty."

But this optical delusion of consciousness is not so easily broken. As we begin to let go of the body and mind, there may arise confusion. "But I've got to be something—I've got to be someone!" the mind reiterates. Because the mind mostly thinks about itself, doubt and confusion arise when it contemplates the possibility of going beyond its imaginings and models. The mind constantly re-creates its existence. Letting go of the mind's insistence that there is nothing beyond, we investigate to find that "I must be someone," is but another impermanent moment in the vastness. We recognize that what the conditioned mind tells us "ain't necessarily so," no matter what credentials it flashes to reassure us of its solidity and ability to protect us from our fears. It is difficult to let go of the security of some imagined "I," and enter into the not knowing of just being.

No longer someone wondering "Who am I?" we become the investigation. At each moment, focusing on the light, we ask ourselves, "Who is it that thinks this thought? Who is seeing? Who is sitting in this chair reading this book?" And there comes a time when the body and mind no longer seem so real and distinct. After surveying all of the evidence, we simply don't know who or what we are. You have let go of who you think you are to become who you really are. Having let go of even memory as real, you find yourself suspended in space without the reference points that mind is so addicted to. As mind withdraws from its habituation, it goes through a kind of cold turkey of doubt and fear. "Where am I?" it screams. The mind grasps at being someone, at being anything. There arises a feeling of emptiness at not having some assurance of who we are. There arises a kind of darkness at not having someone to be, at no longer being certain of the world, or even of our own separate existence. It is like St. John of the Cross's dark night of the soul. We tremble in the silence of having let go of the past, but the future has not arrived yet. This stage reminds me of children swinging across the monkey bars in a playground. Moving across the overhead trellis from one bar to the other with ease, one can see how easily children let go of the last and trust the next. Children seem almost to glide from one end of the bars to the other. But often, I'll notice a chaperoning parent come to play with their child on the monkey bars, attempting that same crossing. They don't move with such ease. They hang stiffly from one bar to the next. They will not let go of the last bar until they've grasped the next, dangling like a herniated chimp before falling to the ground. They don't trust the momentum that allows the next moment to appear as it will, without clinging to the last. We must let go of the last stage before we can go on to the next. We must allow ourselves to be infinitely insecure in order to know the truth. But if we grasp at security, at some mirage of solidity, that is as far as we will go. We recognize the groundlessness of the constantly changing mind, its continual change in point of view. We see there is nothing or no one in there to which we can anchor some sense of "I." It is all just process unfolding by itself.

Letting go of who we thought we were, the mind often angles

for a new self-image, projects imaginings of what it will be in the future. "Soon I'll be enlightened. No more monkey bars. I'll have great peace. I'll have infinite patience. I just can't wait."

The idea of enlightenment becomes just another fantasy in the mind. The ego wishes to be present at its own funeral. It imagines, at last, that it has met a worthy opponent—itself. Thereby reinforcing its imagined existence. But "Who am I?" goes beyond the glib responses of the mind; it is the death of the illusion that there is something or someone separate from the whole. Letting go of being something special. Of specialness itself. The preferences of the mind are seen to be the glue that keeps getting us stuck to the last monkey bar. Immersed in being, we experience impermanence floating in something less affected by conditions. Liberation is not something you get. It is your inherent nature.

"Enlightenment is the final nightmare." The push to be better than you are causes the palms to sweat, the fingers to cramp; the mind becomes timid. We lose our momentum from stage to stage.

A friend, very ill from a degenerative nerve disease that seemed about to cause her death, visited with a Korean Zen master who had just come to this country. After she had told him of her predicament, he smiled and waved his hand, saying, "Don't worry. You won't die." Because he knew that who she was was not her body or her mind, not something impermanent. That who she was never dies. Because awareness simply is.

There is a reality even prior to heaven and earth,
Indeed, it has no form, much less a name;
Eyes fail to see it; it has no voice for ears to detect;
To call it Mind or Buddha violates its nature,
For it then becomes like a visionary flower in the air;
It is not Mind, nor Buddha;
Absolutely quiet, and yet illuminating
    in a mysterious way,
It allows itself to be perceived only by the clear-eyed.
It is Dharma truly beyond form and sound;
It is Tao having nothing to do with words.
Wishing to entice the blind,
The Buddha has playfully let words
    escape his golden mouth;
Heaven and earth are ever since filled
    with entangling briars.

O my good worthy friends gathered here,
If you desire to listen
    to the thunderous voice of the Dharma,
Exhaust your words, empty your thoughts,
For then you may come to recognize this One Essence.

                                        Dai O Kokushi

15

LETTING GO
OF CONTROL

The Chinese poet and sage Chuang-tzu speaks of a man crossing a river in his boat. As he is navigating through the waters he notices another boat coming his way. As he thinks he sees someone in the oncoming boat he yells, "Steer aside!" and gesticulates and swears as the boat continues toward him.

But Chuang-tzu suggests we imagine that same fellow crossing the stream when he looks up to yell at the person in the other boat and discovers the boat is empty. "Even though he be a bad-tempered man he will not become very angry." The boat is being carried toward him by the currents, but since there is no one in the boat he is not threatened or angered. It's just an empty boat. And as the boat approaches he skillfully puts his oar out to steer the other boat aside so that a collision will not damage either vessel.

Chuang-tzu suggests that we empty our boat. That we relate to the world from that openhearted emptiness that flows with what is, so that nothing that comes out of us will be coming from the "someone-ness" which opposes the flow. That we let go of control of the world and come fully into being.

As soon as the mind's conditioning to be someone arises, a

kind of pain comes into our heart. A feeling of being alone. It is the loneliness of our separateness. Our alienation from the universal. But when we sit quietly with that loneliness and let it float in the mind it dissolves into an "aloneness" which is not lonely. But is rather a recognition that we are each alone in the One. It is the great silence of the universe "alone" in space. It has a wholeness about it. But to change the intense loneliness of our personal isolation into an "aloneness with God," we must gently let go of control and stop re-creating the imagined self. We must surrender our specialness, our competition, our comparing minds.

Control is our attempt to make the world align with our personal desires. To let go of control is to go beyond the personal and merge with the universal.

Control creates bondage. Control is the defender of the clinging mind. It opposes the openness of the heart. If our boats are empty, though there is still a vessel carried by the prevailing winds and currents there is not "someone" in it to be misunderstood. There is no one to oppose. There is simply empty space, boat, water, wind. Everything is in perfect harmony. Nothing is pulling against the natural flow. No one in the boat: no one to suffer.

Chuang-tzu wrote of the ease that comes about when we let go of control and tune to what the ancient Chinese called the Tao, the flow, the effortless way of things. Tao also means "just this much."

"When Life Was Full There Was No History."

"In the age when life on earth was full no one paid any special attention to worthy men, nor did they single out the man of ability. Rulers were simply the highest branches on the tree, and the people were like deer in the woods. They were honest and righteous, without realizing that they were 'doing their duty.' They loved each other and did not know this was 'love of neighbor.' They deceived no one, yet they did not know that they were 'men to be trusted.' They were reliable and did not know that this was 'good faith.' They lived freely together giving and taking and did not know they were generous. For this reason their deeds have not been narrated. They made no history."

How often are you so much a part of the whole that there remains no "specialness" that cries out to be recognized?

In the Taoist tradition they speak of becoming invisible. Of being no one special, just the space in which creation is unfolding. Our conditioning on the other hand has been to become as visible as possible. A friend who became a monk in Thailand tells of being encouraged to drop his specialness beginning with the specialness of appearance: his head shaved, wearing simple robes, eating from a simple bowl the food he had been given each day in his alms rounds. Eyes averted in silence. He spent many hours of meditation each day in a secluded forest hermitage with a number of other monks. He relates that as he began to settle into the new way of life, encouraging the mind to let go of its specialness, he started to experience old conditioning arising to resist this anonymity. He said there were periods when he was sitting in the meditation hall with a very agitated mind thinking, "They can't stop me. I think I'll go out and tie-dye my robes. Maybe I'll just paint flowers on my begging bowl." Clearly it is difficult to let go of our specialness. Yet clearly it is that which separates us from the truth.

Our attempt to be special is a pulling back from the natural flow of things; indeed, we are different without having to do anything about it. To make what is different "something special" creates a separation, just more of the judgmental comparing mind. For if we think of ourselves as better or worse than another we break the heart's contact.

In pain and resistance we see how the attempt at control, the "someoneness" in the boat, causes suffering. In a sense our body/mind is like that boat. Who is the helmsman? Is there a feverish tugging against the flow? Does the rudder creak in your hands? Can you feel the current pull against your will? What if the rudder is held loosely, the hand sensitive to the prevailing currents? If the boat catches fire and there is "someone" in it, he burns (death is a tragedy). But if the boat is empty, it just turns to ash silently in the night and sinks without "someone" drowning.

If you are trying to be someone doing something, controlling the flow, then when that which is uncontrollable approaches, your resistance becomes greater and your suffering more intense. As you let go of control, you see as Paul dying of Hodgkin's disease saw, "acceptance is magic." He saw that though there is little in our conditioning, in our personal history, that reminds us that letting go is freedom, it is that opening into the flow that allows the fullness of being. If you are just hanging out, opening to the Tao, to the flow, to that natural unfolding, you see that moment to moment it's just right. Each moment giving birth to the next. There is nothing askew, nothing amiss in that flow. It is perfection. However, if you identify with some bubble in that flow as being "me," in that instant you are removed from the whole. And you watch that bubble of "me" dissolve in your palm.

Because of our long encouragement to be something special, we have lost trust in the universal. That which is common to all seems of no value. We would rather polish the bars in our cage than become free.

As we deepen our investigation of who dies, we notice the tendency to wish that our spiritual practice will make us something special. Yet when we meet quiet beings whose hearts seem to be open, who can listen without interjecting something of themselves that needs acknowledgment, we notice that the quality that most sets them apart from others is not their specialness but the feeling of their being no one special, nothing separate, ordinary. Many of those who met Suzuki Roshi, the Zen master who did so much to bring Zen practice to this country, were often surprised at how ordinary he was. Most who met him admired and loved him because there was nothing in him that obstructed love and understanding. He was a spotless mirror for one's true nature.

Shortly before he died of cancer he said, "If, when I die, the moment I'm dying, if I suffer, that is all right you know. That is just suffering Buddha. No confusion in it. Maybe everyone will struggle because of the physical agony or the spiritual agony, too. But that is all right. That is not a problem. We should be very grateful to have a limited body, like mine, like yours. If you had a limitless life, it would be a real problem for you."

Interestingly enough, the woman who put together his talks for *Zen Mind, Beginner's Mind* also died of cancer. This is what she said about her meeting with Suzuki Roshi (a roshi, by the way, is a teacher): "A roshi is a person who has actualized that perfect freedom which is the potentiality of all human beings. He exists freely in the fullness of his whole being. The flow of his consciousness is not the fixed, repetitive patterns of our usual self-centered consciousness. But, rather, arises spontaneously and naturally from the actual circumstances of the present. The results of this in terms of the quality of his life are extraordinary: buoyancy, vigor, straightforwardness, humility, simplicity, serenity, joyousness, uncanny perspicacity, and unfathomable compassion. His whole being testifies to what it means to live in the reality of the present. Without anything said or done, just the impact of meeting a personality so developed can be enough to change another's whole way of life. But, in the end, it is not the extraordinariness of the teacher which perplexes, intrigues, and beckons the student. It is the teacher's utter ordinariness. Because he is just himself, he is a mirror for his students. When we are with him, we feel our own strengths and shortcomings without any sense of praise or criticism from him. In his presence, we see our original face. And the extraordinariness we see is only our own true nature. When we learn to let our own nature free, the boundaries between master and student disappear in a deep flow of being and joy in the unfolding of Buddha mind."

Many people's motivation for reading books such as this is perhaps to gain something special. I wonder how few come to such a book to let go of their specialness.

But it is very scary to let go, to be free, to be completely empty.

Those who have watched wild life programs, such as "Wild Kingdom," on television have probably seen films of animals being relocated from one place to another where there was a greater chance of survival. A tiger, for instance, in the mountains where it is being hunted out, or where there is very little water or food, might be shot with a tranquilizer dart and put into a cage to be transported to some place like the Serengeti Plain; a lush green veldt rich with gazelle and wildebeests—the perfect place for that tiger to be. But when that tiger comes out of his stupor in the cage, he looks about at this new shimmering green openness and refuses to leave his cage. They will open the gate but the tiger will not come out. Indeed, you could lose an arm trying to get him out of his cage. He will fight to the death to protect his territory, even if that territory is cold hard steel—when all about him glows with the softness of the nature out of which he has evolved. His natural sustenance beckons all about him but his fear keeps him isolated. He is terrified of the freedom of the unknown beyond the bars.

In a manner of speaking we have painted ourselves into a corner. The paint is our models of reality which we use to cover the suchness of things. The corner is our imagined self.

What most people call freedom is just the ability to satisfy desire. Many say, "I want more freedom," and what they mean is they want to be able to have more of what they want. But that is not freedom, that is a kind of bondage. Freedom is the ability to have or *not have* what you want without it closing your heart. Freedom is not to act compulsively on all the contents of the mind, to let the contents flow away and tune to the unfolding. The content of your mind and the content of my mind may be different but the process by which it unfolds is precisely the same. Tuning to that process we enter the Tao.

This, again, is Suzuki Roshi:

"I went to Yosemite National Park, and I saw some huge waterfalls. The highest one there is 1,340 feet high, and from it the water comes down like a curtain thrown from the top of the mountain. It does not seem to come down swiftly, as you might expect; it seems to come down very slowly because of the distance. And the water does not come down as one stream, but is separated into many tiny streams. From a distance it looks like a curtain. And I thought it must be a very difficult experience for each drop of water to come down from the top of such a high mountain. It takes time, you know, a long time, for the water finally to reach the bottom of the waterfall. And it seems to me that our human life may be like this. We have many difficult experiences in our life. But at the same time, I thought, the water was not originally separated, but was one whole river. Only when it is separated does it have some difficulty in falling. It is as if the water does not have any feeling [of being separate] when it is one whole river. Only when divided into many drops can it begin to have or express some [separate] feeling.

"Before we were born we had no such feeling; we were one with the universe. This is called 'mind-only,' or 'essence of mind,' or 'big mind.' After we are separated by birth from this oneness, as the water falling from the waterfall is separated by the wind and rocks, then we have such feelings. And you have difficulty because of such feelings. You attach to the feeling you have without knowing just how this kind of feeling is created. When you do not realize that you are one with the river, or one with the universe, you have fear. Whether it is separated into drops or not, water is water. Our life and death are the same thing. When we realize this fact, we have no fear of death anymore and we have no actual difficulty in our life."*

Letting go of the little mind, of your suffering, is simpler than you think, though it's the hardest work you will ever do. Cultivating that "don't know," we enter the process and become the Tao.

The contemplation of death encourages us to let go of our specialness. The fact of death, of having to leave this world behind, makes us see that we have the opportunity now to let go of all that stays the flow. Or will you try to take your specialness with you? Will death be a struggle and a tragedy? The contemplation of death can be used as an opportunity, even as a technique, to leave specialness behind and dissolve into that which is universal. As you die there seems to be an experience of melting, sometimes gradual, sometimes rapid, that frightens people who want to hold on to who they think they are. But it brings joy to those who wish to go beyond the clinging mind. For some death is the great initiation, an opportunity to let go yet deeper. At death your priorities become very clear. If it is to control the universe, to get all the juice you can, then you will go for the objects of your desires and lose touch with the deathless. Perhaps this is what Jesus meant when he said, "For what is a man profited, if he shall gain the whole world, and lose his own soul." Fear will block the wisdom and unity available in the experience. But if you want the truth more than anything else, your death will be

* If this view seems to conflict with the earlier story of the regressionist allow yourself to draw no conclusions about the unknown—let it all float in "don't know." The truth will present itself to the heart that is prepared for any possibility.

another opportunity to let go of control, to merge with the mystery. Indeed, those who seem most alive are those who want the truth more than life itself. If you want life more than truth, you will seldom touch the truth of your life. But if the truth is the priority, death will dissolve and only the truth will continue.

Our original nature is like a clear water. But imagining that we are something separate from the whole, that imagining seeks yet another body. Yearning for experience we exit the womb. We seek to "fulfill our destiny" rather than empty it.

Born again into a world of wildly changing forms, though having no essential form of our own, we take on the shapes of the containers we are poured into. We become "sons" or "daughters" and are told to think of ourselves in that manner. We are taught to be "responsible." Acculturated, we bend to the curves of that arbitrary modality. Slowly we soldify to fit the "acceptable" shape we are told we should think of ourselves as being. We take on the bends and curves, the hard edge of the container. Slowly we freeze into that shape. The straighter and harder the edge the more we are praised as being "someone" of merit. Eventually the mold can be removed and we stay frozen in that shape—this learned self-image is from that time on applied as the measure of all other forms. We become freeze-dried. Our mind like a wild river, our heart like a desert.

But water is water, no matter what its shape or form. The solidity of ice imagines itself to be its edges and density. Melting, it remembers; evaporating, it ascends.

When you let go of control of the universe, when you let go of everything, only the truth remains. And like a roshi you start responding from the moment. Your actions come out of the present. There is no force. Your boat is empty. The currents move you to the left, "Ahhh, the left." They move you to the right, "Ahh, the right." But you never feel as though you are to the left or to the right, you only feel that you are here now, in the present. Open to all the possibilities and opportunities of the moment. Fully present. Able to respond, not out of personal desire, but out of a sense of the appropriateness of things. You respond from the flow itself, or perhaps better stated, the flow responds to itself. No separation anywhere. Nowhere to go. Nothing to do. No one to be.

A Guided Meditation on Letting Go

[To be read slowly to a friend or silently to oneself.]

Let your attention come to the breath.

Not the thought of the breath, but the direct sensation of the breath, as it comes and goes by itself.

Let the awareness come right to the edge of sensation as the breath enters and leaves the nostrils.

Let the awareness be soft and open, making contact with each breath without the least interference.

Experience the natural tides of the breath, as it comes and goes.

Don't attempt to control or change it. Just observe it.

Open to receive each changing sensation that accompanies the breath, moment to moment.

Let the breath breathe itself. Without comment. Without any attempt to control it in any way. Allow the breath to be as it is. If it is slow, let it be slow. If it is deep, let it be deep. If it is shallow, let it be shallow. Allow awareness and sensation to meet, moment to moment, with each inhalation, with each exhalation.

Let the breath be completely natural and free. In no way held by the mind. Just the breath breathing itself. Sensation arising, instant to instant, in the vast spaciousness of awareness.

If you notice the mind attempting to shape the breath, to control it in even the least way, just watch that tendency and let the breath float free. No holding. No control.

Completely let go of the breath. Let the body breathe by itself. Don't interfere with the subtle flow.

Just awareness. Vast as the sky. Spacious.

The sensations of the breath, arising and passing away within this openness. Nothing to hold to. Nothing to do. Just the breath as it is.

Each breath unique. Sensations changing, moment to moment.

From the body, other sensations arise and pass away within boundless awareness. The hands folded in the lap. Buttocks touching the pillow. Each moment of sensation floating free. Each moment of experience just as it is. No need to label. No need to interrupt anything.

Not naming experience, just contacting it directly. Just being. Experienced in the vastness of awareness.

Sensations of the breath. Sensations of the body. Floating free. Not holding to the breath. Not creating the body. Just moments of experience, appearing and disappearing, within the vastness.

Notice how thoughts arise. Commenting, remembering, thinking. Each thought a bubble passing through the vast spaciousness of mind. Existing for an instant. Dissolving back into the flow. No need for control. Just the vast open flow of change. Just process unfolding, moment to moment.

Thoughts think themselves. Nothing to condemn. Nothing to add. Let go of control in even the least way. Just let things be as they are, approaching and receding within the vastness of being.

Let go of the body. Let sensation float in vast space. Let go of the mind. Thoughts. Feeling. Arising and melting away. Nothing to hold to.

Nothing to do but be. Soft. Open into the vast edgelessness of awareness.

Thoughts that you "own," or are "responsible" for, the mind seen as just more thought bubbles, floating through. Thoughts of "me" and "mine," arising and passing away. Instant to instant. Let them come. Let them go.

No one to be. Nothing to do. Nowhere to go. Just now. Just this much.

Let go of the body. Let go of the mind. Experience being unfolding all by itself. Without the least need of help or control. No judging. No interfering. Just being. Just Flow and Change.

Be silent and know.

Once and for all, completely relinquish control. Let go of fear and doubt. Let each thing float in its own nature.

Dissolve into the vast spaciousness of awareness. No body. No mind. Just thought. Just feelings. Just sensations. Bubbles. Floating in vast space.

An instant of thought. Of hearing. Of remembering. Of fearing. Like waves, rising for an instant and dissolving back into the ocean of being. Into the vastness of your true nature.

No one to be. Nothing to do.

Let each instant unfold as it will.

No resistance anywhere. Let the wind blow right through you.

No one to be—just this much. This instant is enough.

Nowhere to go—just now. Just here.

Nothing to do—just be.

Freedom comes like a thief in the night—holding nowhere, we are everywhere at once.

• • •

Zen Master Yasutani's Encounters with Westerners
(as shared by Roshi Philip Kapleau)

ROSHI (sharply): Who are you? (No answer). Who are you?!

STUDENT (pausing): I don't know.

ROSHI: Good! Do you know what you mean by "I don't know"?

STUDENT: No, I don't.

ROSHI: You are You! You are *only* You—that is all.

STUDENT: What did you mean by "Good!" when I answered, "I don't know"?

ROSHI: In the profoundest sense, we can know nothing.

STUDENT: Yesterday when you told me you were going to ask me who I am, I concluded that I must have some answer prepared, so I thought of various responses, but just now when you asked, "Who are you?" I couldn't think of a single thing.

ROSHI: Excellent! It shows your mind is emptied of all ideas. Now you can respond with your whole being, not with just your head. When I said I would ask you who you are, I didn't want you to reason out an answer but only to penetrate deeper and deeper into yourself with "Who am I?" When you come to the sudden inner realization of your True-nature, you will be able to respond instantly without reflection.

STUDENT: In questioning, "Who am I?" I have come to the conclusion that I am this body, that is, these eyes, these legs, and so forth. At the same time I realize that these organs do not exist independently. If I were to take out my eye and place it in front of me, for example, it could not function as an eye. Neither could my leg function as a leg if it were separated from my body. For walking, my legs need not only my body but also the ground, just as my eyes need objects to perceive in order to perform the act of seeing. Furthermore, what my eyes see and what my legs walk on are part of the universe. Therefore I am the universe. Is this correct?

ROSHI: You are the universe all right, but what you have just given me is an abstraction, a mere reconstruction of reality, not reality itself. You must directly grasp reality.

STUDENT: But *how* do I do that?

ROSHI: Simply by questioning, "Who am I?" until abruptly you perceive your True-nature with clarity and certainty. Remember, you are neither your body nor your mind. And you are not your mind added to your body. Then what are you? If you would grasp the real You and not merely a figment, you must constantly ask yourself, "Who am I?" with absolute devotion.

STUDENT: Last time you said I was not my mind and not my body. I don't understand. If I am neither of these nor a combination of them, what am I?

ROSHI: Were you to ask the average person what he is, he would say, "My mind" or "My body" or "My mind and body," but none of this is so. We are more than our mind or our body or both. Our True-nature is beyond all categories. Whatever you can conceive or imagine is but a fragment of yourself, hence the real You cannot be found through logical deduction or intellectual analysis or endless imagining.

If I were to cut off my hand or my leg, the real I would not be decreased one whit. Strictly speaking, this body and mind are also you but only a fraction. The essence of your True-nature is no different from that of this stick in front of me or this table or this clock—in fact every single object in the universe. When you directly experience the truth of this, it will be so convincing that you will exclaim, "How true!" because not only your brain but all your being will participate in this knowledge.

STUDENT (suddenly crying): But I am afraid! I am afraid! I don't know why, but I am afraid!

ROSHI: There is nothing to fear. Just deepen and deepen the questioning until all your preconceived notions of who and what you are vanish, and at once you will realize that the entire universe is no different from yourself. You are at a crucial stage. Don't retreat—march on!

16

HEALING/DYING— THE GREAT BALANCING ACT

The balance of the mind and heart is reflected in the body. When the heart and mind are not in harmony there sometimes occurs what we call disease (dis-ease). But I suspect this is not the only cause of illness. Many saintly beings have died of cancer (Ramana Maharshi, Suzuki Roshi, Ramakrishna). Some seem to take on illness as a means of purification, or as a friend put it, "Cancer is the gift for the person who has everything." It may be that for some beings illness does not arise out of disharmony but is a "cleaning of the slate," a finishing of old business.

Healing is the title we give to the phenomenon of the mind and heart coming back into balance. When this harmony is restored we say that someone is healed. But often we have a preconception about what healing is. Our attachment to ideas of healthiness obstruct a deeper perspective on what illness and healing may be all about. The deepest healing seems to take us beyond identification with that which causes and experiences sickness.

A woman we know had worked very hard to overcome her cancer. After several months of meditation and deep psychological nit-picking it seemed as though the cancer was no longer present. For some months she felt strong and healthy and clear.

Then one day in meditation she sensed the cancer once again in her body. Tests confirmed her intuition. A healing circle was called. Some of the most respected holistic and Native American healing persons on the West Coast came to her home and formed a silent circle about her. For more than an hour they channeled their energy into her. Some in the room later related that the power was nearly palpable. A week later thirty new metastases, secondary tumors, appeared in different parts of her body. She said the healing had worked. She felt the next perfect step in her evolution had occurred. She prepared for death by continuing to open to life.

It appears that the balancing of the heart and mind can either displace illness from the body or in some cases draw that being into harmony outside the body. In either case, healing occurs. When the attachment to preconceived results is let go of, there is little to maintain imbalance. As our friend wryly noted one day, "Survival is highly overrated."

When the healer's priority becomes that each individual directly experiences their original nature, healing becomes a lens that focuses the potentialities of the moment. But if the priority is to change people, to "heal them," to take something away from them, then perhaps the most that can be expected is that the body may become somewhat stronger, but the weakness in the mind, the clinging that has always obscured the heart, is not affected or encouraged to dissolve.

As long as we are thinking of healing as opposed to dying, there will be confusion. As long as we separate life from death, we separate the mind from the heart and we will always have something to protect, something more to be, another cause for inharmony and illness. When the attitude toward healing is in balance, the attitude toward death is as well.

As my friend said after she discovered the thirty new tumors, "The healing worked. Now I see that for me the perfect healing is to open to whatever happens next with love and awareness. There is nothing for me to do but listen, open, and be."

Sharing with various healers—nurses, doctors, herbalists, acupuncturists, psychics, polarity therapists, body workers, aura balancers, etc.—I have sensed at times a tendency, slight or grandiose, that they believed they were doing the healing. It is perhaps that state of pride and separateness that most obstructs the conduit for the healing powers always available in the universe. But the greater the sense of separateness, of "someone doing something," the more attachment to results. They are not allowing healing, they are clamoring for it. But the heart closes in the presence of such personal force, and harmony becomes less likely. It is by surrendering into the underlying suchness that one seems to be able to make available the essential harmony of being to another. Anything that reinforces the feeling of the "healed" as a separate entity removed from the universe intensifies the separation of heart and mind while it magnifies the fear of death and the disharmony that amplifies disease.

The true healer is invisible. He or she only allows the potential of the moment to come to fruition. Ramana Maharshi, the Indian saint and teacher, was known as a great healer. Thousands had come to him and gone away in balance. There is a story that one day a doctor from the northern part of India came to visit him and asked, "I understand you are a great healer; I would like to know more about how you do it." But Ramana replied with an honesty and pureness, "No, I am not a healer, I don't heal anyone." The visitor said, "I've heard you have healed thousands." Ramana seemed sort of bewildered and said, "No, I don't heal." At that point one of Ramana's devotees turned to him and said, "Bhagwan, what I think the doctor means is that the healing comes through you." "Oh, yes! The healing comes through." He wasn't playing a confrontation Zen game, he was just being who he was. He wasn't doing anything but allowing those energies which flourish in the universe to compassionately focus on any being who came near.

It is not unlike the story of the Tibetan lama Kalu Rinpoche, a much revered meditation master and teacher of incredible tenderness and fierce wisdom, who was visiting the home of a friend one day. He was approached by a number of people who were interested in the occult and various yogic powers that were rumored possible by those who had undergone the initiations of his particular lineage. They asked him, "Can you fly?" "No," he said. "I don't fly." "Can you read the future and the past?" "No, I don't read the future and the past." The group was becoming perturbed and one of them turned to him and said, "Well, just what is it that you do do?" And he said softly, "I simply practice compassion for all sentient beings."

When you are just that kind of space you are not forcing anything. You are not pushing away life or death. You are in reality not even attacking disease. You are just allowing balance to occur by being in balance yourself. Many healers have said to me, "I know God is doing the healing, I am just His stand-in." That is the space out of which healing can manifest.

Love is the optimum condition for healing. The healer uses whatever he intuits will be of the greatest aid, but his energy cannot come from the mind. His power comes from the openness of his heart. He senses something greater than the body's predicament. He goes to the source out of which all healing occurs, not attempting to disturb or obstruct that which may allow the next perfect step. He does not second guess the universe.

Indeed, in many healers, it is the attachment to someone getting well, the attachment to results that limits the depth and potential of the healing. In the Tibetan healing tradition those who have made a commitment to use their energies for the benefit of others, in the beginning course of their training as healers, are first taught to open deeply to death. For the first two or three years of their training they work with the dying so there is a comfort and familiarity with every possibility. They are taught to exclude nothing from their perception of the perfection of things. Life and death are seen as the perfect expression of being, each in its own moment, in its appropriate time. The healer addresses the process of being rather than its separate manifestation. The true healer goes to the root of being and allows it to flower as it will in perfect symmetry to the tendencies that have brought that individual to the teaching known as disease.

This quality of unconditional love and availability to others can be seen in some of those who survived the Nazi death camps. Victor Frankl speaks about a few of those beings who escaped the gas chambers and survived the typhus, dysentery, pneumonia, and despair—the rabbis, nurses, doctors, laymen, and priests who wished to help others, surviving year after year while most others just disintegrated. Reflecting on those times he said, "It did not really matter what we expected of life but rather we had to ask ourselves what life expected of us." It was their selfless love that allowed them to maintain balance when many about them wilted and fell.

Often when we speak of healing the question is asked, "How do you know when to stop healing and begin to prepare for death?" The question once again comes from a partial understanding. In reality the opening to healing and the preparation for death are the same.

When we are differentiating between healing and preparing for death we are forgetting that each are aspects of a single whole. It is all within the attitude with which one comes to life. If we don't use our symptoms as a message of our holding, then any attempt at healing which seeks to suppress that teaching slays a much deeper aspect of being. Is the healing that affects only the body in our best interest? On the other hand, if one welcomes death as an escape, that is a rejection of life, and the same imaginary differences between life and death will occur. In either case we never touch the deathless. We never encourage the exploration of undifferentiated being out of which all healing and wisdom arise.

I have known a few who fought their disease tooth and nail, and only when they prepared to die did their heart and mind come into balance and manifest healing in the body.

Because I do not think I need stress the obvious value of healing, of having a body in which to learn and serve, I do not believe it is necessary to underscore the benefit of physical healing, but I might here attempt to balance some of the misconceptions about the natural form of healing inherent in death. Death is not the enemy. The "enemy" is ignorance and lovelessness. Identifying with the contents of the mind we seldom trust the spaciousness of the heart. Indeed, it may be that much illness is a result of our distrust of our greater nature: the disharmony that results when we pull back from the truth.

For many it may be illness that for the first time causes them to look within. For some it might be the only experience that would get them to pay attention, to begin exploring the mind/body, to develop a sense of wholeness. For many it could be said that sickness is grace, for it brings them into contact with themselves in a way that none of the stumblings of a lifetime's attempt to maintain self-image have accomplished. It causes an examination of that which attempts to protect us from life.

Some have told me they have looked their whole life to find a teacher or a teaching that would bring them into some deeper wholeness and that at last it turned out to be their illness, that it was cancer that became the teacher, the mirror for the truth. For many, disease is the way back into life.

I have seen situations where two people of the same age and similar backgrounds had the same pathology and prognosis. One fought his disease using methods that marshaled his aggression to combat the illness, that encouraged him to think of himself as a victim, to regard illness as an unnatural intrusion. He became tighter and more frightened, grasping at life. In days of lessening symptoms he felt quite "up" and "wonderful." In moments of noticeable illness he felt "down" and "awful." One could see how his self-value was predicated on how well he was able to heal himself. When symptoms asserted themselves his feeling of value diminished and the aggression he was cultivating turned inward in self-loathing and guilt.

The other fellow recognized the disease as a message of work to be done. He strived to come back into harmony, to bring the heart and mind into balance, to improve the quality of his life while harmonizing what seemed out of kilter. Rather than putting his energy into only extending life he went deeper into the richness that made life worth living. He did not hold shallow, "hanging tough" as the other fellow put it.

When the first fellow felt he wasn't healing, he felt all was lost, but for the second there was room for life and/or death. He was investigating life, not fighting it. He saw the value in being healed but that did not disallow the recognition that consciously entering death might be of value. His life deepened as did the beauty of his sharing. There was a touching on the living truth. He was not fighting for life or damning disease; he was investigating "What is sickness? Who is sick?"

One fellow in the process of investigating how healing did not exclude the possibility of his death, examining what it was within him that clung to life, that made healing difficult and dying impossible, said that even though it sounded strange to him, he felt that what was referred to as the "will to live" caused much holding and confusion. "How do you deal with the drive to stay in the body even though the body is dying? Isn't it the 'will to live' that motivates our self-interest, our desire to get all we can? Isn't it 'the will to live' that is the basis for our desire to be someone and becomes the blocked energy that causes disease? In a strange way isn't it the will to live that kills us?"

Is it possible that the self-interest of "the will to live" has a balance in what some call "a homesickness for God," a will toward the truth? If one harnesses the will to live, does it benefit him in the same manner as one who is motivated by "a homesickness for the truth?" Which of these qualities allows life to be meaningful and open to participation in the mystery and wonder of being?

Letting go of the will to live does not mean creating a will to die. Both are attachments to the body, both are based on mistaken identity.

As long as death is the enemy, life is a struggle. Life becomes fractured into heaven and hell. The mind continues its incessant roller coaster of fear and stress which ironically may even cause disease.

I shared some time with a woman whose melanoma had caused various secondary tumors which it seemed would soon evict her from the body. As she experienced the growth of her tumors she had worked hard to finish business with her children and it looked very much as if she would soon die. About that time she heard of the Gerson nutritional method, which is sometimes effective in healing cancer. It is a difficult regimen involving the hourly intake of large glasses of raw vegetable juice and two glasses of Osterized liver each day, as well as three meals a day. She had enjoyed cooking and eating and had a rather sophisticated palate. She said, "I really don't feel like drinking all that stuff. Couldn't they just put it in a chocolate malt or something?" She disliked the taste of the juices so much she found it difficult to believe she could really commit herself to this method. But one day she said, "You know it's O.K. with me if I die but it's also O.K. if I live. I love my children and I would love to be with them. It would be wonderful to see them grow and to grow older with them. I guess I'll try it, there's no reason not to. But how am I who has always loved food so much going to involve myself in a method which takes so much time and energy, and tastes so lousy?"

For months she had been working with the Jesus prayer, "Lord Jesus Christ have mercy on me," which had often brought her beyond the duality of her and Jesus to a place of oneness, the sacred heart shining in her chest. She had learned to tune to the mercy of the universe, to the underlying reality of being, to love itself. A few days later she called to say that she came to realize that the only way she could drink all those glasses of raw juice hour after hour was if she saw each as the Eucharist. So she began to use even her distaste as a means of healing something deeper in herself. A letting go of attachments, pleasures, and pains, a going beyond the hungers of the tongue to the center of the heart. And she said, "You know, even if it doesn't heal my body it is going to do wonders for my heart."

A week later she went to a clinic where the method is intensely practiced, and for the next two weeks immersed herself in the daily regimen. She said that sometimes the Eucharist filled her with a great warmth but that at other times she was just left irritated at the noise coming from the next room. Returning home, she adroitly maintained the intake of these purifying juices and said her body felt much better. A few weeks later, however, she broke out in a rash and called the clinic. She had been told when she applied that her previous medical history didn't offer any assurance that the method would work for her. Much of her immune system had already been destroyed by powerful chemotherapeutic agents. When she told the counselor about the rash there was a silence and then the voice replied, "I'm afraid the rash is indicative that the method is not going to work for you."

She had received her last death sentence and noticed in that moment, to her surprise, that she was rather disappointed. "All this time with the Jesus prayer, surrendering to the mercy of the universe, I guess somewhere I thought that Christ's mercy would be that my body would get better. But I see that you can't second-guess God."

As it turned out, "Christ's mercy" was not to heal her body but to allow a depth of understanding that went beyond her identification with it. She died with ease and the same surrendered love. Her healing was as miraculous as any I have ever seen.

At the moment of her death all that came out of her was a glowing emptiness and love. She did not grasp at life nor did she jump into death. She simply dissolved like a fog of crystals dissipating into the clear air.

Maharaji was known for his extraordinary ability to manifest powers, including those of healing. There are many stories of people coming to him to be healed. In some cases he would give a stick or a piece of fruit or a blessing and the next day the typhus, the cancer, the dysentery would be gone.

But there are other stories of those coming to him with loved ones dying in their arms and he would look at them and shake his head and say, "How can I help if the doctor can do nothing?" Clearly he was unwilling to obstruct what seemed appropriate for that particular person. He apparently saw that for some the perfect healing was the falling away of their body.

One day Maharaji was sitting with some of his devotees in a courtyard when he turned and said, "No, I won't go, tell him I won't go." And the devotee looked about and said, "Tell who? What do you mean?" Just then the servant of one of his devotees came rushing into the room saying, "You must come with me, you must come with me! My master is dying, you must help!" "No, I won't go," said Maharaji, "I won't go." "You must go, you must come with me," begged the servant. "I won't go," said Maharaji, "there is nothing to be done." But the devotees were persistent and implored Maharaji to do something to benefit the dying friend they all knew. "O.K.," said Maharaji, and taking a banana from the basket in front of him, handed it to the servant, saying, "Give him this and everything will be O.K." In India the offering of a piece of fruit under such circumstances is understood to contain the grace of the guru. With great assurance the servant rushed home to his beloved household. The dying man's wife instantly mashed up the banana and slowly fed it to him spoon by spoon. Upon finishing the last spoonful of the mashed banana the man died.

Indeed, everything was O.K. The healing that was appropriate came to pass.

•   •   •

I spent some time with a cancer patient who had worked with one of the currently popular holistic healing methods that encourage the patient to marshal aggressive visualizations to stimulate the immune system to gobble up the cancer. The philosophy behind the method is that cancer is a result of the denial of certain events and experiences that have been repressed that one must take responsibility for. The cancer represents a solidification of long-held resentments, fears, and doubts. But she said because the method didn't show her how to "empty" anger, to investigate it so that its energy might be harnessed as a skillful means, it was geared to "get rid of the cancer," for her to "beat it," which made her feel that in some ironic way she wasn't taking responsibility for the cancer. That this aggression intensified exactly this process of negation that may have caused her cancer in the first place. "It's just more pushing away of some part of myself." Or as another cancer patient put it, after opening to her cancer and long outliving the prognosis for her disease, "I know what my cancer is made of. It is made of the paintings I didn't paint, the sculptures I didn't sculpt, the lovers I didn't love. My cancer is beautiful. It is simply misdirected creative force, energy turned inward and impacted in a cramped space instead of flowing outward into the world."

Another woman opening deeply to her healing said, "How am I to attack my cancer while attempting at the same time to open to all the things in my life which seem so unresolved and embodied in this tumor. It seems to me that what I need to develop is not more aggression but love to dissolve this tumor."

Another patient told us that while meditating one day on the qualities of aggression that would perhaps enable her to destroy her cancer, sending fiery energy to burn away her tumors, she heard a voice within her heart say, "Why are you killing cancer cells, why are you killing anything?" And she saw that what she needed to do was to bring love and harmony to that area, to go to the root instead of treating the symptoms, the tumors, as though they were the problem. And from that point on she generated feelings of loving-kindness, golden light, to wash the cancer, to bring it back into the flow, where nothing is held and nothing obstructs healing in whatever form it might take.

Many are encouraged to "take responsibility" for their illness but are seldom taught the difference between responsibility and blame. Many, when taking responsibility for their illness but finding themselves unable to change its course, feel guilty for not being responsible. "I am deserting my family after all, I never was very together." But responsibility is not blame; it is the ability to respond, which comes out of being present in the moment. As with people in pain who attempt to get rid of their suffering before they directly understand its cause, those who attempt to heal themselves without some understanding of who or what is out of balance only intensify the discomfort. Those who undertake healing with some idea of "body survival" as the only alternative often approach death in deep depression and self-loathing. "Only if I succeed in healing myself am I of value." The self-doubt, the hope born of fear, the aggression cultivated to overcome illness, may be turned against oneself.

During presentations at various hospitals we have on occasion been asked if we would help set up healing and pain clinics. When asked, we suggest that if such a clinic were organized it should be based on cultivating and directing love to illness or pain. Love is the optimum strategy for healing. Nothing is captured and there are no "victims." In love there is the potential to go beyond the holdings manifest as disease. Nothing is held back from the spaciousness of the heart where all opposites coincide in the One. In such openness we melt the dammed-up emotions and come to a state of well-being in which health is a by-product of openheartedness. It seems that some of the methods for healing, including even some called "holistic," do not encourage wholeness but at times cultivate qualities to oppose illness which seem capable of disharmonizing the individual.

One of the therapists who is most successful in the use of aggressive imagery, who has helped many to come from fourth-stage cancer, where all traditional therapies have been abandoned, to a relatively healthy body, calls his most remarkable recoveries his "superstars." He says that some, as they become more and more successful fighting their cancer, seem to develop qualities of separatism and a kind of individualistic ferocity that make them difficult to be around. He says that, indeed, if two of his superstars are in the same room together you can feel the contention between them, their individuality has become so intense, their aggression so finely cultivated.

Though a few using such methods have told me how their heart spontaneously opened and how, instead of aggression, they found themselves trusting their love to cure them.

Which brings us to a question of priorities. What is more important, the saving of the body by the cultivation of aggressive qualities that may indeed go on for incarnations, causing pain and discouraging deeper access to our original nature, or a letting go with love in which the transient body is not the only priority but rather an openness to being that goes beyond death?

Could this be what Jesus meant when he said, "For whosoever will save his life shall lose it; and whosoever will lose his life for my sake shall find it"? In cultivating aggression, if we do not heal, "all is lost." But in the cultivation of love, if indeed what we usually think of as healing does not occur, one has not traded off any part of oneself but rather entered into a greater wholeness. In a sense the cultivation of love is "a no-lose proposition." For if love does not heal the body, its openness and wisdom accompany one into the next perfect moment.

I have no statistics on the power of love to heal but only an intuitive sense of its appropriateness. Love is greater than any emotion: fear dissolves in it, anger disintegrates, pain floats free.

To establish clinics based on balancing the heart and mind, on using love to heal, various meditation practices might be employed.

The first would be the development of the warmth and patience breath: On each inhalation, begin to cultivate the quality of warmth, of openness, the nurturing that so aids the letting go of the encrustations of the heart. On the out breath, develop the quality of patience. Not patience as a waiting for something to happen, for that is impatience. Real patience is an openness, a willingness to be present for whatever is. It is not a goal-oriented expectation that only creates more tension, grief, and restlessness. Just breathing in warmth and developing patience slowly on the out breath. This warmth and patience breath should be practiced for twenty minutes, three times a day, for a week or two, until it is sensed that the second meditation procedure is appropriate.

The second procedure is the self-forgiveness meditation mentioned in the "Finishing Business" chapter—a letting go of resentment and the holdings that armor the heart.

Each meditation it was felt would deepen the investigation of how attachments were capable of closing the heart.

One comes away from the self-forgiveness meditation with a sense of openness and forgiveness of oneself. Our painful separateness begins to dissolve. It begins to balance the inharmony out of which disease may arise.

The third meditation suggested is the development of loving-kindness. (See the "Loving-kindness" chapter in *A Gradual Awakening*.) First generating love for oneself, a wish for one's own well-being. Not an easy thing to do. Then sending that loving-kindness to another and yet another so that as the meditation develops, one eventually embraces all in the love that radiates.

These meditations begin to develop a deeper concentration that will eventually allow one to open the whole body to the universal harmonic of what, again, for lack of a better term, might be called love.

As the heart begins to open, one may begin to focus this universal "lovingness" into the areas of disharmony by just bringing the attention to the sensations there and then directing loving energy right into them. As we feel this love expand, it begins to permeate our whole body and is shared with all we meet. We see how our suffering links us with the suffering of all others, and it brings a deep compassion and understanding, generating feelings of love for sentient beings on every level of existence. Out of such meditations comes a deeper sense of the immensity of the loving energy each being has the potential to direct to himself and all others.

The final meditations, such as the mindfulness meditation would be based on investigation: to acknowledge what is, and to open to it, letting the moment be as it is without contracting around it. A clear seeing of the self-image and the pain and disharmony it generates.

The pain meditations (see the "Working with Pain" chapter) also would be offered so that one could develop a softness and openness even in relation to something as deeply conditioned as aversion to pain.

And always these meditations would be steeped in the investigation of "Who is in pain?" "Who is afraid?" "Who heals?" "Who dies?"

THE BUDDHA IN THE WOMB

Bobbing in the waters of the womb,
little godhead, ten toes, ten fingers
& infinite hope,
sails upside down through the world.

My bones, I know, are only a cage
for death.
Meditating, I can see my skull,
a death's head,
lit from within
by candles
which are possibly the suns
of other galaxies.

I know that death
is a movement toward light,
a happy dream
from which you are loath to awaken,
a lover left
in a country
to which you have no visa,
& I know that the horses of the spirit
are galloping, galloping, galloping
out of time
& into the moment called NOW.

Why then do I care
for this upside-down Buddha
bobbling through the world,
his toes, his fingers
alive with blood
that will only sing & die?

There is a light in my skull
& a light in his.
We meditate on our bones only
to let them blow away
with fewer regrets.

214

Flesh is merely a lesson.
We learn it
& pass on.

Erica Jong

17
SUICIDE

Hamlet wonders, "To be or not to be," but that is not the question. The question is, "How to be?" In a world where so many longings are not met with satisfaction, where so often there is physical and mental pain, how does one survive without becoming deadened before one dies?

A Greek philosopher said, "The tragedy of life, my friend, is not that it must end. But that so many times before our natural demise, we must wish for death." I know very few people who have not at one time or another thought that death was preferable to their present predicament. Indeed, it seems that death becomes an ever-present option within a few years after birth.

Each year, thousands of grade-school children kill themselves.

Among teen-agers, suicide is one of the leading causes of death.

It is not difficult to see that when pain and confusion arise in the mind, they are met by a strong desire for the cessation of that suffering. Indeed, suicide may be an attempt at taking control of what otherwise seems an uncontrollable situation. The only alternative to complete defeat. Suicide often arises not from a hatred of life, but from a lust for it, a desire for things to be otherwise, for life to be full when it appears not to be. Suicide may be for many the manifestation of a thwarted "will to life." For others it may be that the pain has made life not worth living.

I have been with many people dying from degenerative diseases whose physical pain has been so great that they wished only the end of their suffering and seriously contemplated suicide. For many it has been the contemplation of suicide that propelled a deeper examination of life, an investigation of priorities. In fact, it may be for many that the contemplation of suicide is the first instance of their having taken death within, having seriously contemplated the possibility of not existing as they know it.

It seems that there are only two kinds of beings who enter death willingly. One whose heart is wide open, not holding to the body, melting into the next moment, openness to the unknown. The other, whose mind is weary and whose heart is frightened, jumps into death to escape life. The first moves toward the light. The second backs away. They are due equal respect and compassion, the prayers and acceptance of those left behind.

The other day I heard the father of a boy who had committed suicide say, "Everyone has a skeleton in their closet. But the person who kills themselves leaves their skeleton in another's closet." The grief and guilt that arise in the wake of suicide often leave a legacy of guilt and confusion. Each loved one wracks the mind and tears the heart questioning, "What could I have done to prevent this?"

To acknowledge that beings must act within the context of their own life allows compassion for those who kill themselves as well as those left behind. The mind in its queasy rumblings brings up all the insecurity and fear of a lifetime when confronted with the suicide of a friend or loved one. All the moments of thinking we should have been a better person, that we ought to have loved more, float to the surface.

"What could I have done? How could I have made life fuller for my loved one?" A sense of failure arises in the mind, no matter how unfounded. Indeed, those who grieve after a suicide often contemplate suicide themselves. The desperation of "What's the use?" or "Why bother?" is transmitted to those left behind— perhaps the same questions that propelled the poison or pulled the trigger. A feeling of impotence in the face of life's uncontrollable changes.

I think it is skillful, in the wake of a suicide, to practice meditations on forgiveness. Sending forgiveness to loved ones on the other side so they will not be tormented by the pain they imagine they have caused. Encouraging them to forgive themselves so that they will not repeatedly die out of guilt. And forgiveness for oneself, for unknowing; forgiveness for the mind's incessant judgment and self-doubting, which makes each feel responsible for the acts of another.

There is no arguing with the mind. There is only the encouragement to let go, to open around the pain so that we do not recreate another moment of the mental suffering that was reflected in the suicide. Forgiveness of ourselves and others allows life to continue, allows the heart to go beyond the mind's guilt and hellish recrimination.

Indeed, when we work with those whose occupations put them in the position of "suicide counselor," we remind them again and again that if it is not all right with them that others kill themselves, then they are probably in the wrong business. To truly be a suicide counselor, you must have room for every alternative in another's mind. Or you will just be someone else who cannot be trusted, someone trying to impose your will on them. To allow beings to enter into your heart, you can eliminate no part of them.

Our conditioning is that suicide is a heinous act, even a sin. We think we know better than people who contemplate suicide. Yet we never touch the pain in their mind, because we are so frightened of the pain in our own. Our desire to stop people from killing themselves just creates more separation. How will we be there fully for them if we think they are wrong? But if we acknowledge how painful our minds can be at times, we will be able to tune in to the pain of another. We will not withdraw love just because the act that another is contemplating conflicts with our models. We must remember that many wish to die because the love they feel within has never been fulfilled. They are not getting what they want. It is not indifference. They kill themselves out of pain and unsatisfied desires.

Of the hundreds who jump from the Golden Gate Bridge each year, all but a very few jump from the side of the bridge facing San Francisco. Very few leap from the side of the bridge that faces out into the immensity of the Pacific Ocean. Even in suicide, their relationship to the world they wish to leave behind is greatest.

We must touch the desperation in ourselves if we are to encourage another to open to life.

It could be said that suicide is not so much "wrong," as unskillful. Another opportunity for surrender, for letting go of the pain in the mind, not seen nor taken. The long conditioned aversion to the unpleasant acted on and reinforced once again. It is ironic that many who kill themselves after long depressions in which they have many times contemplated, even rehearsed, suicide, but simply did not have the energy or will power to carry it through, do so on the upswing out of that depression. Just as the energy returns, just as the light is beginning to dawn.

Many kill themselves when they feel they are at "hope's end." But hope is born of fear, of wanting. Only when we are without fear will we be able to live without hope. Those who passed beneath the arch in Dante's *Inferno* read, "Abandon all hope, ye who enter here." This was not a curse but a blessing. It says that all holding to future possibilities creates a painful inability to enter the present. Hope causes us to kill ourselves again and again. This is easy to say but difficult to transmit to those who wish to kill themselves. But when you have come to live your life so fully that you can abandon hope, then you will be able to transmit that fearless spaciousness to others so that they may have room in their heart for their suffering. When we have let go of attachment to our fear, then we will become the optimum environment for anyone contemplating suicide. Then we will be the space into which they can enter and let go of their suffering as they wish and take the next small step, the next soft entrance into the unknown.

Our long conditioned condemnation of suicide is put to the test with the image of the Buddhist monk whose picture many saw on the front page of their newspaper in the mid-1960s after he poured gasoline over his body in the streets of Saigon and immolated himself. There is a belief in Vietnamese folklore, quite outside of orthodox Buddhist thought, that the conscious dying of a pure individual can save the lives of ten thousand others. For many, the first recognition of the suffering of the peoples of Vietnam came with the photograph of that being setting himself ablaze in great stillness. He was not backing out of life or lost in some self-conscious heroic gesture. He was attempting to ease the suffering of other beings by allowing his own body to fall away. Is this suicide?

Maharaji said, "Jesus gave away everything, even his body."

The being who commits suicide as a means of escaping life is a manifestation of the pain of us all. Suicide is not the answer. But neither is a life of coping and holding to a hope that things will be different or that survival must be maintained at any cost. Do not ask, "To be or not to be," but only, "What is being?" Investigate the pain in the heart and let it be met by a commitment to serve others, for the cessation of the suffering of all.

Suicide is the killing of the body. Awareness is the rebirth of the mind. Love is the actualization of the unnameable.

18
FUNERALS

The ritual of the funeral was originally a skillful way of saying good-by to a loved one. It was a means of recognizing death. It was meant to encourage that which remains after the body has fallen away to continue with the work ahead: to go on in peace and stillness into the next perfect progression.

A funeral is an opportunity to acknowledge the love we have shared, as well as to remind the departed to continue on their journey without clinging to the life left behind. It is a way of reminding the departed to merge with their original nature, to let go of the particular and join with the universal. It establishes the balance between possessiveness and love, between pulling on the departed not to leave and wishing that being bon voyage. It is a ritual which encourages the heart to open to its grief as well as to trust in what exists beyond the senses. It is an opportunity to express our pain as well as honor the mistaken identity by which we imagined our loved one to be this now empty body.

A funeral is an initiation for those who have gone on and for those remaining. For each the same task is evident: To let go of what binds them to their idea of separateness and to merge in the essential. The funeral is a reminder to go within, to allow the mind to sink into the heart.

The funeral is another opportunity to finish business, to let go of that which separates and recognize the underlying unity of all beings. To recognize that, though the consciousness exists elsewhere and the body lies inert before you, the work on ourselves is always the same: to melt into the brilliance of our original nature, to allow the heart to be torn open in love rather than be protected in fear; to acknowledge our vulnerability and impermanence.

When someone dies in a hospital or at home, instead of instantly removing the body, our group encourages loved ones to make their farewells before death has been disguised by the mortician's art. In the hours that follow death, the body feels cold to the touch, color pales, but the facial expression softens. Peace is clearly evident. The process of grieving and the deepening recognition of love are continued beside the recently emptied vessel.

Often when someone has died at home or in those hospitals where time is allowed with the body, we tidy up the room, put away the medicines and whatever life-support paraphernalia are about, dress the dead body in his or her favorite clothes, comb the hair, put on his or her favorite music, bring in some flowers, perhaps burn some incense, and allow those closest to the departed to come and pay their last respects and recognize how clearly that which they loved is no longer present. To see that who they loved was not just a body. Indeed, standing beside a corpse, one of the most profound recognitions is that what is observing that corpse is precisely what is absent from that empty body. That consciousness has departed, and that is all.

In funeral homes, where corpses are made to look as though they're going to a formal presentation, dressed in their Sunday finest, lipsticked and cosmeticked to appear as though they were just asleep, the experience of death is once more eluded. The opportunity to say good-by, to touch the loved one, is discouraged. The deceased lies in a metal box two or three feet off the floor so that, as you pass, you don't have the feeling that you may touch, hug, kiss, cry, pray. The separation seems unconquerable. But when a body lies in its own bed and the loved ones may come in and the children may sit next to their mother or father, and put their head on their loved one's chest, then death and love meet.

The departure of a loved one becomes very real. There is a wholeness about it.

This society has created few rituals for saying good-by. Perhaps because so much clinging is encouraged by our denial of death, the funeral in this society is of particular importance.

We shared some months with a dying friend who had come to workshops with her husband and would call and visit occasionally. At the time she went into the hospital for her last round of prognosis and treatment, her pain was so great that every two hours massive doses of morphine were necessary to suppress the agony in her spine where the secondary tumors had occurred. After a week in the hospital she asked that I start visiting regularly so that she might enter death with a bit more equanimity. With her family, taking her home the day before Mother's Day, she said that she at last felt she was ready to go on. When we were talking the next day and I reminded her that it was Mother's Day, she said, "Oh, it's my day, let's have a party!" The sandwiches and cookies were spread out on a picnic blanket on the lawn. But by the time the food was ready she felt too weak to join us, so each one of her family and friends went in singly to wish her a happy Mother's Day. Her close friends, her brothers, her husband and daughter all went in to share their feelings and give support for the final hours of her journey.

For the first thirty-six hours she was home she used less pain medication than she had previously used in any two-hour period during the weeks she was in the hospital. As she opened to death, the resistance to pain, the holding to her body, diminished. Because she began to open to the light, in the days she prepared to leave her body there was little pain or confusion. She died three days after she had come home, at six in the morning, with her husband sitting quietly beside her. When I arrived at the house, her brothers and father, who lived some miles distant, had been called and were already on their way. Her best friends dressed her in her favorite long purple dress, as the lyrics of Judy Collins' music filled the room. A feeling of love permeated everyone's activity. Each word was spoken in the presence of the immense unknown.

For those who have never allowed themselves, or had the opportunity, to be with a body in the hours following death a precious opportunity is missed. During the process of the subtle emergence of the life-force, there is a sense of completion. If one observes the face during the hours after death, a greater and greater lightness is perceived. A smile that cannot be attributed to the rigidity of muscles. A softness that may not have been seen in days or months preceding, particularly a painful death. There is a feeling for all about that things are O.K., that the next perfect step has been taken, that their loved one "is in good hands."

About a half hour later, this young woman's father arrived, bereft by the death of his daughter. No matter how many months or even years we have to prepare for the death of a loved one, when death actually occurs, the feeling of loss strikes us as never before. The irrevocability of the departure of consciousness from the body leaves one with a sense of profound aloneness and loss. Her father entered, wishing only that this were not the truth of the moment. Right at his edge to try to keep from breaking down, from crying out for his daughter to return. But the room into which he entered was a room of love. His daughter looked very beautiful three hours after she had died, a smile on her face, her hands clasped over her heart. He was met by an air of acceptance that he'd never associated with death. Her carpenter brother, finishing the coffin which he had begun but had delayed completing in hopes that somehow it would never be needed, was putting on the final touches at home. Her five-year-old daughter, sitting beside her dead mother on the bed, talked quietly to her as she sorted through the box of jewelry left for her to play with and wear as she wished. As the dead woman's father approached the body, he was encouraged to place his fingers very lightly at the top, the crown, of his daughter's head. Because it is often, though not always, the case that one can feel the vibrancy of life as it leaves the body for hours afterward. Though he was told that he might expect to feel something, he made this gesture more out of bewilderment and a desire not to create a scene than anything else. He expected nothing. Laying his finger tips lightly on her head for a moment he just grunted and began to walk away—and then stopped. Gazing at his hand, he looked up and he said, "There's a tingling. What is it?" Returning to place his hand on the crown of his daughter's head, he could feel the life-force as it departed. He was amazed. His relationship to death changed as he stood there experiencing his daughter's energy leaving the body. There was a touching on the essence of their contact that he had not imagined possible. An hour later, when her brothers arrived with the coffin, she was placed gently in it and the coffin was positioned in the middle of the living room, as her family and friends gathered around. But instead of wishing this moment was anything other than it was, we joined together in a prayerful meditation to tell her to go on, that her work here was done, that her only work now was to merge with her pure being, to trust the light, to move toward the light. What a difference for her family. Instead of holding, pulling back, clinging, there was an acknowledgment of the moment's perfection, painful though it might be to those left behind. It was a ritual of the heart that seemed to heal all those present.

To be able to be around the body of one who has just died for four or five or eight hours afterward allows an understanding of the process of death unparalleled in our experience, a touching on the lightness of that being's floating free from the body, a touching on the depth of the feelings of separation, of the pain of our holding and the sweet encouragement to let go gently into the light, for ourselves and for all others.

For an increasing number of people cremation has become an acceptable means of disposing of the body. In Asia it is among the most common means of dispersing the elements of the empty corpse. Some Asian teachers say that cremation is preferable because it helps the departed immediately recognize that the body had little to do with their real nature or their present necessities.

Often, after the loving encouragement of the departed to go on, attended usually only by those closest, there can, at some later date, be a memorial service. In some memorial services the ashes of the cremated body are dispersed on the wind from some favorite glen or beloved beach. It is a time when those who wish somehow to participate in that passing may come together. In such memorial services we often hear the lyric wisdom of Kahlil Gibran, songs sung by a lone guitarist, poetry, group meditation, perhaps even some silent dance that acknowledges the continuance of all things.

A memorial service is not just a time to remember the departed one, but to remember our shared essence as well. It puts death in context. It brings death within.

Another practice that many have found useful is to put a photograph of the departed loved one on a table, perhaps with a candle and some incense next to it, so that each day for the first week or two after death one may sit for a half an hour or so with the loved one and speak to him of the love that has been shared and the need for him to continue on his journey. After ten days or so (as the heart dictates), the practice may be carried out only on a weekly basis, on the anniversary of the death, for a total of seven weeks. This is a skillful means both for the departed and for the individual who may be in grief, for it allows a letting go and a sending on that is skillful for both. It allows the finishing of business while a recognition of death and loss is fully acknowledged.

We have a friend in Montana whose work as a carpenter is to make cradles and coffins. He also conducts very simple funeral-burials. Often, in the back country, a hole will be dug and the body, in a plain pine coffin or perhaps just wrapped in tie-dyed cloth, will be lowered into the ground. Instead of a tombstone, a fruit tree is planted over that body. The roots nourished by the return of that body into the earth from which it was sustained. And in years to follow eating the fruit from that tree will be like partaking in that loved one. It touches on the ritual of the Eucharist.

The funeral is a skillful means to remind the departed as well as those left behind that they are not simply a body. That there is so much more to life and living.

At memorial services, the following reading inspired by the Heart of Perfect Wisdom Sutra may be appropriate.

226

Funeral Reading

Go on now. The universal always remains the same. Yet is constantly changing.

Here, in the clear mind, in the open spaciousness of non-clinging, in the vastness of original mind, of no separate personality, see the emptiness of all the senses and the attachment to the body. Know now that form is only emptiness. Emptiness only form. Form is no other than emptiness. Emptiness no other than form.

Feeling, thought, and even the choices that seem to be ours, consciousness itself, are all composed of the same essential emptiness. Each moment empty, as the primal vastness of being.

Within this edgelessness of being it can be seen that none take birth or die. Nor are they stained or pure. Nor in reality do they come or go. Only the body arises and passes away. That which we are remains, beginningless, endless.

In this luminous emptiness our essential nature is experienced as beyond form, feeling, thought, or choice. No eye, ear, nose, tongue, body, mind. No color, sound, smell, taste, touch, or what the mind takes hold of. Nor even sensing. In this essential emptiness all these things float, but none define the vastness.

Go on now. No ignorance nor end of it. Nor all that comes of ignorance. No withering. No death. Nor is there pain or cause of pain, or cease in pain, or even liberation to lead from pain. For what your true nature is, is beyond ideas of liberation. Nothing to attain, nothing to be, nowhere to go. What we call life is an illusion. What we call death is a dream. We are never separate from the One. The nature of the One is emptiness. The nature of emptiness is love.

Give it all away. Hold to nothing whatsoever. Enter the spacious heart, free of delusion and hindrance. Rid of the fear bred by old yearnings. Though there is in truth nothing separate, allow the illusion of separateness to enter the shimmering light of your original nature by which all things are seen.

Go on now. Do not mistake what is seen for the light by which it is recognized. Go beyond all doubt, beyond such imaginings as "mind" and "body" and know the truth for what it is.

Gone, gone, beyond gone, altogether beyond gone.

Enter deeply the light.

19
RAMANA MAHARSHI
(1879–1950)

"Sri Ramana Maharshi was born in India in 1879. In his seventeenth year he attained enlightenment through a remarkable experience as if undergoing death of the physical body while remaining in full consciousness. Following this transformation, he left his home and was drawn irresistibly to the sacred hill of Arunachala. He never left it. In the ashram which was formed around him he taught the purest form of Advaita Vedanta (nonduality) through the supremely simple discipline of Self-Enquiry."

Arthur Osborne

At seventeen he experienced his first opening: "It was about six weeks before I left Madura for good that the great change in my life took place. It was quite sudden. I was sitting alone in a room on the first floor of my uncle's house. I seldom had any sickness, and on that day there was nothing wrong with my health, but a sudden violent fear of death overtook me. There was nothing in my state of health to account for it, and I did not try to account for it or to find out whether there was any reason for the fear. I just felt 'I am going to die' and began thinking about what to do about it. It did not occur to me to consult a doctor or my elders or friends; I felt that I had to solve the problem myself, there and then.

"The shock of the fear of death drove my mind inward and I said to myself mentally, without actually framing the words: 'Now death has come; what does it mean? What is it that is dying? This body dies.' And I at once dramatized the occurrence of death. I lay with my limbs stretched out stiff as though *rigor mortis* had set in and imitated a corpse so as to give greater reality to the enquiry. I held my breath and kept my lips tightly closed so that no sound could escape, so that neither the word 'I' nor any other word could be uttered. 'Well then,' I said to myself, 'this body is dead. It will be carried stiff to the burning ground and there burnt and reduced to ashes. But with the death of this body, am I dead? Is the body I? It is silent and inert but I feel the full force of my personality and even the voice of the "I" within me, apart from it. So I am Spirit transcending the body. The body dies but the Spirit that transcends it cannot be touched by death. That means I am the deathless Spirit.' All this was not dull thought; it flashed through me vividly as living truth which I perceived directly, almost without thought-process. 'I' was something very real, the only real thing about my present state, and all the conscious activity connected with my body was centred on that 'I.' From that moment onward the 'I' or Self focused attention on itself by a powerful fascination. Fear of death had vanished once and for all. Absorption in the Self continued unbroken from that time on. Other thoughts might come and go like the various notes of music, but the 'I' continued like the fundamental *sruti* note that underlies and blends with all the other notes. Whether the body was engaged in talking, reading, or anything else, I was still centred on 'I.' Previous to that crisis I had no clear perception of my Self and was not consciously attracted to it. I felt no perceptible or direct interest in it, much less any inclination to dwell permanently in it."

By the time he was eighteen he went to the holy mountain, Arunachala, where he spent the rest of his life meditating and teaching.

Some years later a Hindi gentleman asked Ramana how the fear of death could be overcome.

M: Find out if you were born before you think of death. Only he who is born can die. You are as good as dead even in sleep. What fear is there of death?

If a man considers he is born he cannot avoid the fear of death. Let him find out if he has been born or if the Self has any birth. He will discover that the Self always exists, that the body which is born resolves itself into thought and that the emergence of thought is the root of all mischief. Find wherefrom thoughts emerge. Then you will abide in the ever-present inmost Self and be free from the idea of birth or the fear of death.

When a man dies the funeral pyre is prepared and the body is laid flat on the pyre. The pyre is lit. The skin is burnt, then the flesh and then the bones until the whole body falls to ashes. What remains thereafter? The mind. The question arises, "How many are there in this body—one or two?" If two, why do people say "I" and not "we"? There is therefore only one. Whence is it born? What is its nature? Enquiring thus the mind also disappears. Then what remains over is seen to be "I." The next question is, "Who am I?" The Self alone. This is contemplation. It is how I did it. By this process attachment to the body is destroyed. The ego vanishes. Self alone shines.

Mr. Ranganatha Ayyar, a devotee of fourteen years, asked, How long is the interval between one's death and reincarnation?

M: It may be long or short. But a liberated being does not have any such changes; he merges into the universal Being, so says the *Brihadaranyaka Upanishad*. Some say that those who after death pass into the path of light are not reborn, whereas those who after death take the path of darkness are reborn after they have enjoyed the fruits of karma in their subtle bodies.

But in fact, there is neither birth nor death. One remains only as what one really is. This is the only Truth.

DEVOTEE: Is it possible to know the condition of an individual after his death?

M: It is possible. But why try to know it? All facts are only as true as the seeker.

D: The birth of a person, his existence and death are real to us.

M: Because you have wrongly identified your Self with the body, you think of the other in terms of the body. Neither you nor the other is the body.

D: But from my own level of understanding I consider myself and my son to be real.

M: The birth of the "I"-thought is one's own birth, its death is the person's death. After the "I"-thought has arisen the wrong identity with the body arises. Thinking yourself the body, you give false values to others and identify them with bodies. Just as your body has been born, grows, and will perish, so also you think the other was born, grew up, and died. Did you think of your son before his birth? The thought came after his birth and persists even after his death. Inasmuch as you are thinking of him he is your son. Where has he gone? He has gone to the source from which he sprang. He is one with you. So long as you are, he is there too. If you cease to identify yourself with the body, but see the real Self, this confusion will vanish. You are eternal. Others also will similarly be found to be eternal. Until this truth is realized there will always be this grief due to false values arising from wrong knowledge and wrong identity.

D: Are intellect and emotion, like the physical body, growths with the birth of man; and do they dissolve or survive after death?

M: Before considering what happens after death, just consider what happens in your sleep. Sleep is only the interval between two waking states. Do they survive that interval?

D: Yes, they do.

M: The same holds good for death also. They represent body consciousness and nothing more. If you are the body, they always hold on to you. If you are not the body they do not affect you. The one who was in sleep is now in waking state just speaking. You were not the body in sleep? Are you the body now? Find it out. Then the whole problem is solved.

Similarly, that which is born must die. Whose is the birth? Were you born? If you say you were, of whose birth are you speaking? It is the body which was born and it is that which will die. How do birth and death affect the eternal Self?

Ask, "To whom do these questions arise." Then you will know.

M: Look, the Self is only Be-ing, not being this or that. It is simple Being. Be—and there is an end of the ignorance. Enquire for whom is the ignorance. The ego arises when you wake up from sleep. In deep sleep you do not say that you are sleeping and that you are going to wake up or that you have been sleeping so long. But still you are there. Only when you are awake you say that you have slept. Your wakefulness comprises sleep also in it. Realize your pure Be-ing. Let there be no confusion with the body. The body is the result of thoughts. The thoughts will play as usual, but you will not be affected. You were not concerned with the body when asleep; so you can always remain.

D: Do not one's actions affect the person in after-births?

M: Are you born now? Why do you think of other births? The fact is that there is neither birth nor death. Let him who is born think of death and palliatives therefore.

M: That which is born must end. The delusion is only concomitant with the ego. It rises up and sinks. But the Reality never rises nor sinks. It remains Eternal.

When Ramana was dying of cancer his devotees asked him to heal himself. "Why bother? This body is all worn out, why hold on to it, why keep it going?" he said. To which they implored, "Oh, master, please don't leave us!" Looking at them as if at young children, he softly replied, "Leave you! Where is there to go?"

"On Thursday, April 13, a doctor brought Ramana a palliative to relieve the congestion in his lungs but he refused it. 'It is not necessary, everything will come right within two days.'

"At about sunset on the next day Ramana told the attendants to sit him up. They knew already that every movement, every touch, was painful, but he told them not to worry about that. He

sat with one of the attendants supporting his head. A doctor
began to give him oxygen; with a wave of his right hand he mo-
tioned him away.

"Unexpectedly, a group of devotees sitting on the veranda outside of the hall began singing 'Arunachala-Siva.' On hearing his
favorite song, Ramana's eyes opened and shone. He gave a brief
smile of indescribable tenderness. From the outer edges of his
eyes, tears of bliss rolled down. One more deep breath, and no
more. There was no struggle, no spasm, no other sign of death;
only that the next breath did not come."

20
STAGES OF DYING

During the 1960s Elisabeth Kübler-Ross, while working with terminally ill patients in a hospital near Chicago, noticed what seemed to be certain common states of mind and formulated generalized stages that those who are confronting dying seem to pass through. These stages have become popularized, indeed have become a model, used often by those working with the dying, as a means of comprehending the experience of those they wish to serve.

The concept of the stages of dying has changed the way many look at this process. Probably most are familiar with the five stages of denial, anger, bargaining, depression, and what is generally called acceptance. These are the scenario of loss. Not just the loss of one's body, or a child or a mate or a parent, through death, but the loss of the child leaving the home upon maturation or of a divorce. It is also the loss of one's position in society, the loss of a job, or the inability perhaps as a result of old age to continue driving or walking or communicating in the manner that one has become accustomed to. It may be the loss of an arm or the loss of self-confidence.

The stages begin with the denial, anger, and bargaining of the mind and the darkness that ensues when things don't turn out the way we wish. And the light that often follows when we surrender into the present moment. Not the surrender we fear is defeat, but the strength and power of the heart to open even in the most adverse circumstances. These are the stages of passing from hell to heaven, from resistance to acceptance.

However, in reality there are no stages but only the incessant changes of the mind. A moment of denial or anger opening into acceptance until a moment later the mind curls back on itself in depression and fear, trepidation and confusion. It is the roller-coaster mind constantly changing, opening and closing, fluttering in the face of reality. These stages aren't happening to someone else. They are the process of our most ordinary day. They are the stages of dying that occur during our acknowledgment, opening and letting go of that which blocks our original nature.

These are the stages of converting our predicament from tragedy to grace, from confusion to insight and wisdom, from agitation to clarity. They are our pilgrimage toward the truth. The process we go through confronting the loss of some security we can no longer run to for reassurance. It may be the disintegration of your self-image, the desperate clinging to the old before the new presents itself. Indeed the stages of loss, of dying, clearly parallel the stages of spiritual growth: The erratic, often confusing, changes of the death of our separate self as we merge with the whole—moments of denial, of resistance to how things are and anger at their not being as we imagine they must. Moments of desperation, opening to how things are, of getting caught again. It is not A to Z or one, two, three, four, five, it's not that easy or neat. And even the idea of stages is a confusion of the truth because it makes solid something that is actually flux and flow. These stages, instead of being swallowed whole as an absolute reality, can rather be used as a means of focusing, a way of encouraging recognition of the impermanence of all things so that one may go beyond seeing others as what they are becoming and instead experience them as they are. To touch the living truth of their being, to share in the reality that goes beyond death.

For some the stages of dying have been a way of not touching the living truth of death but instead disguising it in ideas and models. For many, such concepts, rather than bringing them deeper into the experience of another, have allowed a certain quality of disconnectedness with the process by concretizing the flow. How many times at nursing stations have I heard, "He's in denial," or "He's in the anger stage," "He's hitting depression now." People are not stages, they fit no model for long. Each being is a process moving constantly toward fulfillment. Each consists of the same ever-changing baby flesh and stillness of being.

Denial is important to recognize because everyone is in it. It is the hiding, the resistance to life, the grasping at the old. When one contemplates denial in oneself or in another, one sees the unfinished business of a lifetime. "Oh, I'll do it later," though you have not the least guarantee that you'll ever see anyone you love ever again. That you'll ever leave this place alive.

There is no later. You are already dead.

Denial is the resistance to acknowledging our grief, our feelings of loss that we carry with us and add to daily. Is it any surprise that the mind denies a prognosis of death when it has hardly acknowledged that it is alive? How could it be otherwise? Can a mind that has seldom opened to the truth of the moment, unwilling not to know, allow itself recognition of the unfolding as it is? Indeed denial tries to stay the loss of who we think we are, of how we thought it should, and would, be.

Many cultures have made a big business of denial. The multibillion-dollar cosmetic industry, hair dyes, toupees, corsets, "corrective" plastic surgery, are all denials of decay, bargainings with change, depression that the body moves constantly from birth to death.

How ungrateful we are for the lessons of decay; the perfect teachings that this body we are born with is constantly aging and someday must be left behind to rot. The flesh and ligaments falling away from the bones. The bones disintegrating to dust. The dust blown by a gentle wind through the trees and vines of the forest. As this empty form disappears back into that which has nurtured it.

We usually think of "the stage of denial" as relating to a patient who upon discovering a malignancy says, "There's got to be some mistake, this couldn't be happening to me. There is some mix-up in the lab analysis. That's got to be someone else's biopsy." We seldom recognize denial as our mind's incessant pulling back and withdrawal from the truth of our impermanence. Not recognizing denial keeps us stuck in the same old pains and fears, tribulations and loss. It is like being jostled in an old train along corroded tracks while dishes rattle and the luggage falls from the overhead rack, while continuing to insist that all the time we are on a quiet ride through the countryside or have never left the station at all. The mind denies the present inconsistencies with our models of how things "should" be.

It is our examination of the denial in our mind that opens us further to life: that allows us the investigation of who lives, who dies, and what indeed this process may be all about.

Denial is a pushing away of the present. Indeed the slogan for the great waste producing industry of the mind might be, "Denial is our most important product."

The other day I received a call from an old friend who told me her favorite aunt had just died and asked me if the meditation group might take a moment of silence for her. I said, "No, really, death is nothing special." While you are reading this page hundreds of people are dying. We don't mourn that aunt, we don't mourn our children. Who we mourn is ourselves. We mourn *our* loss: someone we related to isn't on the other side of the net for the game of life that we have become so used to playing. Honor that loss and trust the feelings that arise when the mirror for your love has been shattered. Know that it is you who you are mourning and make room in your heart for yourself. It is the pain in your heart that you feel, not the pain of another.

Ironically the whole funeral industry is based on the denial of death. Stuffing cotton in the pale cheeks of the dead man to make him look robust, stitching a contented smile on his face, all attempt to make death appear as if it were going to a party. Even in death, death is denied.

The anger stage is one I suspect all are familiar with. It is part of the confrontation with the truth, the fearful opening to reality. "Damn it, it's true but why does it have to be so painful?" Anger is not to be judged but simply recognized and opened to. Things often aren't the way we want them to be. There is desire blocked and from that frustration arises anger and a fearful tightness. "Why am I going to die, why not the bastard down the street? He doesn't mow his lawn, he yells at his kids, he cheats on his income tax. Why me?"

And there is the rage against God. "How could You do this to me? I have been so good. I go to church every week. I give to charity. I am a good person. I even work with the dying. How could this be happening to me? How unfair." And though we rail against God for such "injustice," how often do we thank Him for the bounty with which we are so often provided?

Anger arises from that feeling of impotence that has always been there, and becomes focused in that moment. "Why is it so damned hard? Why is life so confusing and frustrating?" The impotent rage of a lifetime. Anger is such an isolating painful experience. To be with someone who is enraged with the "unfairness of things" is to become soft and yielding to our own frustrations, an open space into which that storm can spend itself. That is the work on yourself.

States of mind are contagious. To be able to be with someone who is on fire with anger and not get caught in those places where you too cry out at the seeming injustice of things. To let go of your suffering so that you are not consumed by the fire of another. To let go of the righteous pride which maintains the force of anger so that your compassion is not blocked. To be able to acknowledge your own anger, your own rage, willing, without judgment, to be present for another as for yourself.

"Everything happens to me!" the mind screams out when the job you wanted so much is not offered, when your new car is sideswiped by a steam roller, when your left arm becomes numb and you sense that your cancer has metastasized. "Screw this world, screw everyone!" Can your heart stay open in the face of such a storm? Or are you demolished when the denial of your own fear and anger is shattered by the confusion of another? None of this is very far from home.

In the stages game the next stage that is often spoken of is bargaining. In the terminal patient it might be, "If only I could stay alive, I would build a new wing on the hospital. I would give all

my money to charity. I would stop eating chocolate. I would
meditate two hours a day, really I would!" But the actuality of it
is that most people who make bargains don't keep them. Our bargains are a trade-off for what we want. They do not arise out of a
pure motivation of giving. "I will do this if only I can become
that." It is the motivation to receive rather than to give. It is at
the basis of many of our relationships and most of our spiritual
practice. Indeed it is in the stage of bargaining that we clearly
perceive the "if-only mind" that leads to the deep depression to
come when things aren't the way we bargained for. "If only I
hadn't worked in that asbestos factory, I wouldn't have cancer
now"—but you did! "If only she hadn't gone out that night, she
wouldn't have had that accident"—but she did! "If only I didn't
feel so lousy, I would be able to do my exercises and get my body
strong"—but you do! "If only the guy next to me wasn't scratch-
ing, I could meditate more deeply"—but he is! The false encour-
agements of the if-only mind keep us in hell. The quadraplegic
lying unmoving in his bed thinks, "If only I had two good arms
and legs I could go to God." But of course there is nothing in any
moment that obstructs us from investigating the truth. There is
nothing absent in any situation that keeps us from our potential,
"if only" we can fully open to it.

Much spiritual practice is based on this kind of trade-off. I'll
sit, pray, sing, if only I can see the light. How seldom do we act
just in the perfect present. Doing what we do for its own sake
without some idea of return, some reward for what we imagine to
be our "good deeds." How much does this quality of bargaining
in our lives lead to the "keeping of accounts" that causes so many
relationships to become unfinished business. How often are we
"collecting merit" like a ragpicker going through the trash cans?

When the bargaining mind begins to melt, to fade away, we become more open, and things become more workable. When bargaining ceases we become present to the truth. Each act comes
out of a sense of its appropriateness rather than a gambling on results. We begin to let go of the fruits of our labors and instead
allow each moment its fullness. We are no longer trying to buy
our way out of hell, we are no longer attempting to bribe God.

But the bargaining doesn't gain the result we wish; it's all so
much work and we find ourselves at the end of our tether with

nowhere to go: this is the stage of depression. Most are afraid of depression and yet there is in depression a potential for great healing, an opportunity for new beginnings. It is a confrontation with the truth that we cannot buy or yell or deny our way out of. There may be a deep seeing of "how powerless I am." Though many view depression with alarm, a creative process may be going on. We have nowhere to turn, nothing is working in the way we wish. We have come to a place where we are beginning to see how things really might be. Seeing that we cannot control the universe, depression has the power to lead us to a new openness. It is a painful process of shedding the parts of us that are dying away at each moment. We become depressed at our vulnerability and powerlessness in the face of change. Indeed, it may be in depression that one begins for the first time to take responsibility for the way we respond to change. Depression can have almost an alchemical quality about it when we begin to investigate the dross, the fear, the withdrawal, the anger in our lives and transmute them into a new richness, a deeper understanding. From this understanding a new fearlessness arises, a new loveliness. For some, depression can be an initiation into a new life that is no longer a struggle with difficulty but is instead workable and at last exciting.

Though these stages are not sequential, it should be added that we need to honor each of these stages, because they are the work we are doing on ourselves.

You don't try to talk people out of depression, you just open your heart to them. You don't try to rationalize them out of it: "Everything is going to be O.K." Everything *is* going to be O.K., but one must see that for oneself directly. The touch of your hand on another's is more important than all the words you can say. If your words come from a place in your heart where you can touch and go beyond your own fear of depression, then there will not be a separateness. Depression is not a very verbal state. It is a space of deep feeling and the presence you manifest when you are with someone in depression will communicate to him the okayness of things even if it isn't acknowledged.

Opening to depression takes us beyond depression as opening to hell takes us beyond hell. It is the beginning of our ability to resolve the aloneness of the constantly created separate self with the vastness of being. In being there is neither a pushing away nor a reaching out. There is no duality. You no longer feel separate from life, you open to it and become encompassed within it. There is "no one" separate. Even to "open" to anything. You are the openness. This is a relatively deep level of the state of acceptance. However, in my experience, much of what is called acceptance is actually resignation. A tie with life, that quiet desperation with which so many live so much of their lives. It is the bargaining of "if nothing makes it too bad, I won't expect it to be too good" come to fruition. The depression of a stalemate with life.

Certainly there are various levels to the stage of acceptance. But it seems this is the least understood of all the stages. Elisabeth Kübler-Ross defines acceptance as "A patient who does not want visitors anymore, who does not want to talk anymore, who has usually finished his unfinished business, whose hope is no longer associated with cure, treatment, and prolongation of life. It is a feeling of inner and outer peace." Indeed it is a feeling of peace, but this example seems to me more a kind of "preparatory grief," a withdrawal that may denote a kind of depression. It seems a rather limited understanding of the capacities for letting go and surrendering that I have seen manifest again and again. People in "acceptance" are often very present for those about them. They do not necessarily stop speaking or wish to be alone. The mark of their acceptance is that their heart is open, their words soft and direct. Elisabeth goes on to say, "The stage of acceptance simply means that people have faced that they are finite, that they learn to enjoy today and not worry too much about tomorrow, and that they hope that they still have a long, long time to enjoy this kind of life." Here we find some of the confusion that surrounds this stage in the contradictory statement that those in acceptance don't worry too much about tomorrow, yet "hope that they still have a long, long time to enjoy this kind of life." When I am with people whose state is really one of peace, I see few preferences, little isolation, little "hope," because fear has dissolved into a kind of confidence in the process.

One morning a fellow who most in the hospital thought was "in acceptance" said, "I feel like I am sinking into the bed. I feel like

I could sleep forever." And I asked, "Do you think you're going to, are you dying?" Softly he said, "Oh it'll be O.K. when it happens; I just hope it's not today." That is not acceptance, that is resignation. It is just a more verbal form of depression which verges on "there is nothing I can do, I am just stuck with it." Resignation is another fearful coping, the death before death (and the least lucky of the two).

Yet in the word "resignation" we see the concept of a re-signing, of a recommitment, a new contract with life possible as we open to our fear of dying as well as living.

A woman we know had some years before been given a terminal prognosis and spoke of going through the ups and downs of these various stages for some time before she experienced a spaciousness in which she saw that there was nothing of intrinsic value to be lost. That openness allowed old blockages to fall away; bargainings were seen as empty fears. Depression was no longer an enemy but the logical outcome of old holdings. Day after day she opened to the uncontrollability of things. She experienced a new freedom, a spaciousness she had never known. She said that even more important than death becoming more acceptable, life had become acceptable. A few months into that openness she had a complete remission. She suspected that it was her opening to death that allowed life to come back into balance. She said, however, that as she looked back at those years when she was considered terminal, "I was never so alive as when I was dying." She was never so awake, there was little bargaining or denial. Frustrations were dealt with as they arose and didn't mire into resentment. But as her death receded, she noticed that in her worldly preoccupation with life, the daily bargaining, denial and anger slowly reasserted themselves. Her confrontation with death had taken her from hell to heaven but gradually the old conditioning and ways of being had allowed life to slip by unnoticed, had allowed hell to re-establish itself. Life was not as worth living as when she was dying. She said she now saw herself going through the stages of dying in relationship to the loss of the peace she felt when she was letting go into the unknown. The acceptance she felt had slipped away in a fog of old fears and resignations, the rumors of the mind, the gossip of the separate self.

Dying out of becoming anything at all, we enter what is.

These five stages are predominantly psychological. They deal with the content of the mind, thoughts, emotions, feelings, and relate to death as something outside of ourselves. Indeed, to over-simplify it greatly, the difference between the psychological and the spiritual is that the spiritual relates not only to the contents but to the space in which these contents are unfolding. The five stages deal with death as though it were outside of ourselves. Perhaps real acceptance is the first time we take death within. Where death is not the enemy but instead becomes the great teacher that directs us toward our fear and encourages us to relate *to* it instead of *from* it. Death's teaching is to relate to your life as a whole rather than some fractured reality from which you wish to escape.

Each one of these stages expands upon the last, leaves a little more space. Denial is a tightness and a closedness that, as it begins to open, feels the frustration of life arise as anger. But there is a little more room in which to investigate. Then opens the bargaining table: "How can I see deeper?" "What must I do to make the pain go away?" And even there we find a bit more space in which to understand. As the space expands, depression begins, the darkness of sensing how far we are from the truth. Seeing that our fear maintains the darkness, in acceptance we allow our protective walls to collapse, leaving a new spaciousness. We stop becoming someone, anyone at all. We stop being "someone" dying and enter into the spaciousness of being that has room for it all. We take death within and experience the wholeness we have always been.

Guided Meditation on Dying

[To be read slowly to a friend or silently to oneself.]

Find a comfortable position and close your eyes. Bring your attention to the level of sensation, feeling in the body.

Just feel that which sits here.

Feel this vessel. Feel the substance of it. Feel the weight of the head as it is balanced on the neck. Feel the musculature of the neck, its strength and its thickness. Its substantialness. Feel the long bones of the shoulders and the sockets that form to receive the arms.

Feel the weight of the arms as they rest on either side of your body. And your hands.

Feel the torso. Its thickness, its weightiness. The earthen quality of this body.

And your buttocks, as they rest against the pillow or chair. Feel those points of contact, how it supports your weight. Feel the pull of gravity on this substantial form.

Don't grasp at sensation. Just allow these sensations to be received as they arise in this body we inhabit.

Open to the sensations in the legs, their thickness, heaviness. Feel the solidness of this body. The feet. Earth. Solidness. Weight.

And feel the sensations that are arising here and there, in the palms, the back of the neck, the buttocks, the soles of the feet. Tinglings. Vibrations. Heat. Multiple sensations arising here and there.

Feel these sensations, and notice how they seem to be received by something subtler than this heavy form. Something lighter. Awareness itself seems to experience these sensations in the solid body, receives these tinglings and vibrations.

Feel this lighter body, this body of awareness within the heavier vessel.

Sense within this heavier body a lighter body, a body which receives all the experiences that enter through the senses. It receives sound as hearing, experiences light as seeing, tastes, knows life as it is experienced.

Enter the light body of awareness.

See how each breath, entering into the heavy body, is received as sensation by the lighter body. Each breath entering the heavy body sustaining this lightness, maintaining the balance that allows this body of awareness to remain.

Feel how each breath maintains this connection.

Let the awareness settle very alertly, very carefully, on each breath as it is breathed in, as it breathes out. Feel this contact between the heavy body and the light body. Feel how each breath sustains the light body, balanced within.

Experience each breath: feel life in process in this body.

Just awareness and sensation. Each breath. Experience this delicate balance, moment to moment, as sensation, as awareness itself.

And take each breath as though it were the last.

Experience each inhalation as though it were never to be followed by another. Each breath the last breath.

Each breath ending without another to follow. The last breath. The connection severed between the heavy body and the light body.

The end of a lifetime, the final breath.

Let go. Don't hold on to it. Let each breath go, finally and forever. Don't even be attached to the next breath.

Let go. Let yourself die. Don't hold on. Don't clutch at life.

Let go. Gently. Smoothly. Let it all go. Let it all float free. Let yourself die.

Each breath disappears. Each thought dissolving into space. Don't hold. Let go once and for all. Let go of fear. Let go of longing.

Let yourself die. Open into death. Nothing to hold to. That's all past. Die gently into this moment.

Holding on to nothing. Just let yourself die.

Let go of thoughts. Let go even of ideas of dying or living. Let go completely and at once, gently into death.

Go on, now. Die gently into the light. Float free from that heavy body, free from thoughts. That body is so heavy. Each thought so heavy. Go beyond now. Float free. Altogether beyond, altogether free.

With an open heart. Let go of all the things that pull on you, that hold you back. Let go of your name. Let go of your body. Let go of your mind. Just float free, beyond holding, beyond clinging. Let yourself die now.

Don't be afraid. There's nothing to hold to. Moment after moment, the light body free now. So go on. Gently into the light. Free from this dense body. Free from this incarnation now.

Let go into the light. Into the pure, open luminosity of your original nature. Just space. Space floating in space.

Let go completely. Die gently into the light.

Just light, floating in vast space. Float free in boundless space.

Let go of your knowing. Let go of your not knowing. All that comes to mind is old. Any thought is just old thought. Nothing to hold to now. Just the clear mind dissolving into the open heart. Free at last.

Just awareness dissolving into the light. Light experiencing itself within itself.

Space within space. Light within light.

Altogether gone. Beyond gone. No inside. No outside. Just is-ness, just edgeless being in endless space.

Open into it. Floating free of the body, free of the mind. Let yourself die into pure space.

Gone beyond the denseness of the body, of thought. Die into the open light of your essential purity.

Vast space. No boundary. Just being floating free in the vastness.

Open endless space. Vast edgeless space.

And from across that space notice that something gently approaches. Watch each breath approaching as if from far away. Watch it entering the body.

Each breath the first. Each inhalation the first breath of life. Each breath completely new.

Birth.

Consciousness experiencing the body once again. Space within space.

Pure awareness reinhabiting pure form. Born again.

Awareness continuing, moment to moment, just as ever. Experiencing what is the breath of life once again in the body.

Gently that lightness once again animates the heavier form. Once again takes birth to fulfill its karma, to learn what is to be learned, to share what is to be shared. To be with things as they are.

No death. No birth. No life. Just is-ness. In the body. Out of the body. Just being. The formlessness within form.

No life. No death. Just now. Just this much.

Each moment new.

Entering each moment fully awake. Each moment so precious. All there is. All there ever will be.

Lakshmana's Death

From the *Ramayana,* the bible of many in India, comes the story of Lakshmana's death. Lakshmana is the brother of Rama, who is an incarnation of God, of essential being. As it is stated in William Buck's inspired translation, "One who sees Rama even for a moment gains heaven, he is Narayana, identical with the souls of all creatures. He is the oceans and the forests and the air I breathe. He is more subtle than an atom. He goes everywhere by illusion, without beginning or end, unchangeable, unconquerable . . . so let us remember him when we are in difficulty from inside or out." Gandhi's "Ram" at the moment of his death is just such a remembrance. In India thousands live and die with the name of Ram or Rama on their lips and their heart at one with God.

"Rama looked at Lakshmana. 'Farewell, my brother.'

"Lakshmana made no answer. He walked three times around Rama and left the palace. He went half a league to where the Sarayu River swiftly flowed. Lakshmana sat by the running river. With open eyes, he looked around him and saw all things as Rama, thought of them as Rama. He rinsed his mouth with the clear water and stopped his breathing. The luminous person within Lakshmana's heart, the soul no bigger than a thumb, made ready to leave this world behind. The life center stopped spinning and went out and Lakshmana's energy, the fourth part of Lord Narayana, rose step by step up along his backbone, seeking flight out the crown of his head where his skull bones joined their seams.

"Lakshmana shut his eyes and watched the lights of his life slowly die. The lights of war long ago, the lights of his first love and marriage . . . the lights of his childhood . . . , And he thought, 'It's like something that I made once. . . . All of us.'

"In heaven, Lord Indra heard empty stone vault doors closing one after another in echoes. Sight was closing, hearing closing, mind turning away. Spirit was rising and leaving empty rooms. The ether space within the heart was empty, fires and lamps turned off, locks and threads snapped and untied, and all released.

248

"Indra swept across Kosala invisibly. He took Lakshmana's soul into his own heart and flew to heaven, carrying him and bearing light. Indra, the bright King of the Sky, took him away. Lakshmana's body fell into the water and was gone."

21

CONSCIOUS DYING

"Lightly, my darling, lightly, even when it comes to dying. Nothing ponderous or portentous or emphatic. No rhetoric, no tremolos, no self-conscious persona putting on its celebrated imitation of Christ, or Goethe, or Little Nell. And of course, no theology, no metaphysics. Just the simple fact of dying and the fact of the clear light."

A. Huxley

● ● ●

To let go of the last moment and open to the next is to die consciously moment to moment.

When we take death within, life becomes clear and workable. One of the remarkable things about confronting death is the depth at which it gets our attention. If you could fully experience even a moment of being in its totality, you would discover what you have always been looking for. We don't pay attention to most things, but death catches our eye.

In a sense all of this talk about death is really a ploy. Because what we think of as death only occurs to the body. It threatens our seeming existence only to the degree that we imagine and pretend it does. It makes us pay attention. Focusing on death is a way of becoming fully alive. Because wherever the attention is, wherever awareness is, that is where our experience of life arises. Indeed, the recent interest in "danger sports" such as mountain climbing, hang gliding, and sky diving may all be ways we have of tricking ourselves into being present. Many say they "feel so alive" when doing these sports because they make them pay attention. The more attention, the more alive we feel. Perhaps that is why so many who are dying also say that they have never felt so alive. When we take death within we stop reinforcing our denial, our judging, our anger, or continuing our bargaining. We don't push our depression away. We ask ourselves in truth, "Who dies?" and surrender our resistance and knowing because we see that it blocks our understanding.

Perhaps the first recognition in the process of acknowledging, opening, and letting go that we call "conscious dying" is when we begin to see that we are not the body. That consciousness is constantly in a process of unfolding. We see that we have a body but it is not who we are. Just as one may have an overcoat but that is not you. One honors the overcoat because it is a given of the moment and because it wouldn't be very satisfactory to revile it or let it go to rags when it could allow one to continue on one's long winter's journey of wisdom and love. When it is spring one doesn't need the overcoat any more. One puts it aside or sends it to the dry cleaner.

One fellow remarked that he could see that he was "creation constantly in the act of becoming." He saw the perfect unfolding of each moment and that there was nothing he had to *do* about it, that all his doing to *become* something or someone just "dulled the wonder of it all."

The stages of becoming, of our constant goal-oriented someoneness, dissolve into the stagelessness of just being. It is the end of stages. It is like entering a room only to find it has no walls, no door, no one inside. Awakening from a dream to find we were never asleep (that sleep too was just part of the dream). It is a going beyond creation and destruction. You are neither the dancer nor the dance, nor even the ground on which the dance is played out, nor the music, nor even the electrons or the space between them, nor the perception of them, nor the consciousness that you are none of them, nor the feelings that meet this recognition, nor even the "don't know" that allows it to be seen so clearly. You recognize that you can't know who you are, you can only be it.

Our perception of the universe changes. "Who dies?" changes as the old is seen not to be real in the way we imagined. Each "thing" is seen to be more real than ever before. Not something you trip over at night on the way to the bathroom. Not as related to you but in its own vibrating suchness. Not the separate reality of "this" and "that" but the unifying thusness out of which all things are composed.

Letting go of old thought, perceptions, models, concepts, the whole world dissolves as a new world begins to form moment to moment on the screen of consciousness. It is not the old worn movie we are used to, that poor cartoon replica of the truth. And though at first we lament its loss, the loss of the familiar, we let go of the false security and pain which have defined our imagined territory of the body and the mind. The new emerges as we uncover deeper and deeper levels of "don't know." Not becoming something or someone, just opening to it all, not becoming, just being.

The death of the body is accompanied by less agony than the death of the ego, the separate self. The death of the self is a tearing away of everything we imagine to be solid, a crumbling of the walls we have built to hide behind. Letting go of the self-protection which is constantly bargaining with the suffering of the mind, there may arise a dizziness and a nausea, like coming out of a tiny cave into the endless vistas of the Himalayas. It means the death of everything we have learned to be, all the thoughts and projections that so enamored us in the past and created someone for us to be in the future. All is allowed to die back into the flow of life.

When all we have imagined ourselves to be is allowed to die, all is seen in its essentially empty, impermanent nature. And we experience the superficiality of the separate self we have clung to so long. As we see the nature of this dreamlike separateness, we recognize that there is in reality no one to die and that it is only the illusion of this separate someoneness that takes birth again and again. Then when loneliness or insecurity or fear arises, we recognize them as the longings that have driven us from incarnation to incarnation. All is seen as just a coming and a going. It is as though we hear the wisdom and compassion of the Buddha or Jesus, our original nature, for the very first time.

Then physical death is honored and respected as a wonderful opportunity in the passing from the body to recognize the relativity of everything we imagine to be solid. Passing out of a body, we see all that we thought of as us, the mind and body, to be other than we imagined. And we approach the truth beyond the mind.

"How come you trust your thoughts so much when you see they hardly stay a moment and often conflict?" "Who is thinking?"

The mind/body no longer struggles to protect itself. The stages of becoming are created by the momentum of our struggle for satisfaction. Perhaps even by what some people call the "will to live." But letting go of our becoming reveals our underlying being, the deep satisfaction of no one to protect and no one to be. A life of greater ease and quiet. All that we have conjured to distract us from our pain, even the subtle attempt to control and possess the world in our minds that what we call "understanding," is seen to be just more suffering.

"It is enough just not to misunderstand, understanding will take care of itself."

The pain of "trying to understand," to resolve our relationship to the universe, to find out "where we stand," is based on the idea that we are separate. Thought can never encompass reality, because it is such a small part of it. Then even our precious partial understanding is relinquished so that we may directly experience the truth instead of attempting to hold it captive in the superficial mind.

Maharaji one day turned to a devotee and said, "Don't even be attached to your next breath."

When the mind and heart coincide in loving surrender and clear acceptance of what is, that's when conscious death starts to become possible. Watching the process we have always mistaken for "I," we see that all that arises passes away, that everything ends and is instantly replaced by the next moment—that time itself is constantly dying.

Death is an illusion we all buy into, so we must be aware that "conscious death" can become a still greater illusion when we imagine we know what death is.

We hear of the death of Zen masters, of saints, of those we imagine are "remarkable people" dying without the least resistance, and it seems like all this may be beyond us. Yet I see many people, as they approach confusing death, become one with the process. They seem to go through what almost could be called "incarnations" in the last few months of life. They deepen the work that they perhaps may have taken birth to complete. They are no longer someone separate, someone "dying consciously," they are merely space within space, light within light.

Robin was thirty-three years old when I met her. For the last two and a half years she had been working with her cancer. When she received her diagnosis, working in an insurance company as an adjuster, she was "pretty square" as she put it. Trying to understand the process of healing, letting go of the stagnation that may indeed have caused her illness, she began to investigate life itself. For the year and a half that followed the first diagnosis, she deepened her participation in life with meditation and prayer and the reading of spiritual texts which up until then had little or no meaning for her.

"What a teaching this cancer has been," she said as she began to relate an experience she had the night before. She told of feeling that she was approaching death, and as she opened her heart in prayer, she felt herself move down a great tunnel and land in a huge golden palm. For the first time in months she was without pain and as she lay there in the palm, luxuriating in the peace of it all, she began to wonder if she wasn't being a bit lazy by not taking this opportunity to look about. So she got up on all fours and padded over to the edge of the palm and looked out into what was an endless star-filled sky. She said there were tens of thousands of stars glittering and that somehow she knew each one of them intimately, and indeed was but another of those stars. She didn't know how it could be, she only knew that it was. One of

the stars approached and it was Jesus, then another came forward
and it was Ramana Maharshi. Then each receded into the starry
field, and became the same as all others. At this point she said
she "knew beyond knowing" that the essence of all things was the
same. A moment later, the sense of things dissolved and she
found herself back in her painful body. She said that the experience left her with a feeling that death was nothing special.

A year later it seemed she had come to "end game" and that
death was rapidly approaching. Having heard of the many instances in the Native American and Eskimo traditions where a
dying person calls his or her family together, waiting sometimes
weeks for all to arrive before saying good-by to each one individually and wishing them well before returning to a quiet room and
a peaceful death, she thought that she too would practice this
kind of conscious departure. She had done much work in the past
years and thought this would be the perfect manifestation of the
consciousness she had worked so hard to bring to the months of
pain and bewilderment. She invited her family to come to her
home on March 10 to be with her on the evening of her death. As
the tenth approached she said that at times she had to hold on so
as not to die before the "allotted time," and the deep sharings
that she felt were appropriate for that moment. On the afternoon
of the designated day, her ex-husband and her six-year-old son,
her sister (a nurse), her brother, her sister-in-law, and I arrived
to share in this final good-by to the being we had loved so much.
As evening approached, a large meal was served, but few ate. The
moment was full of the energy of this final good-by. At about
eight, Robin was helped by her sister and brother from her bedroom to the living room. It was a powerful moment. She was very
clear and shared the okayness of her death and the satisfaction it
gave her to be able to be with those she loved and to leave this
body without qualms or any feeling of unfinished business. After
an hour and a half of sharing she was becoming weaker and was
helped gently back to her room. Each left sitting in the living
room looked into the eyes of the others around with both a sadness
and a fullness. Each had said his good-by and had wished her
well on her new journey. As the door closed behind Robin each
wept for the friend they would never see again.

At about five the next morning, Robin opened one eye and said, "Oh, shit." And we spent much of the day speaking of what might be holding her back, of her wish to "die consciously" and of the uncontrollability of things as they present themselves. That night each person came individually into her room to say their last good-bys on what assuredly seemed to be her final hours on earth. As we read to her that evening from the Bible, she seemed quiet and at peace. And it was decided that it might be useful if I slept on the floor next to her in a sleeping bag so that I could be there for whatever might be appropriate in the final moments as she died.

At four in the morning we both opened our eyes looking at each other with bewilderment and began to laugh at how nature has its own timing. This process continued for days. For the first few days, we spent an hour or two first thing in the morning coming back to ground zero, letting go of any preconceptions, opening to the process as it was. By the fourth day our sharings at dawn lasted only about half an hour. We began to share more silence than concepts. Our work at night, for perhaps an hour before she went to sleep, was spent opening to the image of Jesus, which was gradually presenting itself in her heart more each day.

Slowly, day after day, her ideas about who she was, even as a "conscious person," her ideas about opening to death, her ideas about what death might be, began to melt away. She wasn't even being allowed to be someone dying consciously. She was getting weaker and weaker, no longer taking food, wide open to death, yet somehow not allowed to die. At times she was a bit confused, but more often all that one felt from her was love.

Everyone settled in to be with Robin during her dying and about a week into the process she woke up one morning and in her bird-thin voice said, "In the middle of the night I thought I was going to leave my body. Jesus was standing right next to me and I asked him if he would take me but he said no, that it was all all right. That this was all a teaching for me to learn trust and patience. And here I am."

As the days went by, she had to let go of even her understanding of how things were. She had to let go of all of her knowing and just be there. A few days later, upon awakening, I asked her, "What's happening?" and she said with extraordinary clarity, "I don't know." But this "I don't know" had within it a deep satisfaction that I hadn't heard before. At last she didn't know and it was wonderful for her not to second-guess the process but simply to surrender into it. It allowed her to be yet more present. She was letting each day be as it was. Just trusting the moment with an open-ended patience that was no longer expectant of things being any way at all—soft, open, yielding to whatever truth might arise, surrendering to God. All that we imagine is lost in dying: the personality, our sense of history, our goals, our concepts, and models were being relinquished as she lay there. Each day she became a bit more translucent. Trust and patience.

For the first few days, surrounded by her family each evening, she prepared for death. But as the weeks continued there was no longer any self-conscious preparation but just a humorous bewilderment at the way of things. Sometimes it felt more like she was being born than dying.

Here I would like to interject that in all such stories of "conscious dying," no matter how picturesque, there are still times when the old mind surfaces. That even with patients who are quite clear, still there are moments of confusion along the way. Instances when the mind closes around some slight fear or desire. But the self-forgiveness and unattached chagrin at the uncontrollable unfolding of things that meet this denseness in the mind soon allow that sense of spaciousness to return once again.

When we had come together, nearly two weeks earlier, for Robin's death, none were prepared for the long unfolding that ensued. When I had gone to her home on the day before her planned departure, I had expected to be back in a day or so. But now, twelve days into her opening to death, I was long overdue for a meditation retreat I was to be at. It was obvious that she and I had done the work we needed to do. She was slowly melting beyond herself and whatever little balancing might be necessary could be done over the phone. Before I left to drive the five hundred miles to the retreat, we agreed that I would call each day to sort of "check in" and make myself available in whatever way might be useful. As I said good-by to her, knowing we would probably not see each other again in this form, it was clear how little attachment, how little holding, was in her mind and heart by the way she winked and the lightness with which she let go of my hand.

Arriving at the retreat, I called to see how things were going to find that the process continued in its own natural course and that all was well. Each day I called her from the retreat, it was clear that there was little she needed from anyone.

If any slight confusion arose, we would share and often laugh at how the mind addictively clings to the old. It always came back to trust and patience. I watched the ease with which she returned to balance. One day, a week into the retreat, I called to find Robin quite agitated and disturbed. "Maybe I'm losing it. I don't know what's happening, but my mind is bouncing all over the place." I asked her if anything had changed in her environment and she said no, only that because she was no longer able to swallow the Brompton's mixture she had been using for the past few months to deal with the pain, the doctor had instead suggested morphine suppositories, which seemed to be adequate for the pain. After a moment's thought, I had to smile. "Robin, is it any wonder that after taking a medicine which contains a bit of cocaine five times a day, that upon discontinuance you might be experiencing a little good old drug withdrawal." "Aha," she sighed and we laughed. "Of course," she said. "I guess I even have to do that one. Something else to surrender into."

A few days later at five in the morning, during the first group meditation, I started to feel a pain in my chest. As I watched the sensations getting hotter and deeper, after a few minutes I thought perhaps I was having some sort of dying hallucination. Not surprising, I thought, considering all the people I have been with as they died. I did not know where it was coming from but all I could do was stay open to it to see what the next moment held. It felt like some kind of pressure was displacing my lung capacity. I had to concentrate on each breath. It almost seemed as though I consciously had to draw in the oxygen almost at the molecular level to keep from fainting. As it became harder to breathe and the pain in my chest spread I could feel the tendency of the body to tighten with each breath, but as long as I could stay open to it I had room for the experience. So there I was with whatever seemed to be happening, not labeling or even trying to understand it, just attempting to stay open to it, when about ten minutes into the experience I heard Robin's voice saying, "We've been so close, we've shared so much, and there is really nothing I can give you, but I know you want to know what it is like to die, so I am sharing my death with you." I mused to myself, "Well, that's an interesting thought, true or not, whatever it is, it's just a thought, who knows?" More "don't know," but it felt as though I was in the process of dying, whatever the reason. It was getting harder to breathe and I watched the body starting to vibrate with a sense of emergency. The red light was on. There was definitely something happening that the body was treating like a threat. Fear was arising as I watched the body trying to hold on. It was almost as though the body was involuntarily trying to encapsulate the fire inside, trying not to let it out, but the fire was burning its way through. I was trying just to breathe, not thinking of anything else, because I sensed that if the attention wavered I was going to pass out. In my body there was only the pain and the slow hiss of my breath, drawn in and released under pressure. Perhaps twenty-five minutes into the experience, the pressure in my lungs felt as though it was evicting me from my body and I watched the body trying to hold on. The body was on alert, the mind was trying to think its way out, but there was no room for control. I sensed that I must just give it space, that any control would cause it to burst. I felt like a tube of toothpaste being squeezed with its top still on. But all of a sudden the mind said, "Stay in? Why?" and no answer came. Suddenly there was great peace. The priorities had instantly changed, leaving the body seemed entirely appropriate, no reason to resist or hold on. It was as though I had remembered something I had forgotten a long time before, perhaps since birth. Then the pressure in my chest seemed perfectly natural and was doing exactly what it should to eject me. Right! Death was no longer a threat. In fact, it became just another inconsequential bubble in the flow of change and the sense of joyous expectancy at the next moment. It was like, "Why stay in the body? How could I have been so foolish as to hold on to this thing? Everything is perfect." There was a pervasive knowing that everything was just as it should be which converted the pain and pressure that were ejecting me from an enemy into an ally. It was very satisfying. It suited my goal rather than obstructed it. The priority had changed to, "Let it happen, go on out, go on out, let it all go." The pain was there, but the expansiveness was immense. I was no longer contracted around my life. My life was expanding beyond my body. "Ah, this is just right, it is all happening just perfectly." And again I heard Robin's voice in my heart, this time saying, "It's time to stop being Robin and become Christ dying," and the experience then became other than identification even with someone dying, with my dying or her dying, it was just a process unfolding perfectly. I was not relating to myself as body but more as the karmic bundle, a process in its next perfect stage, the consciousness dissolving out of its vessel, dying is just another part of living. Silence.

As the bell that ended the sitting rang, the mind wondered, "What was that all about? An interesting hallucination to be sure, who knows?" And as I got up, my chest still ached. Going to breakfast I was just about to begin to eat when I was called to the phone. It was Robin's brother. Robin had just died.

This experience has left me with an insight and confidence in the work that we share. It has allowed me to understand why people who were dying and seemed to be having a difficult time often in the last moments went through a considerable change, a seeming opening beyond all the unfinished business and fear and holding that led up to that moment. For some this "knowing" seemed to happen days or sometimes weeks in advance of death. For others it seemed to happen just moments before they left the body. I had always marveled at photographs of the dead at Auschwitz in which there seemed no suffering in those faces. It was a phenomenon that I could never understand before, but that now seemed very clear: at some time, perhaps just a split second before life leaves the body, the perfection of that process is deeply understood. Indeed this might be a universal experience; that even those who have held most tightly encounter the perfection and fearlessness of the moment of death.

Robin had to let go of everything. She had become just open space. Her death was no longer something added to her personal history, it was instead her merging with that part of herself which was the open heart of Christ. Beyond the mind's ideas of death, no matter how "conscious," she let go into the brilliance of the truth.

As we look through the plethora of spiritual literature, the biographies of saints, the death poems that were part of the Zen tradition, the dying of roshis with their infinite humor and lightness at death, we see again and again examples of the conscious dying of beings who honor their body but had no remorse at leaving it behind; whose business was finished from moment to moment; who lived their lives as Suzuki Roshi put it, "without leaving a trace."

It is this leaving of no trace, this complete finishing in each moment of what arises, that allows us to leave our body or to go to sleep each night with the same equanimity and fullness that there is nothing to do and nothing that remains undone. It is perhaps bordering on another statement by Suzuki Roshi which says, "Even if the sun rises in the west, the bodhisattva (the being of wisdom in service to all) has but one way."

Basho, the great Japanese poet, wrote, "From olden times it has been customary to leave behind a death poem and perhaps I should do the same. But every moment of life is the last, every poem a death poem! Why then at this time should I write one? In these my last hours I have no poem." Just as when Master Ta-Kuan was dying, his disciples asked him to write a death poem but he refused. When they insisted, he wrote the Japanese character for dream, and died.

When we hear such stories we fear that this degree of consciousness, this spaciousness in which to die, is beyond our capability, and yet that is not what I have seen. Death often brings out the best in us. For many, a lifetime's yearning for the truth holds them in good stead.

One day I received a phone call from a woman who asked, "Do you help people die consciously?"

A few days later Pam drove down for a visit. She said she felt it was time to go deeper; her melanoma was rapidly spreading. She had been working with the illness for a few years but now it seemed to be getting worse. She said she had done a bit of meditation and since it looked like she might be dying, she would like to work with us. She said she wanted to use her death as a means of generating the peace she felt was missing. It seemed she might find her way through by concentrating more on the opening of her heart, so we recommended that she begin repeating in her heart the Jesus prayer, "Lord Jesus Christ, have mercy on me."

Slowly, her heart began to soften to the prayer.

A few days later she went into the hospital for a minor bladder operation to remove a tumor which was causing discomfort. She had experienced this operation before and found the hospital a very difficult environment, but this time her heart was so full she was quite at ease with it all and she said the hospital felt like a temple. The experiences in her body were reminders to stay present. The fearful ramblings of her mind interrupted her meditations again and again. "My mind keeps interrupting my heart," she said. "Are they different? Are there two inside of you?" I asked. "Only when I identify with the fear in the mind," she replied. She persevered and slowly her mind began to quiet. At last her mind was becoming the servant of her heart. "There is nothing separate from God except that our mind makes it so," she said.

For months we worked together sharing the process of our unfolding as she experienced at times the sacred heart of Jesus beating within her own frail chest. Sharing with her four children the process she was going through in whatever manner felt appropriate in the moment, she continued her doctor's recommendations without much attachment to their being "successful" in the way he hoped. She said it was all successful as long as she paid attention to the changes and noted how the mind grasped at the possibility of the body's healing. At times when she felt better she said she could see how the mind automatically constructed some false logic about what Christ's mercy was going to be. But she maintained her openness, her "don't know," and let such thoughts float free in the warmth and patience of the heart. She just continued to open to the oneness that includes life and death. When fear would occasionally arise, it was met with a humility and surrender that allowed great growth. There was little resistance anywhere.

A few months after our first meeting, she attended a five-day retreat we were offering in Santa Cruz, California, about eighty miles from her home. A day and a half into the retreat, she began to experience considerable head pain. She had been getting a little aphasic and in fact she said she had awakened one morning a few days earlier and found that as she started to speak, her words were like "alphabet soup thrown out into the air." "How wonderful," she had said at the time. "Me having just become a lawyer you know, what they call 'a mouthpiece,' and here I am, my words making no sense at all. Talk about Christ's mercy! That's a good one to get done with. I won't have to do that again," and she laughed heartily.

As the pain in her head began to increase she lay down in her room with a few friends around and went into what seemed a light coma. Lying on the bed, writhing back and forth, no one could relieve her pain. Even the pain medication which was brought seemed to have little effect. She was in extreme discomfort, her mouth dry, beads of perspiration on her forehead, her body vibrating with extreme pain.

Sitting next to her bed, I found myself praying that somehow she might be released from this viselike pressure that seemed to be making her whole body contract. But the pain continued and all in the room had to surrender into its intensity. Returning to lead the group in the afternoon session, I was soon called away because, "Pam seems to be in a lot of difficulty. She may be dying, you'd better come down." As I entered the room, I sensed something I had not noticed before and as I knelt next to her bed I heard myself say, "Pam, Christ is here." Suddenly her whole expression changed and the heaviness seemed to leave her. She went into what seemed pure ecstasy, which for the next couple of hours was so intense that one could not be near her without being flooded with an effusive joy. It seemed almost as though her body was glowing with compassion and transcendent love. People were coming out of the room saying, "I'm a little embarrassed to say how high I'm getting from hanging around her. I know I could be sad because I love her so, but somehow I just feel wonderful."

After a few hours Pam settled a bit deeper into coma but there continued a feeling of great joy and peace about her. A doctor came in with more pain medication but said she seemed so remarkably whole in her soft silence that he didn't want to disturb the balance. Which reminded me of the physician a year before who visited when we were working with a patient in considerable pain just as her body began to soften in surrender and her heart let go of its resistance. "I came here to do something about her condition," he said, "but I think I am learning the laying off of hands."

One of Pam's friends, concerned that she might be dying, called her husband and family to come take her home. A few hours later her ex-husband walked into the room with an understandably protective air, quite unsure what to expect from these "deathies." With his ex-wife were a half dozen people whose faces were radiant with the energy that could instantly be felt upon entering the room. He sat down next to her, almost wordless, surrounded by strange company, probably wondering how he could get his dear friend out of this strange environment. But there was such peace in the room—such quiet. There was no emergency, clearly nothing was the matter. She was just dying. Within an hour he accompanied me outside and said, "You know, five years ago I stepped off the path. I lost God. But being in there now I'm just coming back into seeing what it is all about."

Soon after, her children arrived and were sitting by the bed much like anyone else. Part of a precious process that all were honored to share. The thirteen-year-old twins found it much harder than the older daughters. It had been difficult for them to relate to the illness before and now it was little easier. But no one was reinforcing their suffering and no one was pushing it away. Their sadness was O.K., their confusion too. They could do whatever they wished. They didn't have to be holy about it. They didn't have to be like anyone else. And soon they too were becoming part of this mandala of love and acceptance that surrounded Pam as she lay so peacefully on the bed.

Pam's family decided that this was the best place for her and for them as well. A room was found for the family to stay in so that they could accompany Pam on the journey that was evidently underway.

Two more days passed as Pam continued in this semi-comatose

state. The room filled with a soft joy and the sense of the perfection of things. But the retreat was to be over the next day and it was unclear whether or not she was going to die. So on the last evening at the retreat when everyone went to supper, I sat next to her and said, "It's Thursday night, my friend. The retreat is over tomorrow. I think if you are going to die, now is the time to do it because tomorrow the circus leaves town." Soon after that she came out of the coma and began talking a bit. She said she felt fine, "really quite light," and that there was no pain at all. Leaning over her in my most professional manner, thinking there might be some unfinished business, I asked, "Is there anything you want to do before you die?" "Yes," she laughed, "live ten more years."

The next day she went home with her family.

A few days later I visited her at her home. As I walked into the room there was a feeling of great space all about her. My thoughts were like bowling balls, each seemed so awkward in this vast silence. My mind was so weighty in comparison to this soft space because she appeared not to be caught anywhere in the mind. There was just space. And I recalled a friend telling me of a retreat with a Zen master where he kept getting the uneasy feeling during interview sessions that the Zen master knew what he was thinking. One day, coming into the Zen master's room, he asked, "When I walk in here I feel like you know what I am thinking." The roshi looked up and said with a smile, "Well, I'm not thinking, so that must be you." She wasn't clinging anywhere. It was as though she were no longer "someone." There was a feeling of unity in the room. She seemed to have no edges.

She looked up softly at me and said quizzically, "You know the other day when I came out of that coma, Maharaji was sitting at the end of my bed and he was just laughing and laughing and laughing."

I was a bit surprised by this spontaneous connection with Maharaji when it seemed for so many months that her touch point had been Jesus. No one had encouraged her to focus on Maharaji. It seemed to have been something that arose by itself. So I asked her, "But what about your connection with Jesus?" "Well," she said, "Jesus has to do with suffering and I'm not suffering any more and Maharaji is just pure joy."

In the next weeks on two occasions she went into similar two-and-a-half-day semi-comatose states. What she called "vacations" that she said she could not adequately describe but which reminded her very much of the Greek Orthodox choral music which a friend had given her on tape. She said, "The closest I can come to describing that space is the fullness of that chorale music." Each time she went into this seeming coma it appeared as though she was having pain but each time afterward she said that there was no difficulty, no problem at all. Each time she came back clearer and lighter. Which is not to say that there were not difficult moments. Periods of getting lost here and there. The pulls of dying with one's mother and children about. The occasional confusion of the bedside melodrama. But more and more she was becoming just space. Her only reading a short treatise by the third Zen Patriarch.

Tara, one of the people who had supported and shared so much with Pam in the months preceding, later told us that "one day during one of these coma-like periods, Pam's eyes were wide open as she looked into the distance. In whispers she continually repeated, 'Sun, sun, done, done,' tears streaming from her eyes, both hands over her heart . . . Even after she became incontinent it was a pleasure to do the most seemingly unpleasant work. No complaints, only how could we purify ourselves more to let her innocence touch our hearts."

Christmas morning Pam was helped downstairs to be with her family for a last bit. As she returned upstairs, it seemed clear that she was beginning to pass out of her body. What was interesting about it, the people around her noticed, was the lack of personality. As the hours passed she seemed to open more and more, becoming just space, just a process unfolding in an awareness that was not separate. As someone said, "She is no longer a noun, she has become a verb."

A day or so later, with friends sitting on either side of her, she gave birth to herself. She was like space dissolving into space. There was not the least feeling of any pushing or pulling. It seemed as though she too was looking on quizzically at the process. As Tara mentioned later, "The room was filled with a feeling of love and gentle peace. Everyone was silently aware of the stillness. Pam stopped breathing very quietly and just slipped out of her body. A tear rolled down her cheek and she was gone." Just a dissolving out of temporary form, a going on.

A contemporary Zen master, Roshi Taji, approached death with his senior disciples assembled at his bedside. One of them, remembering the roshi was fond of a certain kind of cake, had spent half a day searching the pastry shops of Tokyo for this confection, which he now presented to Roshi Taji. With a wan smile the dying roshi accepted a piece of cake and slowly began munching it. As the roshi grew weaker his disciples leaned close and inquired whether he had any final words for them. "Yes," the roshi replied. The disciples leaned forward eagerly. "Please tell us." "My, but this cake is delicious," and with that he died.

When such beings die they expand beyond themselves. They just go on and the rest is left for the sweeper.

Who's dying?

We're all stir crazy—
been in the body so long.

And on the day he died
Maharaji whispered,
    "Today I am released from central jail forever."

But we are not in the body,
the body is in us,
depends on us for life
(not us on it).

Jesus said,
    "I am the Light."
Us all.
The Evershining.

22
THE MOMENT
OF DEATH

From our experience with many patients at the time they are dying, we have come to see that the moment of death is often a moment of great quietude and peace. That often even those who have approached death with trepidation, in the moments before death, have an opening. As with the experience of Robin's dying, where suddenly something was remembered that seemed long forgotten. The relationship to death, to dropping the body, seems to change in the moments preceding death. Somehow there is an okayness that is felt. The mind and the heart gradually seem to become unified. Or as one being put it who had died and come back to tell the tale, "Death is absolutely safe."

Having seen the final ease with which some people are able to die, I come to this subject with a certain confidence, but even a greater amount of "don't know." It seems that in the last moments, for many, their experience is converted from hell to heaven, from resistance to an openhanded ease, a floating out.

We can only speculate on the experience of dying. However, in the Tibetan Buddhist tradition, there has developed a considerable technology around the experience of death; several meditations encourage one to familiarize oneself with this precious moment; to practice dying as a means of a deeper insight into that which causes us to misperceive life. An insight into how the automatic, essentially impersonal processes of the mind are mistaken for some separate self, something to lose, something to protect from death. [See Appendix II.]

What can be sensed from such meditations is the process of dissolving, which appears to be the predominant physical experience in the transition we call dying. It seems that the process of dying is like a melting, a dissolving. Each stage seems to expand beyond the last. The boundaries become less defined. What is external and internal become unified. Dying is a gradual process of withdrawal. It is said in the various traditions that it may take from twenty minutes to several hours for the consciousness element to withdraw from the body. The internal process of dissolving out of the body is accompanied by certain external phenomena that physicians recognize as the shutting down of various life functions. As the energy that animates certain systems withdraws, the energy in those systems becomes less and less evident. At one moment they are measurable, at another they are not, though the process of withdrawal may still be occurring. It is this phenomenon of measurability on which we predicate our idea of "a moment of death." But death does not occur in a moment. It is a gradual process that continues for some time after instrumentation is unable to measure its presence. In reality it is not that death has occurred in that moment but that life is no longer accessible to instrumentation and gradation.

The process of dying seems to be an expansion beyond the forms in which it has always been measured. The following is a scenario for the physical experience of dying as based on the ancient concepts of the body being composed of the four elements of earth, water, fire, and air, as felt within the aggregate of form:

As death approaches the earth element, the feeling of the solidity and hardness of the body, begins to melt. The body seems very heavy. The boundaries of the body, its edge, are less solid. There is not so much a feeling of being "in" the body. One is less sensitive to impressions and feelings. One can no longer move the limbs at will. Peristalsis slows, the bowels no longer move without aid. The organs begin to shut down. As the earth element continues to dissolve into the water element there is a feeling of flowingness, a liquidity, as the solidity that has always intensified identification with the body begins to melt, a feeling of fluidity.

As the water element begins to dissolve into the fire element, the feeling of fluidity becomes more like a warm mist. The bodily fluids begin to slow, the mouth and eyes become dry, circulation slows, blood pressure drops. As the circulation begins to thicken and stop, blood settles in the lowest extremities. A feeling of lightness ensues.

As the fire element dissolves into the air element, feelings of warmth and cold dissipate, physical comfort and discomfort no longer have meaning. The body temperature drops until it reaches a stage where the body begins to cool and becomes pale. Digestion stops. A feeling of lightness, as of heat rising, becomes predominant. A feeling of dissolving into yet subtler and subtler boundarylessness.

As the air element dissolves into consciousness itself there is a feeling of edgelessness. The out breath having become longer than the in breath has dissolved into space and there is no longer the experience of bodily form or function but just a sense of vast expanding airiness, a dissolving into pure being.

●   ●   ●

It will be noticed that each stage is accompanied by less solidity, the edges less defined; less external input is received and there is an increasing feeling of boundarylessness. Death or the process of dying seems to be accompanied by a sense of expanding beyond oneself, of dissolving out of form, of melting into the undifferentiated.

But imagine attempting to resist this dissolution, this feeling of edges melting away. Imagine trying to hold on to the solidity as it melts into the fluidity. Of trying to push against that liquidity, to grasp back at something solid, only to experience the fluidity become lighter and more flowing as it dissolves into the fire element, feeling the temperatures of the body cool and, like heat dissipating, to melt into the vastness of space as the air element and the energy expand and dissolve into consciousness itself. Imagine trying to push against this, trying to halt the incessant progression of this process. If you go with it, opening into it, there is an experience of expansion, a melting out of solidity, a dissolving into the underlying reality. Imagine trying to hold on to that which is melting away. Perhaps this is what some call purgatory. The hellish holding back from the next unfolding, resistance to what is?

All apparently come to a point where they are evaporating out of the body and the body must be left behind. All experience the elements merging into their essential energy. Their separate qualities of solidity, fluidity, temperature, and flow are no longer predominant and there is just consciousness floating free. For a few moments, awareness shines more brilliantly than a thousand suns and there is the experience of the one reality out of which all creation arises. The duration of the experience of the light seems to vary for different people, perhaps depending upon the willingness to open into the truth and the trust and reverence in which you hold your original nature.

This is a thumbnail imagining of the moment of death but according to the teachings of various belief systems this is only the first part of the process before the unconscious tendencies re-establish themselves to create as many realms after death as the mind created before. After hearing of this ongoing process, one fellow asked, "Are these after-death realms real?" To which one must reply, "They are as real as you are. But no realer! In fact, they are only as real as you think you are."

Many find it useful to "practice" dying. I have rehearsed with several the experiences that might arise during the process of dying so that they can meet them with clarity and love. Any such rehearsal, of course, must be done with the lightness of "don't know" so as not to program what will occur later. Certainly our approach to the present is the same in death as in life: an acknowledgment, an opening, a letting go. Learning to die is learning to dissolve past the holdings of this moment, opening fresh to the next without clinging anywhere. We are each day, each moment, learning to die: to dissolve into the ocean of pure being.

23
EXPLORING
THE AFTER-DEATH
EXPERIENCE

Some time ago we received a letter from a woman in New York City who said she was thinking of going over to the Brooklyn Convalescent Hospital, in which her mother was dying, to sit by her bed and read her *The Tibetan Book of the Dead*. I called that day to tell her she might be making an error of judgment. Consider the likely reaction of an eighty-five-year-old Jewish woman in considerable pain and fear, dying in a strange environment, who has to lie there and hear that when she dies she is going to confront swirling lights and thunderous roars coming from harukas and demons in circumstances she has perhaps never confronted in life. Death is frightening enough but to put it in terms so unfamiliar would cause her yet more anxiety and fear. *The Tibetan Book of the Dead* was intended for Tibetan monks, not for old Jewish ladies dying in Brooklyn. Since we do not share this same conditioning in life, why expect the mind to project such conditioning after dropping the body? Instead we suggested she sing old Yiddish love songs to her mother.

The Tibetan Book of the Dead (also known as the *Bardo Thodol*) is a tract written for and by Tibetan monks and devout lay people to incorporate a lifetime of practice into the moment of transition we call death. It is meant to make the unfamiliar familiar. To reinforce visualization techniques that may have been practiced for years. It is perhaps the best-known example of the literature that exists in almost every culture on the contemplation and possibility of wise navigation through the after-death states. It is part of a long practice to keep one on the mark even under the most divergent and uncommon circumstances. By constantly recognizing and reaffirming that the observed is the observer, that everything one perceives is a projection of the imagined self, that all one sees is one's mind, the text attempts to liberate one from clinging to old desires and separatist feelings that cause fear and self-protection. It encourages one to merge with one's original nature. To surrender the false and merge with the real. [See Appendix III.]

To this end states of mind are personified as celestial beings as a skillful means, a technique, to make states of mind larger than life by incorporating them into forms of angelic and demonic entities recognizable by their garments, colors, ornamentation, and costume. Personifying such states, compassion becomes the shimmering figure of Avalokiteshvara; fear becomes a six-armed blood-soaked warrior demon; the quality of cutting through the attachments that bind us to the mind becomes the sword-wielding discriminative wisdom of Manjushri. It is a means of demagnetizing the power of heavy emotions. But we have not been raised with a long familiarity with such ornate personifications and forms. They do not represent to us our feelings as they might to a Tibetan monk. Perhaps for the Western mind these qualities are better described simply as love, fear, jealousy, envy, or a recognition of unconscious tendencies which have always caused clinging and confusion, which have always reinforced fear and self-doubt.

The moment-to-moment acknowledgment of states of mind, the daily noting of feelings and thoughts as they occur, accomplishes much the same goal as such personifications and perhaps more directly for the Western mind. Opening to these states of mind allows one to go beyond them, to pass through a mind that does not close around them or become identified with them.

Indeed, if after leaving our body the mind does continue to create its world, if indeed we are confronted by all that we held in life, projected about us by a mind whose concentration has greatly increased by the diminishment of the distractions of bodily input, we may see not Avalokiteshvara but perhaps Mother Teresa or some kind friend who has helped us at one time. Rather than some wrathful deity arising in our path, it may well be that anger is personified as some enemy we have made, some bit of unfinished business from the past. Wisdom might appear as some spiritual teacher we have known. Jealousy or envy might appear as the fierce green-eyed lover jilted years before. Fear might be a great serpent threatening to swallow us. Still, the attraction or repulsion to those images would be the same whether they were clothed in Tibetan garb or in the familiar conditioning of the old mind projected from the depths of imagination. Indeed, the work is the same for the Tibetan monk and for us: to acknowledge what is happening, to open to it without the least clinging or resistance, and to let it go so that we can see beyond the mind's imaginings, goals, and fears.

At this moment or at the moment of death the work is always the same: to go beyond to the truth, to merge with the Evershining.

"It is your self-image that continues after death." To the degree you have related to yourself as the body, why should you imagine that the fear of death, of the dissolution of that body, should halt at the moment of transition out of that body. It is interesting to note in the navigational schemes of the various texts that exist in widely divergent cultures, that even after leaving the body one is still motivated by the fear of death. A demon or tiger approaches and you find yourself attempting to escape as though this body needed to be protected. For what other reason would one pull back from a red-eyed demon coming at you with a broad ax? It is because we still tend to identify with the body as being who we are even when we no longer have a body. Those who think of themselves as a body have much to protect. But those who identify with the spirit cannot be assaulted by a tiger, by a red-eyed demon. Being cannot be threatened; only the self-image causes fear, creates something to protect.

To the degree that you would kill to protect those possessions you cherish, that is the degree to which you may well fear being killed. To the degree that lust can drive you past any sense of compassion for another being, that is the degree to which you may fear that others will not be so compassionate with you. If you are constantly searching for security, how will you relate to an environment in which you are infinitely unfamiliar and insecure? How, if a lifetime has been built on the acquirement of a much protected title and reputation, will you as a statusless being be able to find the ground of your true nature? Where will you take refuge?

The poet Kabir states, "What is found now is found then." The way you relate to experience now, that is most probably how you are going to relate to that same state of mind in the future. The future may be tomorrow at work or it may be tomorrow as you float out of your body after the crumpling of steel and the screeching of brakes. Your unconscious tendencies, your mental accumulations, seem to continue from moment to moment and death is not a barrier to this continuance. To the degree you identify with states of mind as who you are now, that is the degree to which you will be frightened or attracted by what your mind projects in the next moment, wherever that moment may occur.

How do you stay aware in situations that are disorienting? Do you open to what seems unusual and frightening or do you withdraw in an attempt to hide in the first safe place that arises? What does it take to make you veer from the path of truth in an attempt at self-protection and deceit? When danger arises now, do you soften and open and try just to be with what is happening, using all your facilities to penetrate deeper into the moment, to see the next appropriate step, or does everything become an emergency, the body tense, the mind compulsively attempting to escape from the present? Are you like one who runs from a barking dog only to take shelter in a pit of vipers? Or are you one who recognizes your humanity, the fear and doubt, and gives it room so that the dog does not become the personification of all the fears of a lifetime, but instead remains just a dog, a workable reality, something one can deal with spaciously? What do you do when you find yourself in the midst of a reality that is unfamiliar and recognize how poorly prepared you are for the truth? But to the degree that we start looking now into the mind and begin to recognize the awareness by which all is known, that is the degree to which no matter what arises you will be present; "Even if the sun rises in the west, the man of wisdom has but one way." To what degree can you make who you think you are the object rather than the subject of perception, recognizing all that arises as momentary phenomena? To the degree you recognize that you are the space in which it is all happening now, that is the spaciousness you will bring to whatever circumstance arises in the future. The mind is constantly translating amorphous reality into a manageable, self-defined mass so that we can hardly touch it, smell it, taste it, feel it; instead we only touch, smell, taste ourselves. We are constantly eating ourselves, smelling ourselves. We can hardly look into another's eyes without the mind interposing a self-protective filter for the reality of the moment.

That suchness which departs the body upon what we call death is called by some people "soul," by others "the karmic bundle," by others "the consciousness element." But it doesn't matter what you call it, only that you investigate it directly and remain open to the dissolution of the connection that maintained life in the body. To recognize with much "don't know" that there seems to be a continuing on, not of "someone" but of the energy out of which that someoneness was mentally constructed. As long as there is any attachment left to take incarnation, it will. To the degree the illusion seems real it will draw awareness back into itself.

When you are asleep, the sleeping consciousness says the waking state is false and that only it is real. However, when we awaken we look back at our dreams and say, "This one is real, the other one is false." But if both are acknowledged as transitional dream states where all that appears to be real is only relatively so, we can open to each transition as a process and let go of the "I" that holds reality captive. Experience is only as real as you imagine yourself to be. When you start investigating awareness itself, you see the origins of consciousness. You experience first hand that out of which the idea of "I," of "someone" to die, to be born, to be enlightened, arises. And the "I" pales by comparison, floats in the immensity of the truth.

In many traditions, and by those who have been pronounced clinically dead and have been eventually revived, it is said that the actual process we call dying (third and fourth bardo) is not unpleasant or even frightening.

One being said it was like taking off a tight shoe. There is a potential at the moment of dying unlike almost any other that arises in an incarnation because in that transition, as the body falls away, awareness can be seen within consciousness as the clear light it is and there exists the possibility of breaking the illusion of "I am this body and this mind." At the time we drop the body, the potential exists for us to see how mind forms the world. How the world is in us, not us in the world. Mind is addicted to and conditioned by its seeing, hearing, smelling, tasting, touching, and thinking; so identified with itself that each moment of sensory awareness continues to turn the Wheel of Becoming. But there you are with no body, eyes, ears, nose, and yet the senses continue. It is not dissimilar from sleep. In sleep you are not seeing with your eyes, hearing with your ears, or smelling through your nose; however, consciousness continues such experiences. Indeed some dreams are so powerful that they change our life. Dying may also offer the possibility of recognizing the immensity of the light of our original nature revealed for a few precious moments. And to see how identification with such thoughts as "I am not the light," or feelings of lust or doubt, can pull us away from the simple experience of being.

"What is found now is found then." Your difficulty in opening to the light now is directly proportionate to your ability to enter into the open arms of Jesus, into the compassion of Buddha should they appear after death. It is our unwillingness to surrender past our holding that keeps us caught in shadow. When there is anger or guilt or fear now, do you open to it and give it space? Or do you contract, creating more of the same, increasing the deep imprinting which colors each perception in the future: another investment in Karma Savings and Loan.

Even those who have spoken of their experiences approaching the light during clinical death seldom seem to have recognized that the light was their true nature, their essential being. Either they were frightened by it or supplicated. But I have never heard anyone say that he or she sought to merge with it, to let go of all that was separate, including the pleasure of that moment of freedom from the body and the denseness of the mind. All that is so precious as our individuality seems somehow to be held to. The "experiencer" did not dissolve into the experience. It is not unlike the ego wanting to be present at its own funeral, the dandy living his life before a mirror. Yet enlightenment is the complete and final eradication of the illusion of separateness. We just come back to who we always were. And all the superficial becoming of the past dissolves into the light of the underlying reality.

QUESTION: I have read so much in the works of Raymond Moody and Elisabeth Kübler-Ross and others of the after-death experience of people leaving their bodies and meeting a being of great light. Does everyone meet Buddha or Jesus or whoever they personify as "the soul" after death?

ANSWER: Please remember that all of these so-called clinical experiences are only of the early stages of death. What might be called the first bardo after death. What occurs after the primary ease of the act of dying and the coming into the luminosity of being is the basis for hundreds of cosmologies and writings on the after-death experience. *The Tibetan Book of the Dead* and many other such texts indicate that after meeting the primary light, if we are unable to surrender wholly into it, to become one with it, the light breaks into its individual components as through a prism and the various inclinations which create duality reassert themselves. The shimmering silence is disturbed by old tendencies which agitate the mind like the mirror-smooth surface of a quiet pond rippled as the creatures within swim to the surface. Then one may go through a whole other process of purification, a meeting of one's mind in a way that allows surrender and conversion of obstacles into allies, an ongoing opportunity to meet such old imprinting with wisdom and love, entering as one can the essence shared by all.

Some years ago I spent time with a teen-age boy who was dying of a brain tumor. We hadn't talked much until he asked, "What is it going to be like when I die? What do you think death is like?" And I told him I didn't know what death was like but that there seemed to be certain kinds of experiences spoken of in the writings of various sages as well as in the outcome of recent research with those who had been clinically dead and then resuscitated. Moody's book *Life After Life* had just been published and I related to the boy some of the experiences that those who "died" mentioned about the first stages of death. How they viewed the body as from above and had some recognition of not being that body. Sharing with him some possibilities of how to stay open to this process, we went through the whole scenario. Occasionally an "Ah!" would escape his lips. "They speak of being outside their body," I told him, "and able to move as fast as thought." He frowned and asked, "Could I create thunderstorms and lightning?" I said, "I don't know if you could or not but I sense that once you are outside this body that has been giving you so much trouble you might have a different perspective on all this. You might have a different take on how these troubles that anger you so much now have actually brought you a kind of compassion and maturity. You might not even be angry. It might not even occur to you to create thunder and lightning." He wasn't so sure about that. "You know, a few minutes after you die you are going to know more about death than any of the so-called experts like me. Many people speak of moving down a corridor or across some barrier like a river and coming into the presence of a great loving light, and there may be a being of great wisdom there to guide you who some have seen as Jesus and others as Buddha." "Wow!" he said. "It will be like meeting Spock!"

I wonder how many young people upon leaving their bodies meet Spock. It doesn't matter what the personification of wisdom is; it's the relationship to wisdom itself, to the shimmering disguised in form.

QUESTION: What about someone who dies suddenly? Is his experience any different from those who have a long time to prepare?
ANSWER: I was brought up to think that when people died in their sleep that was the best possible death. If you ask your parents how they want to go, they will probably reply, "In my sleep." I now see that a sudden death may not be as fortunate as we have been conditioned to believe. I see that there is often grace in

somebody having a year-long illness in which to begin investigating the mind and opening the heart.

Someone who is suddenly popped out of his body without much preparation, like a teen-ager in the fullness of life who has a fatal accident, may after the smoke clears wonder, "What the hell was that all about? What happened to my body? I can't be dead because this is all still happening to me." To the degree we think we are our body, that is the degree we may be confused upon removal from that vessel. A friend spoke of hovering above the mangled wreckage of his Porsche as he watched police and firemen cut his bloody body from behind the steering wheel and put it in the ambulance. He said that the last thing he could remember was trying to decide whether he should get in the ambulance with it or not. Apparently he decided to go for the ride.

For the individual who dies suddenly there may not even be the recognition that he is dead, because "How could I be seeing all this if I am dead? It must be a dream." If indeed you see your body lying there and you are floating around near the ceiling, you are going to be a little puzzled. In fact in the case of those who have died suddenly it seems skillful to picture them in your heart, and say to them something like, "My friend, you have died. Your body is no longer a suitable dwelling for your spirit or your consciousness. Just look around you with love, there is nothing to fear." Trying to find the words that will be most useful for that individual. "Now there is a light shining near you; move toward it. That light is your own pure nature; let go of any thought or feeling that keeps you from it." It is the same process we share with patients who are preparing to die: you just offer your sense of the truth whenever it seems timely, before death if possible, after death if necessary. Reflect with the departed on the preciousness of the opportunity to see that they are not the body, to participate in the pure light of being. If a person has passed out of the body and is confused, you can ease that by saying, "Okay. Just that you hear my voice, that you can view your body, means that things aren't the way you thought they were. You've died and it's O.K. It's probably not the first time."

If there is a meditation practice the person used when they

were alive, remind them of that practice. If they had a relationship with a teacher they admired encourage them to make
contact with that devotional quality in their heart. I wouldn't
remind them of personal loves. I wouldn't say, "Think of your
girl friend." That is just going to stimulate the desire to get back
into the body, which must be left behind.

The more you can remind them of their underlying being, to
melt into the light, to trust and open and go into the next perfect
moment, the greater the support. The more confused a person is
the more likely he is to be around to hear it all. The deeper the
preparation, the more likely he is to relate openly to his experience and go on. You may even sense the reception of these words
by the other person. But don't get caught in being occult or mystical about it. There is really nothing exceptional about death. You
are in a body one minute and leaving it the next. Don't put in
"something extra." Just trust "don't know" and let your heart express its love without some limiting definition of who is receiving,
much less who is sending, this love.

QUESTION: All of this guidance for the dying seems more suited to
someone dying at home. What about those of us who work in
hospitals?
ANSWER: A doctor friend was telling me that he had pronounced
nineteen people dead that month and that it was getting to be a
bit much for him. He said he was conditioned to help patients, to
"do something," but that there was nothing he could do under
these circumstances, that they were "already dead." "Only their
body is dead," I said. "There is still something that might be useful to them." So now to every patient he works with who dies, he
says silently, from his heart, "Let go. Go on. You have only died.
Don't be confused. Let love guide you. Let go into the light." He
says he doesn't know if it does them any good, but it does something very useful for him.

A nurse's aide in a Texas hospital told of working one day in
the emergency ward when they brought in an alcoholic from skid
row who had been treated several times before. He had been injured and was having a massive heart attack. There was a flurry

of energy and machines around him as they attempted to resuscitate him, to no avail. The doctors pushed away the equipment and said, "That's it for him," and left the room. There were blood and vomit all about. It was a mess. The nurse's aide was to clean up and send the body to the morgue. Normally he would hurry through this process with his mind agitated and angry. "Damn it! Why am I always stuck with the shitty jobs?" Mopping up the vomit and sponging the blood from the table, he wanted to get the "stiff" to the cooler as soon as possible. But as he started to work, he thought, "Hold it. This is a human being whose life has been very difficult. How little dignity he has known. Why should I add to that?" So he sat for a moment next to the corpse to quiet down from the urgency of a few minutes before. Then he went over and got a basin of warm water and a sponge and began mindfully to wash the battered old body, all the time speaking softly to that fellow. "What a life this must have been for you! A difficult one, huh? You have been on the streets for years but you are out of all that now. Be kind to yourself. There is nothing to be frightened of, it is all going to be O.K." Looking at the sores and scars on the dead man's body as though they were the scourge marks on the body of Jesus ("Christ in his distressing disguise," as Mother Teresa puts it), he washed him and sang to him of freedom, saying, "What a difficult life, rest easy now, that one is over, just try to use what you have learned, to see what pain you have caused yourself and forgive it and forgive yourself, let go lightly, don't hold back from the light, go on now, now is the moment for freedom." He later said he didn't know how it was for the fellow who had died but for him it was the most conscious death he had participated in.

Whenever we think we have done all we can there is always one more thing to do and that is just to send love and to encourage trust in our own great nature.

24

AFTER-DEATH MEDITATION

The following is a guided meditation inspired by *The Tibetan Book of the Dead* and similar texts. It is not offered as *what will be* but only as a "scenario of investigation."

It is suggested that rather than simply reading this meditation to one who is preparing for death or to one who has already died, that one instead internalize these words by meditating on them oneself, so that the transmission that comes at this most precious and sensitive moment does not come from the intellectual mind but rather from the caring heart. It is an indication of what might be shared with another in a time of that person's possible bewilderment, if your heart connection is strong enough and your concentration sufficiently directed. Make this material your own so at the time of another's need it can come forth of itself. Let it pour out of your heart; let it come forth as it will in combination with your own intuition and love, trust that the loved one will find his way through with your compassionate encouragement.

If you intend to use this meditation with someone who has just died, it is suggested you start by just absorbing and repeating the first few paragraphs or pages as soon after death as possible and to continue sharing during the next days as feels appropriate. Indeed if you trust your intuitive sense of it all you may wish to repeat, even several times a day, certain paragraphs that you sense are useful. Just stay in loving contact and sense the connection you might share with that being, so that what comes out of you will be in harmony with that person's needs.

Let your concentration come from the heart, focused in concern for another's liberation. It is the heart energy that directs this meditation to another. Don't use it paragraph by paragraph or word by word, concept by concept. Let it be the heart's rendition of what feels appropriate in the moment so that you are not so much reading it as you are just reminding yourself out loud and sharing that remembrance with an individual in ways he might use to open his heart and let go lightly. Allow yourself to amplify and expand on any part of the reading you sense is particularly useful to that individual. Make the connection the medium for a deeper love and trust of your own inherent nature.

Guided After-death Meditation

[To be read very slowly to a friend or silently to oneself.]

Imagine that your body no longer has the strength, the energy, to maintain its connection with the life-force, with the body of awareness within. And imagine now that you are beginning to experience the process of dissolving out of that body. Slowly, the earth element begins to melt. The feeling of solidity falling away, melting into the water element, becoming a flowingness. The edges less defined. The water element dissolving, dissolving into the fire element. Sensations from the body no longer so distinct, melting away, leaving just a spaciousness. Dissolving out of the body. Leaving that heavier form behind. Dissolving into consciousness itself. Just space floating in space.

My friend, listen now, for that which is called death has arrived. So let go gently, gently, of all that holds you back. Of all that pulls you away from this most precious moment. Know that now you have arrived at the transition called death. Open to it. Let go into it.

Recognize the changing experience of the mind as it separates from the body, dissolving.

Dissolving now into the realms of pure light. Your true nature shining everywhere before you.

My friend, the clear light of your original nature is revealed now in this release from heavier form. Enter into the brilliance of the light. Approach it with reverence and compassion. Draw it into yourself and become what you have always been.

My friend, maintain an openheartedness, a spaciousness of being that does not grasp. Let things be as they are without the least attempt to interfere. Pushing away nothing. Grasping at nothing.

Enter the essential nature of your own being shining there before you, a great luminosity. Rest in being. Knowing it for what it is. This light shining, luminous. Your true self.

My friend, at this moment your mind is pure luminous emptiness. Your original mind, the essence of being, shines before you. Its nature is compassion and love, vibrant and luminous.

This is the light that shines from the open heart of Jesus. It is the pure light of the Buddha. This essential mind is inseparable luminosity and emptiness in the form of a great light. Holding to nothing, let go into this vastness. Dissolve into the light of your true being.

Let go, gently, gently, without the least force. Before you shines your true being. It is without birth, without death. It is the immortal light seen shining in the eyes of newborns. Recognize this. It is the Evershining.

Let go of all which distracts or confuses the mind, all that created density in life. Let go into your undifferentiated nature shining there before you. You have always been this light now revealed.

Go gently into it. Do not be frightened or bewildered. Do not pull back in fear from the immensity of your true being. Now is a moment for liberation.

My friend, listen very closely, for hearing these words as you pass through transition can liberate you from the clinging which has caused you such pain in the past.

These words can free you from the confusion that may arise, from whatever illusion of separateness you held most precious in this life just passed.

Listen without distraction, for what is called death has arrived. You are not alone in leaving this world. It happens to everyone. Do not desire or yearn for the body you have just left behind. You cannot stay. Indeed to force back into this life will only cause you to wander in bewilderment and confusion, stumbling in the illusions of the mind. Painting wonders that do not exist. Creating terrors that are unreal. Open to the truth. Trust in your own great nature.

My friend, if the light should fade or you should begin to feel faint, recognize whatever yearning pulls at you. The light of the one mind shines before you. It is the luminosity of the wholeness of being before it divides into the ten thousand separate images of thought and personal preference. This is the light of oneness, the underlying nature of all things.

Merge with it, letting go of all that has kept you separate. This is the light whose pure reflection is the truth.

Do not allow old pulls to shatter this oneness into the separate and fearful, experiencing as seemingly real the ten thousand beautiful images and the ten thousand horrible images that the mind has carried for so long. Do not be confused or bewildered.

Recognize whatever object that comes between you and the light to be only the empty projections of mind, emanations of old desires and yearnings.

Now, reaching this most crucial point, do not cling to the peaceful or wrathful states of mind that you have experienced so many times in the past. Allow yourself lovingly to let go of whatever resistance might hold you back.

Now is the time for holding nowhere, for melting into the great light of your original nature. Melt, dissolve into the luminosity of being.

Observe it all from the still point of the heart, wishing all the forms that appear before you the great joy of liberation as they arise and pass away.

Go forward. Stay nowhere in mind, letting all that arises pass away as it does.

See each image distinctly. Remember each to be only the projections of the old mind, seemingly solid, seemingly existing outside of you. But they are just empty shadows. Dreams of mind accumulated through birth after birth.

Let nothing distract you. Let nothing draw you away from the light of your true nature.

My friend, when the body and mind separate, the clear light appears shining with such an intensity that old fears may cause you to withdraw, to attempt to escape its incredible brilliance.

Do not be led by fears or yearnings of the past. Do not be faint or bewildered in this most precious moment. It is the natural radiance of being that shines before you. Recognize it. Enter into it.

A great sound may come from within this light. A thousand thunder claps, the roar of ten thousand lions, this is the great sound of your natural being.

You no longer have the physical body which you so often may have mistaken for your true being. You now have what is called a mental body. A shining body of awareness that experiences thoughts as though they were external objects. The unconscious tendencies which throughout life have directed and driven you can create whole realms of pleasure or fear if the mind does not take rest in its true nature.

Know yourself to be the pure edgeless awareness of being. The very suchness of the truth. Trust in this truth, let no mind state obscure it.

You have no physical body of flesh or blood; sounds, colors, lights, and projected mental creations cannot hurt you. Indeed, you cannot die, for what is called death has already occurred to the body. And now you move through the realms between births.

Do not hold to your old fear of bodily harm in these realms beyond life. Though the body has fallen away, still the mind may hold the fear of death. See the illusion of such thoughts.

Old fears. Old bindings. Let go. Let go into the light. Experiencing the unfolding with openness and love. Holding nowhere.

Dissolve into the light that shines from the sacred heart of Jesus, from the vast brow of the Buddha. Let go into the shining truth.

Recognize the sounds, the lights as just states of mind. See them as you would flickering fires, ever-changing shapes and forms, momentarily existent, then gone, of no solidity, of no substance. Do not be afraid. But like a moth, be drawn to the luminosity of your being, there, shining everywhere before you.

My friend, if you are frightened or withdraw, you may continue to wander on, separating the One into the many. Forgetful of your own great nature.

If you are seduced by the forms of your sexual desires as they brush by, or are threatened by images of old fears, you may be drawn by a yearning for pleasure to softer lights that appear more enticing, that seem to offer greater satisfaction. Know that the brightest light is your deepest nature, and enter into it. Let yourself become what you have always been.

My friend, as the days go by, the images projected from your mind may change. These images are the elements of your mind spread before you. They may appear dazzling and luminous as they approach. Let go of all that seeks to defend you, that keeps you separate, that identifies with you as form, a body, something to protect.

Within each moment, within each object, the One exists.

If feelings of anger or aggression arise as in the past, mistakenly attempting to protect you, recognize these obstructions to your essential freedom. Let go of aggression and fear. They are passing moods which float like clouds through the vast sky of awareness.

Do not take pleasure in any path that invites old habits to satisfy themselves but gently and with great compassion acknowledge the pull of old feelings and desires to draw the mind away from the light. Gently let go of all that obscures the vastness of being.

Know all thoughts, all sights, all feelings to be but the emanations of mind.

Let go of false knowing. Let go of old models and superstitions. Merge back fully with yourself. Open to the totality of being. All that is seen, is one with the mind. Melt into that oneness. Become the essence of all that is. Feel yourself beyond the mind's forms. Beyond form itself. No longer clinging to old addictions of pleasure and pain, let your mind go and rest in the pure light, relaxed, resisting nothing.

When the knower merges with the known, all that remains is knowing, being itself. When the separation dissolves, just the light remains.

Do not let old desires drag you once again into the muddy swamp of constant unknowing rebirth, of constant becoming. Let your mind be soft and open, trusting the heart's devotion to the truth.

Do not be wearied as you travel through these shining realms, perhaps so different from what you imagined. You are the essence of awareness itself.

Know yourself as awareness present in each moment of consciousness, experiencing as it does whatever arises.

If you should be attracted by old thoughts, visions of old friends, feelings that draw you toward old situations, know that all these separate incidents are but the shadow play of the one mind whose radiant emanations move toward you. Merge with the space which holds all forms, luminous and shining, endless.

If one has not merged wholly with the light of being and feels pulled after many days to once again take incarnation choose carefully the birth that seems appropriate, birth that encourages the openness you now see as so precious. Recall the essence of being so that you will not be tossed headlong into a new birth without awareness. Stay awake and sharp. Allow your heart to experience its great compassion. Be altogether patient. Watch the magnetic quality of old tendencies that may attempt to pull you into action. See them for what they are, just empty bubbles floating through the vast spaciousness of your original mind.

My friend, you see now that even death does not exist. That who you are, awareness itself, does not depend upon a body for its existence.

My friend, what you see is the spontaneous play of mind. So rest in your supreme state, free from activity and care, free of separateness and fearing. Rest in the deathlessness of your great nature, free of judging, free of the duality which causes forgetfulness of being. Enter into the essential spaciousness of being which is no longer pulled by thoughts of near or far, of inner or outer. No longer pulled by distraction or forced by resistance. Draw yourself into your own true nature, vast, luminous space.

My friend, all of these things which you see about you are your pleasures and your pains, your memory and your desires, each is an opportunity for great understanding. Notice your desire for control and the painful contraction it can cause. Let go of such solidity, take advantage of this most wonderful opportunity.

Float free in the vast spaciousness. Your devotion to the truth will carry you through.

Recognize whatever images arise, large or small, perfectly proportioned or ugly, as only the movements of mind. Do not let a beautiful body or a beautiful voice or a beautiful statue or a beautiful home, or whatever it is that desire projects about you, distract you from the luminous light path which shines before you.

Move with devotion and openheartedness toward the light. Become the pure edgeless spaciousness within which the flow continues.

My friend, many days have passed now since you left your body. Now know the truth as it is and go on, taking refuge in the vastness of your original nature. Know that you are well guided by your compassion and love. You are the essence of all things. You are the light.

25
END GAME

As one person put it, "Death is just a change in lifestyles"—an opportunity to see the cause of suffering, our clinging, and to discover the surrender that opens the way to our essential wholeness. Death puts life in perspective. A great gift which if received in love and wisdom allows the clinging mind to dissolve so that nothing remains but the truth. And we become just the light entering the light.

It is as Walt Whitman wrote,

> *"All goes onward and outward,*
> *Nothing collapses*
> *And to die is different from*
> *What anyone supposes*
> *And luckier."*

The Buddha when dying was asked by his followers what they should do to maintain their practice after he was gone. He said, "Be a lamp unto yourself."

From the Lotus sutra he suggests, "Thus shall ye think of all this fleeting world: a star at dawn, a bubble in a stream; a flash of lightning in a summer cloud, a flickering lamp, a phantom, and a dream."

DYING AT HOME

Some years ago a friend called from the hospital to say that his mother's illness had worsened and that the doctor had suggested he make final preparations for his mother's death. He asked, "Should I take her home to die? Or will that just cause more suffering for the rest of the family?" As we spoke it became clear that the most loving and supportive place his mother could be was in her own bed surrounded by loving faces and familiar objects.

The next day he took his mother home to die. Living in an upper-middle-class neighborhood for many years, all knew Mrs. Sylvan was "upstairs dying." If the house had been painted red and green stripes it could not have stood out more in the minds of the neighbors. Death was too close for comfort.

In the first days occasionally a neighbor would come to the door with a casserole or some baked goods, sending "good wishes," peering inside for the gloom they imagined must exist in such circumstances. But each time a neighbor came to offer some support in the form of a cooked meal or kind words they were surprised that rather than being met with some lugubrious heaviness they were greeted with warmth and love by the husband, sons, and attending nurse, who seemed a bit tired but very much at peace with it all. As the weeks went by, the neighbors seemed drawn to the house.

As the neighbors slowly ventured across the threshold of the house and entered into the kitchen and living room, they sensed something different. They felt a warmth and patience, a compassion and peace they had not previously experienced to such a degree in this household. Slowly the house, instead of representing death in the neighborhood, came to represent love and care. Many came to visit, investigating their own humanness, experiencing within themselves some new ease with death they had not previously imagined possible.

Mrs. Sylvan died in love and quietude, surrounded by a caring family. All had grown immensely in the six weeks preceding her final, soft breath. Each had finished business in service and love. All had worked very hard to support and maintain Mrs. Sylvan's care and each had clearly joined in the freedom of the passage. Though there was a weariness in the body from the intensity of the service, there was an openness of heart that brought a sense of fulfillment and completion to the passing of their beloved friend, mother, wife, and fellow being.

In a recent survey, four out of five people said they would prefer to die at home, though in practice four out of five people die in institutions. To die at home is to die in the midst of life. In the midst of love. Indeed, many of the people we have taken home to die have found a much diminished need for pain relief, because of the support and relaxation available in such a home environment. There is often less resistance to the unknown when one is surrounded by the familiar and can work day by day to open to his or her predicament, to discover the strength and spaciousness that lie within, that allow a deeper participation in the next unfolding. Bringing a loved one home to die often brings a family together as never before. All the petty quarrels, jealousies, and resentments are brought within the purifying fire of the intense confrontation with loss and the unknown.

Seeing a loved one in pain or having difficulty breathing may at first seem to be too much to bear, but in reality it is often the opening to our profound helplessness, to the uncontrollable nature of change which allows one to go beyond oneself and touch the essence they share with another. To recognize their own fear and the fear of a loved one and to sit in loving-kindness with their hand lightly touching that other being, allowing them to move through whatever they must in love and openness.

Many have said in the last weeks of some loved one dying in a hospital, "I wish I could do more." And I think to myself, "Well, if you take them home to care for them in their last weeks, don't worry, you will!" To give a loved one round-the-clock support and care may draw on energy reserves that have gone unexplored, while feeding some place deeper than bodily fatigue. To bring one home to die is like accompanying one on his last pilgrimage. There is no experience more intimate than to be with someone during the process of death. To share that time with another, to encourage a loved one to let go gently while we ourselves practice what we preach, brings beings together as almost no other situation allows.

Indeed, a whole book could be written about the art and science of dying at home and the skillful means which allow that process to be yet more deeply experienced. Here, however, I would just like to mention a few things that might make the home experience more workable and easier on all involved:

One of the most useful devices to have near the bed of one who is seriously ill is a cassette recorder so that person may listen to the wide variety of music and guided meditation tapes available that might encourage investigation and letting go. Speaking of the process of letting go at two in the afternoon when the patient feels relatively well and is not particularly open to investigating dying may not seem appropriate or even well received. But a tape about working with pain or preparing for the moment of death, left at the bedside may be appreciatively absorbed when the patient feels it is the right moment. Perhaps at four in the morning when sleep has become impossible and the pain in the body has intensified, that individual may then feel prepared, open, to hearing what earlier in the day may have seemed beside the point or frightening. Indeed, those who think others "aren't conscious enough" need push none of their philosophy but only be open-heartedly available to them—just allow them to come to their own understanding, support the love within them, remind them of the good they have done.

A rope and a bell hung beside the bed are also useful, so the patient can always feel in contact, able to summon help.

An "egg crate" mattress and many pillows may increase the patient's comfort as well.

For women it should be remembered that female urinals are often most appreciated. Plastic bedpans are often useful, since they aren't as cold to the touch as metal. Keeping bedpans warm is a kindness.

Turn people frequently if it does not cause them too much discomfort. Bedsores and the like occur mostly because a patient remains in one position, as does contraction of the muscles, which can cause a secondary difficulty and yet more discomfort. Bedsores most usually occur at the heels, base of the spine, buttocks, and elbows, wherever the body lies static against the bed. The watchwords for guarding against bedsores are "clean and dry." The areas that are most in contact with the bed should be massaged with oil regularly if that is comfortable. If one is watchful, there is no need for bedsores to arise.

Daily baths also aid in this protection against bedsores, while allowing human contact and much loving caress in the doing.

Massage is a very useful means of decreasing tension and anxiety while deepening the contact between beings.

Some people develop difficulties with dry mouths, fissures in the tongue, bleeding gums, and the like, which cause other, secondary problems. Be mindful of oral care.

Don't force someone to eat. Your push for someone to stay alive might be noticed in your "need" for him to eat. But that is not the process you are sharing. You are sharing an openness and ease with what is. If one wishes not to eat, so be it.

For the majority who wish to take nourishment, a blender can be very helpful when one does not wish to take in much bulk at one time. High-caloric foods rich in cream, ice cream, milks or whatever that individual wants should be offered. The use of high-protein powders, brewer's yeast, fruit, etc., may allow the individual to drink "smoothies" that are high in nutrition and quite palatable. Give the person what he wants to eat.

A hot plate in the room of the patient will allow one to keep him company without having to leave the room for a cup of tea or some light repast.

Water and juice should always be available. There is usually no need for intravenous feeding at this time. This is a time for the support of the heart and the clearing of the mind during the gentle care of the diminishing body.

Those wishing to have a loved one home to share death might find it useful to call the visiting nurse association in their town for additional support and information on how to make bathing, sheet-changing and the turning of the body more skillful. How to use "draw sheets" may well be useful information to have.

In the course of the slowing down of the body, in the process of dissolution, often bowel movements are sluggish and inconsistent. It is suggested that one not allow waste to build up in the body for more than two or three days. Routine enemas, if comfortable, may be useful as well as gentle natural laxatives that are not too abrasive. Herbal laxative teas are often very helpful.

Nausea, too, may become a problem, depending on the physical condition and the types of medication used. It is useful to investigate with your physician what pharmaceuticals and natural medicines might be available to decrease the discomfort of nausea while not decreasing or dulling consciousness. Marijuana seems useful for many as an antiemetic. It seems to deal very well with nausea as well as act as an appetite stimulant. It is often also used to balance the side effects of certain medications. Once again, one might be mindful of the balance between the alleviation of uncomfortable symptoms and the unnecessary blocking or dulling of awareness. But again it's up to the patient. If used properly marijuana seems to aid in the decrease of physical symptoms while deepening a sense of okayness with the process through which the individual is passing.

For anxiety a cold washcloth on the forehead and a long-held hand may be sufficient. However, an option should always be available if the individual's anxiety is not pacified by touch, soft music, and loving care. Allow the patient to decide for himself what degree of anxiety medication might be necessary. Even though you may disagree or think it unnecessary, allow that person his sense of it. Conversely, if you notice a "need" within yourself to tranquilize that individual, be mindful of your own feelings of fear, of not wanting that individual to experience the present reality.

If an individual is having difficulty swallowing, liquid foods can be fed slowly with a syringe, or even frozen into a popsicle. Water can be offered as ice chips or as a damp sponge placed against the lips.

If one is having difficulty with breathing or any breath anxiety, it is often useful to have a small tank of oxygen about. Though a hand touching the heart or gently rubbing the forehead may do as much to relieve anxiety.

A hospital bed with side rails is often quite useful for comfort, because it can be adjusted in so many ways. And the side rails can act as protection during the night so that one does not restlessly or absentmindedly fall from the bed. Though a hospital bed is very useful, many prefer to die in their own bed and would rather use a foam wedge for support and a few extra pillows than the up-and-down motorized movement of a strange bed.

Chux and opened Pampers are often useful as absorbent padding for keeping the bed clean.

Comfort is the primary goal of physical care. Give the individual what he needs as often as he needs it without projecting any need of your own. Be flexible; no rules, just be tuned to the moment and trust your own heart's sense of what is appropriate. Unless asked, the fewer opinions the better of how one should die. Just allow that being his own process. Be sensitive to the constantly changing condition of the individual. Sometimes someone might want to be held or massaged. At another moment only medication will be sufficient. One needs to be sensitive to another and to oneself so that one's own fear does not close around one.

Pain medications should be given routinely and as the individual wishes. Do not push your own ideas of how someone should work with pain.

Guided meditations are very useful for opening past certain states of holding and for experiencing deeper states of being. Feel when such meditations and sharings are appropriate.

There is nothing to sell, no philosophy that need be inculcated, nothing to do but be with that person in love and go to the door with him, remembering that he must pass through that door alone.

Indeed, if someone goes into a coma, stay with that person and talk with him. He is present. Indeed, coma is like being on the mezzanine. You are not yet on the second floor but you have a whole different perspective of the first floor. Talking with that person either aloud or silently through the heart seems to give a relative point by which they can see that they are not who they imagined themselves to be, that consciousness is not limited to the body. Reading holy books and talking with someone who is in coma may be very useful to him. Music too may be of aid.

Just be there.

For many, instead of using the bedroom, the living room may be the best place for the hospital bed and the paraphernalia necessary for the care of a loved one. Allow the individual, as he wishes, to be in the midst of life. It is always useful to put the bed in close proximity to a large window so that the individual can maintain contact with the familiar in the process of opening to the unfamiliar and the unknown. Putting the bed in the living room may be particularly skillful in the case of a child who is dying, as the bedroom may have a slight connotation of separateness, children perhaps having experienced being sent to their room as a means of punishment.

It is not uncommon for people who are dying to somehow feel that their illness is a punishment for previous actions. Any supportive measure that can dissolve that guilt and doubt should be encouraged.

In the Japanese Pure Land School of Buddhist thought, as one is dying it is a common practice to put at the foot of the bed a painted lacquer screen that depicts the joy and purity of the realms to which he will soon have access. We have found that in hospital rooms and at home it is quite useful to place a picture that depicts some sense of his original nature on the opposite wall, where the patient's eyes most often rest naturally. For some it may be a picture of Jesus, for others, Buddha. For others it may be a beautiful sunset or the moon rising over the sea. A photograph or picture placed appropriately can allow the patient an object of concentration that both reduces anxiety and intensifies a deeper sense of being and connectedness. Personalized pictures of the family and such, though they may be desired on the bedside table, are not usually the best sort to be posted as a meditation or contemplation object, in that they may intensify personal attachments and a greater longing to remain in the body.

Dark curtains should be made available on the windows so that the person may modulate the environment to fit his state of mind.

A mirror, if requested, is sometimes useful. Some wish to watch the process of bodily change as they note the growth of their spirit, which seems for many to give confidence in the process, though for others it might be quite frightening. Once again, be sensitive to the needs of the individual and recognize too that those needs may be in change.

Indeed, if the room in which the individual is resting can have an adjacent bathroom that is ideal.

Room temperature should be relatively constant, with no drafts. For those who are still ambulatory, warm floors are often appreciated, with nonslip rugs that will not cause the individual instability while using a walker or tenuously moving toward the bathroom.

Don't forget the old comforts of the hot water bottle, heating pads, and the like.

Also a removable phone in the room may allow that individual contact with the world as he wishes. The ability to remove the phone may also suit the individual's needs and desires at certain times.

Many find it useful to write in a journal the process they are moving through. Pens and loose paper should always be available so one can write what he feels both as a process of investigation and as a sharing for those left behind.

Plants are very good company. To have half a dozen plants in the room, if it can accommodate them comfortably, may give a yet more vibrant feeling to the room. Plants are silent and ever-giving in their love.

Be sensitive.

Be creative.

SKANDHA MEDITATION

One of the elements of the Tibetan understanding is their delineation of the process of dying defined in the "Dissolution of Aggregates" meditation (also known as the Dissolution of the Skandhas). It is an examination of the dissolution of the combined mental processes that we mistake for "I" as they come unglued (and can each be seen as not being the basis for any real separate entity we can call "me"). It describes the "actual" experience of dying as the dissolution of these groups of experiences we identify as ourselves. The dissolution of perception, of feeling, of the unconscious tendencies, of volition, and of consciousness itself. These five groups are spoken of as the basis for experience, the phenomena on which we base the idea of "I." They are the experience of our "someoneness" as it melts into the unity of all things, the tension of the separate reality dissolving, participating in the essential spaciousness of being.

Skandha Meditation

This variation on the classical Tibetan meditation is actually a description of the death evolution as given by Buddha. It pictures the dying process of an ordinary person, not a saint, in an ordinary, nontraumatic death.

Dying is described in terms of the dissolution of the aggregates which comprise our experience of "reality," the groups of processes which compose what we call personality.

There are five such aggregates: form, which is the five senses and their objects; feeling, such as pleasant, unpleasant, and indifferent in the body and mind; perception, which includes memory; unconscious tendencies or the accumulated imprints whereby previous desires, feelings, and thoughts create our present mental state; and last, consciousness itself.

Though these processes produce the thought "me," we believe it is the "me" that creates these processes. We take the experience of these qualities as they intertwine and alternately predominate as something personal. The ever-changing underdream we call "I." As we observe how these qualities form our experience we penetrate the illusion of a separate solid self and realize that even this "I" is but a reflection of the awareness by which these processes are seen.

● ● ●

Find a comfortable sitting position and allow the attention to come to the breath.

Let the mind and the body be still.

Imagine that this is a description of your dying. Observe, visualize within yourself these processes as they unfold.

Imagine yourself approaching death. Feel consciousness withdrawing from one level of experience after another.

First the aggregate of form begins to be absorbed. The physical body becomes weak and thin. It is quite evident to those around the bedside that the body is deteriorating.

As the earth element dissolves, your arms and legs lie loose and heavy at your side. They are no longer in your control. A feeling of heaviness weighs them down, a feeling of sinking into the bed.

You cannot move or focus your eyes. Blinking ceases.

The gross and subtle form is absorbed and the physical body loses its color. There is no strength left in what once seemed so solid a body.

The sense of sight fails.

There arises the inner vision of a shimmering silver blue mirage like water in the heat.

Next the aggregate of feeling is absorbed. The physical body ceases to experience pain or pleasure or even indifference. Feelings of happiness, suffering, and indifference are recognized as being of the same nature. One no longer remembers or differentiates between physical and mental impressions.

The water element dissolves. The bodily fluids—blood, urine, saliva, semen, sweat, begin to dry up.

The sense of hearing fails. The ear ceases to hear outer sounds. Even the buzzing in the ears is no longer received.*

An inner vision of smoke arises.

Next the aggregate of perception is absorbed. You no longer recognize family or friends.

The fire element dissolves. The heat of the physical body disappears. The capacity of the body to digest food ceases.

Breathing in becomes weaker and breathing out becomes stronger and longer.

The sense of smell dissolves.

A vision of fiery sparks trembling like distant stars arises.

Next the aggregate of unconscious tendencies, of conditioned mental impressions, of volitional formations, is absorbed. The body can no longer move at all.

That which recalls past worldly work, success, and "significance" dissolves. You lose all idea of the purpose and meaning of such worldly work, it all seems so empty.

The air element dissolves. Breathing stops.

The sense of taste dissolves. The sense of touch is lost. You can no longer distinguish between textures.

A vision of a dim blue-red light arises like the last light of a candle sputtering in a dark room.

Finally, the aggregate of consciousness is absorbed. This dissolves the delusions of a separate reality of what we call "my mind," "my con-

---

* It is interesting in this classical Tibetan meditation that it notes the end of hearing so soon in the process of dying. Yet *The Tibetan Book of the Dead* is based on the ability of the deceased to hear during and after death. It is widely acknowledged that hearing may be the last faculty to go.

sciousness." The superstitions of the gross delusive mind, the dualistic, the conceptual, dissolve.

At this point the various depths of the aggregate of consciousness dawn in stages as a number of inner visions arise: first you experience a vision of great whiteness like a clear night sky in autumn bright with the full moon.

As the brightness fades you experience a vision of redness—as a coppery red reflection like a vast sunset filling the sky.

The red vision gives way to a vision of darkness as though of a darkening sky.

Gradually your vision becomes of the clear light dawning. A vision of clear luminous empty space like the bright sky after a long hard rain. This is the clear light of death. What is called the "dying process" is completed.

Without grasping at any thought, without rejecting any thought, merge the perceiver of this clear light vision with the clear light itself, so there is only the awareness of clarity, luminosity, and infinite space.

Maintain this vision as long as you can—the vision of final death.

When the clear light vision is lost to perception, the "individual," the conditioned clinging to the five aggregates as a separate self, begins to re-establish itself, moving toward ultimate rebirth in the opposite order to that in which the death process occurred; starting with the dark vision, to the red vision, to the white vision, volitional formations, perceptive faculties, emotional responses, to the conception in the womb, acquisition of the sense organs and their contact with their objects.

Birth, a lifetime, and death once again.

●   ●   ●

THE TIBETAN BARDO SYSTEM
(Variations on a Theme)

There are many translations for the Tibetan word *bardo,* but essentially it means a passageway, a point of transition. Some define it as a gap, a space; others, as a portal. It is, it seems, another evolutionary stage, like the metamorphosis between phyla, a stage of transition from one moment to the next. Generally we think of the bardos as occurring after death but actually this moment is a bardo. We tend to think that such portals will become evident only after we drop the body but that is only part of it. You are in bardo at this very moment. Awareness and thought meet to produce consciousness whether one is in or out of a body. In sleep, when the body lies relatively inert, awareness continues meeting thought after thought, feeling after feeling produced from the momentum of mental energy. Clearly the activity of the body is not necessary for the experiences of consciousness. When the life current that is produced by consciousness inhabiting a body departs, the body instantly collapses. The body depends on the presence of consciousness/awareness for its existence though we have been given to believe that it is precisely the other way around.

There are six bardos. The first of which is the Bardo of Birth; it is a moment of birth, an emergence bardo, if you will, the transitional experience of consciousness within a body moving into its own independent existence in this realm. The second bardo is the Lifetime Bardo; a bardo of becoming; the growth from child to adult; a bardo of learning and aging and the changes of a lifetime. This interval may be much shorter than the first or a hundred years longer. The bardo of life may also be thought of as the "empty-handed bardo"—a following of accumulated desires and goals, becoming what one wishes to be. The third bardo is of dissolution. It is the Bardo of the Moments Before Death. It is the transition out of the seemingly solid, a spacious withdrawal, a melting out of physical form into subtler realities.

The fourth is again a bardo of emergence. It is the Bardo of the Moments After Death. You will notice that there is no such thing as death but only the moments before and the moments after. The concept "death" has no basis in reality. For the body there is a moment when it is animated and a moment later when it has become a nonreturnable empty.

Indeed, in this case, only the contents are returnable while the container is not. It is like a light bulb which is lit one minute and dark the next because the current running through it is withdrawn and leaves it gray and empty. The light bulb is the same—only the current which made it functional has departed. There is no moment in between. Only the body dies. From the body's point of view this bardo occurs when death is recognizable. But the body was never alive on its own, only the life-force (whatever that reflection may be) is withdrawn. As one person pointed out, in actuality the body is never so active as after death, supporting myriad microbes and a multitude of creatures which obtain sustenance from decomposition.

In *The Tibetan Book of the Dead,* it is in this fourth bardo, the transition after death—the emergence—that we often hear of the appearance of the great light called the Dharmata, where the essence of being, no longer identified with the confines of the body, shines before us. It is considered by many one of the most important and opportune times of an incarnation.

The fifth bardo, the Deathtime Bardo, is another of the roaming bardos, where we are in the transition to the next learning, aging, and growth that occurs as our mind runs off its conditioned content from a lifetime of holding and maneuvering for safety and security. It is an unraveling of the past, another opportunity to relate directly to the forms that arise in the mind and create our ways of seeing. It is in this bardo that many of the peaceful and wrathful deities are encountered. It is here that it is said that one meets the ten thousand loving and the ten thousand wrathful aspects of the mind. But, of course, these qualities are observable in our present bardo as well.

Like the second bardo, the Lifetime Bardo, this bardo of "death" may be seen to be of some duration to the time-oriented mind.

The sixth bardo, the Bardo of the Moment Before Birth, is again of dissolution. It is a moment of selecting a new birth, the choosing of incarnation. It is the moment when you are attracted to your next stage of becoming, when desires lead you to a new womb out of which to emerge into a world that most often seems too big or too small.

The use of the concepts of the bardo is a skillful means of pointing out that the illusion is happening right now wherever we are holding. It is also interesting to note that these bardos follow a certain process of arising (emergence), existence (a roaming), and dissolution; precisely the same as each state of mind that we notice arising, existing for a moment and passing away to give rise to the next emergence, existence, and dissolution. Watching the moment-to-moment birth and death of the mind prepares us for whatever the next incarnation may be. It is watching this process of creation and dissolution that frees us from our sense of solidity, of "someone" to protect. It is clear that the bardos of emergence are interchangeable. That birth and the moments after death are the same. That the bardos of existence roaming, of "life" and "death," are comprised of the same elements of consciousness and old tendencies. That the bardos of dissolution, of the moment before death and before birth are also interchangeable. Relating to each transition as it arises, we die from moment to moment into the Deathless.

MUSIC LIST

Music is a particularly useful tool for the centering of consciousness. In times of pain, restlessness, or anxiety, listening to music can quiet the mind. Indeed, if one concentrates on the music from note to note, it can allow the mind a profound stillness.

Ron Dexter, Golden Voyages, Vols. I–III, Awakening Productions, 4132 Tuller Avenue, Culver City, California 90230

Steven Halpern, Ancient Echoes with Georgia Kelley; The Rain Machine with Sunil K. Bose; Spectrum Suite; Starborn Suite; Eastern Peace; Halpern Sounds, 620 Taylor Way, Belmont, California 94002

Paul Horn, Inside, Epic BXN 26466; Inside II, Epic KE 31600; Heru Records, P.O. Box 954, Topanga, California 90290

Georgia Kelley, Rainbow Butterfly (with Emmett Miller); Sea Peace; Tarashanti; Heru Records, P.O. Box 954, Topanga, California 90290

Iasos, Interdimensional Music, Unity Records, P.O. Box 12, Corte Madera, California 90425

Sachdev, Raga Bhupali, Unity Records, P.O. Box 12, Corte Madera, California 90425

Tony Scott, Music for Zen Meditation, Verv, V8634

Joel Andrews, The Violet Flame, 245 E. Mountain Drive, Santa Barbara, California 93108

Joel Andrews, Kuthumi, Group Incorporated, P.O. Box 673, Daytona Beach, Florida 32017

Jordan de La Sierra, Gymnosphere Song of the Rose, Unity Records, P.O. Box 12, Corte Madera, California 90425

Gary Burton and Chick Corea, Crystal Silence, ECM 1024 ST

Henry Wolf, Nancy Hennings with Drew Gladstone, Tibetan Bells I & II, Island Records, 7720 Sunset Boulevard, Los Angeles, California 90046

Jean Michel Jarre, Oxygene, Polydor Records

Tomita, Snowflakes Are Dancing; Cosmos; RCA Records

Pachelbel's Canon in D

A Treasury of Gregorian Chants, Vol. II, Monks of the Abbey of St. Thomas, VOX Records

Carl Orff, Carmina Burana

Pablo Casals, Bach, Columbia Records

Ravi Shankar Family and Friends, produced by George Harrison, Vols. I & II, Dark Horse Records

A Bell Ringing in the Empty Sky, Goro Yamouchi, Nonesuch Records

Chopin Waltzes and Études

Joseph Haydn, Symphony No. 67 in F Major and Symphony No. 69 in B Major

Haydn's Concerto for Violin and String Orchestra No. 1 in C Major and No. 2 in G Major

Mozart, Haffner Symphony, Concerto for Violin and Orchestra No. 7 in D Major, Concerto for Piano and Orchestra No. 18 in B flat Major

Songs of the Humpback Whale, CRM Records, Del Mar, California 92014

The Environment Series, Environmental Sounds, Countryside, Birds, Seashore, Nature, the Atlantic Label, Syntonic Research series

Jai Gopal, Crystal Tears, Hanuman Tape Library, P.O. Box 61498, Santa Cruz, California 95062

Also please remember the music of the Beatles, John Denver, and Judy Collins

BOOK LIST

There are thousands of books and articles about death and dying; even a 120-page bibliography is available about books dealing just with this subject. So rather than mention all the fine books by such knowledgeable beings as Elisabeth Kübler-Ross, Philippe Ariès, Karl Osis, Peter Koestenbaum, Edgar Jackson, Edwin Schneidman, and Raymond Moody, I have just mentioned a few of those books I have found useful along the way.

There are also books like the Bible, the Dhammapada, the Tao Te Ching, the Ramayana, and the Bhagavad-Gita that are recommended to be read aloud to one who is trying to gather the mind and open the heart in preparation for the next transition. (Though any of these books may be suitable reading for the appropriate person at the appropriate time.) It is suggested, if one wishes to take this exploration farther and has not already read the author's *A Gradual Awakening* that one do so for a more complete explanation of the mindfulness method that is the basis for the investigation encouraged in this book.

On Death

The Wheel of Death, Roshi Philip Kapleau

The Tibetan Book of the Dead, Trungpa and Fremantle

The Human Encounter with Death, Grof and Halifax
Beyond Death, Grof
Dialogue with Death, Eknath Easwaran
Meditation and the Art of Dying, Pandit Usharbudh Arya
The Facts of Death, Simpson

On the Investigation of Being

I Am That, Vols. I, II, Sri Nisargadatta (an Indian publication available from Bodhi Tree bookshop in Los Angeles)

Zen Mind, Beginner's Mind, Suzuki Roshi

Freedom from the Known, Krishnamurti

The Journey of Awakening, Ram Dass

Grist for the Mill, Ram Dass and Levine

A Gradual Awakening, Levine

The Way of the Pilgrim, French (translator)

The Last Barrier, Reshad Feild

The Invisible Way, Reshad Feild

The Art of Prayer, Ware

Miracle of Love (tales of Maharaji, compiled by Ram Dass)

Talks with Sri Ramana Maharshi (published in India, available in Bodhi Tree bookshop, Los Angeles)

Journey to Ixtlan, Castaneda

The Myth of Freedom, Chögyam Trungpa

The Lazy Man's Guide to Enlightenment, Thaddeus Golas

The Way of Chuang Tzu, Thomas Merton

The Three Pillars of Zen, Roshi Philip Kapleau

The Experience of Insight, Joseph Goldstein

Living Buddhist Masters, Jack Kornfield

The Zen Teachings of Huang Po, John Blofeld (translator)

The Teachings of Ramana Maharshi, Arthur Osborne, editor

Zen Flesh, Zen Bones, Paul Reps

Dropping Ashes on the Buddha, Seung Sahn (compiled by
    Stephen Mitchell)
The Hsin Hsin Ming (teachings of the Third Zen Patriarch)

Poetry from the Journey of the Heart

At the Edge of the Body, Erica Jong
The Kabir Book, Robert Bly (translator)
Four Quartets, T. S. Eliot
A Gift for God, Prayers and Meditations, Mother Teresa
The Prophet, Kahlil Gibran

On Dying at Home

Care of the Dying, Lamerton
Last Letter to the Pebble People, Virginia Hine
Counseling the Dying, Bowers, Jackson, Knight, and LeShan
Until We Say Goodbye, Elisabeth Kübler-Ross
Home Care, Evelyn Baulch

INDEX